Schizophrenia

Kevin Silber

PALGRAVE
INSIGHTS IN
PSYCHOLOGY

SERIES EDITORS:
NIGEL HOLT
& ROB LEWIS

Aim higher with *Palgrave Insights in Psychology*

From phobias to research methods and relationships to sport psychology, our fantastic range of *Insights* titles take you on a tour of the field, providing a comprehensive, readable introduction to key areas of study within psychology.

Whether you're studying at A-level, university, or have a keen interest that you want to take further, you're sure to find what you need with our *Insights in Psychology* series.

Visit **www.palgrave.com/Insights** to explore our full range of books.

More titles in this series:

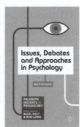

9780230249424

9780230249882

9780230272224

9780230295377

PALGRAVE INSIGHTS IN PSYCHOLOGY
Series Editors: Nigel Holt and Rob Lewis

The Palgrave *Insights in Psychology* series provides short, readable introductions to a wide range of topics across the field of psychology. Accessible and affordable, each book offers clear, up-to-date coverage in a manageable format. Whether you're studying at A-level, university, or have a keen interest that you want to take further, you're sure to find what you need with our *Insights in Psychology* series.

Heather Buchanan, Neil Coulson *Phobias*

Graham Davey, Suzanne Dash, Frances Meeten *Obsessive Compulsive Disorder*

Ian Fairholm *Issues, Debates and Approaches in Psychology*

Leanne Franklin *Gender*

David Giles *Psychology of the Media*

Simon Green *Biological Rhythms, Sleep and Hypnosis*

Leo Hendry, Marion Kloep *Adolescence and Adulthood*

Nicola Holt, Christine Simmonds-Moore, David Luke, Christopher C. French *Anomalistic Psychology*

Chris Irons *Depression*

Amanda Ludlow, Roberto Gutierrez *Developmental Psychology*

Nick Lund *Intelligence and Learning*

Antony C. Moss, Kyle R. Dyer *Psychology of Addictive Behaviour*

Karen Rodham *Health Psychology*

Adrian J. Scott *Forensic Psychology*

Kevin Silber *Schizophrenia*

David Tod, Joanne Thatcher, Rachel Rahman *Sport Psychology*

Ian Walker *Research Methods and Statistics*

Julia Willerton *The Psychology of Relationships*

For more information, visit www.palgrave.com/insights

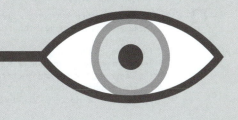

Schizophrenia

Kevin Silber

PALGRAVE INSIGHTS IN PSYCHOLOGY

SERIES EDITORS:
NIGEL HOLT
& ROB LEWIS

palgrave
macmillan

First published 2014 by
PALGRAVE MACMILLAN

Palgrave Macmillan in the UK is an imprint of Macmillan Publishers Limited, registered in England, company number 785998, of Houndmills, Basingstoke, Hampshire RG21 6XS.

Palgrave Macmillan in the US is a division of St Martin's Press LLC, 175 Fifth Avenue, New York, NY 10010.

Palgrave Macmillan is the global academic imprint of the above companies and has companies and representatives throughout the world.

Palgrave® and Macmillan® are registered trademarks in the United States, the United Kingdom, Europe and other countries.

ISBN 978–0–230–29986–3

This book is printed on paper suitable for recycling and made from fully managed and sustained forest sources. Logging, pulping and manufacturing processes are expected to conform to the environmental regulations of the country of origin.

A catalogue record for this book is available from the British Library.

A catalog record for this book is available from the Library of Congress.

Typeset by MPS Limited, Chennai, India.

Printed in China

To Mum and Dad, and my three lovely grandchildren,
Josh, Isabella and Zackary
Thanks also to Dominic Howard for some of the drawings.

Also by Kevin Silber

Instant Notes in Physiological Psychology (with H. Wagner)
The Physiological Basis of Behaviour: Neural and Hormonal Processes

Contents

List of Figures and Tables

Figures

Tables

Acknowledgements

The publisher and authors would like to thank the organisations and people listed below for permission to reproduce material from their publications:

Box 1.1 reprinted from Schizophrenia Research, 150 (1), Rajiv Tandon, Wolfgang Gaebel, Deanna M. Barch, Juan Bustillo, Raquel E. Gur, Stephan Heckers, Dolores Malaspina, Michael J. Owen, Susan Schultz, Ming Tsuang, Jim Van Os, William Carpenter, Definition and description of schizophrenia in the DSM-5, 3–10, copyright 2013, with permission from Elsevier.

The extract on page 10, reprinted with permission from Kyle Reynolds

The extract on page 11, reprinted from Schizophrenia Bulletin, 21 (3), Jordan, J. C., *First person account: Schizophrenia–adrift in an anchorless reality*. 501–3 copyright 1995, reprinted with permission from Oxford University Press.

Figures 3.1 and 3.2 copyright Dominic Howard

Figure 6.1, reprinted from Schizophrenia bulletin, 30 (4), Combs, D. R. & Gouvier, W. D., *The role of attention in affect perception: An examination of Mirsky's four factor model of attention in chronic schizophrenia.* 727–38, copyright 2004, reprinted with permission from Oxford University Press.

Figure 6.2, reprinted from Schizophrenia bulletin, 32 Suppl 1, Couture, S. M., Penn, D. L. & Roberts, D. L., *The functional significance of social cognition in schizophrenia: A review.* S44–63, copyright 2006, reprinted with permission from Oxford University Press.

The extract on page 112, reprinted with permission, from Cochrane Database of Systematic Reviews, 2005, Tharyan, P. & Adams, C. *Electroconvulsive therapy for schizophrenia.* Copyright © 2009 The Cochrane Collaboration. Published by John Wiley & Sons, Ltd.

Figure 9.1 reprinted from Schizophrenia Bulletin, 32 Suppl 1, Roder, V., Mueller, D. R., Mueser, K. T. & Brenner, H. D., *Integrated psychological therapy (IPT) for schizophrenia: Is it effective?* S81–93, copyright 2006, reprinted with permission from Oxford University Press.

Note from Series Editors

Schizophrenia is a very misunderstood mental health condition with a great number of complications. It is extremely poorly described in many places and the myths surrounding it are many. This book begins with a description of the most common of these and a clear and unequivocal explanation of why these are just that, myths. This book is an invaluable addition to the literature in this area of psychology. It is at the same time informative and interesting, entertaining and educational. This is a neat and difficult trick to achieve and the author has done it seamlessly.

Kevin Silber is a fascinating character. With great experience in many levels of psychology, from A-level to the most learned of journals, his enthusiasm and tenacity are contagious. When the Insights series was conceived a number of years ago he was in our wish list of contributors from the very start. Sadly his commitments to research, teaching and researching teaching allowed him to commit to this very significant project only now and the book has been worth the wait. The text is very easy to follow, and extremely well organised and we are certain the reader will not be disappointed with this most clear explanation of such a very emotive and tricky topic.

- *This book may form part of your pre-university preparation or as general reading.* It may be that you have come to this book because you are interested in finding out more about schizophrenia because you yourself, or an acquaintance has been identified as having the condition. Whilst clearly not a diagnostic tool, the book does however set out schizophrenia clearly and with great care and we hope you find it illuminating and useful. If reading as part of your pre-university preparation you should consider this as the most up to date, and clearest introduction to the topic there is. If it whets your appetite to issues of mental illness consider the book on *Obsessive Compulsive Disorder* in this series also for a similarly clear and fascinating account.

- *This book may form part of your university reading list.* In many psychology courses schizophrenia will fall into a general course on 'psychopathology' or 'abnormal psychology'. As lecturers at university we are aware of all textbooks in the field and directed the publishers to develop this book with Silber because we know that there is a need for this in the literature at this level. The book provides both an introduction and an extension to the topic, perfect for introductory reading and for more focussed research in the area.

- *You may be using this book while studying for a pre-university course, such as A-level.* Silber is only too aware of the needs of those preparing for University. With many years of experience at that level he is very used to preparing material for those focussing on examinations at that level. The book has been written with this in mind, both for the very best students and for those preparing to teach them.

The breadth of coverage in this book is exactly what the *Insights* series is designed to provide. It fits perfectly with the others in the series. For many people 'textbooks' are not bedside reading, but we are confident that the way this book has been constructed and presented will make it hard for those with curiosity and enthusiasm for our magnificent subject to put down. We are delighted to introduce it to the *Insights in Psychology* family.

NIGEL HOLT AND ROB LEWIS
Series Editors

Reading Guide

This is one of the books in the *Insights in Psychology* series. There are a range of topics covered in the books, and these have been chosen to carefully reflect the subjects being studied in psychology at a number of levels.

Whether reading for interest, for your degree study or for pre-university courses, such as A-level or other courses where you may find psychology, the material in these books will help you reach the very best of your potential.

The authors of these books have written their books to include material from the specifications of all relevant A-level examination boards in the United Kingdom, these include:

- The Assessment and Qualifications Alliance (AQA)
- The Welsh Joint Education Committee (WJEC)
- Oxford, Cambridge and RSA (OCR)
- EDEXCEL

To keep the qualifications fresh and focussed on the workplace and further education destinations, and to respond to the very latest research and trends in our subject, the examination boards regularly update their curricula. To ensure you have the very latest information we have chosen to include a reading guide online at: www.palgrave.com/insights.

Chapter 1

What Is Schizophrenia?

It is hard to imagine any other term in psychology that has been as misused as the term schizophrenia. When Bleuler conjured up the label in about 1908, I doubt he believed that he was describing a condition that would come to be feared more than Mary Shelley's Frankenstein. So my mission for this chapter is simple; I will try to dispel some of the myths around schizophrenia and set you, the reader, up for an excursion into what we understand about this most disturbing yet fascinating mental illness. Throughout the book, we will explore the debates about causes and the alternatives regarding treatment. We will explore the views of neuroscientists, psychologists, therapists and, most importantly, the people with schizophrenia themselves in an effort to comprehend the many perspectives on this intriguing topic. Whilst I, myself, am a biological psychologist by training, my aim here is not to convince you that one argument stands head and shoulders above another. Instead, I aim to provide you with the questions you should ask of the data and the doubts you should have about the evidence so that you can come to your own conclusions about the nature of this spellbinding condition.

Probably the best place to start is with some of the myths about schizophrenia.

◉ Myth 1

Schizophrenia describes people with a split personality

This is, by far, the most common myth and, in all probability, it derives from the term schizophrenia itself. The term schizophrenia comes from two Greek words:

Schizo – meaning split

and

Phrene – meaning mind

It is not surprising, therefore, that the insertion of personality for mind has become an interpretation of the term. This has led to numerous misunderstandings about what schizophrenia is. So we see people believing that those with schizophrenia have dual personalities, one that is quite unaffected and pleasant and one that is a psychopath – real-life versions of Dr. Jekyll and Mr. Hyde. This is reinforced even in people who know that the term actually means split mind as they relate it to 'being in two minds', a common, everyday phrase. When I say that I am in two minds about something I sort of imply that there is one me that wants one thing and one me that wants another. From here it is easy to see how the error of equating split mind with being in two minds, and so with having a split personality, comes about. However, as this book will very clearly describe, this label could not be further from the truth.

Myth 2

All people with schizophrenia are dangerous

It is true that a small proportion of people with schizophrenia are prone to violent outbursts, especially if they are also fuelled by drugs or alcohol or are not taking their medication and are experiencing voices at the time. However, this is a small minority and really doesn't warrant the myth. Most people with schizophrenia are withdrawn and unlikely to do any harm to others. Indeed, they are more likely to harm themselves and are infinitely more likely to be the victims of violence against them from a media-frenzied, uninformed public. Certainly our Western society is pretty intolerant of anyone suffering from a mental illness.

Myth 3

Schizophrenia is untreatable

There are a wide range of **antipsychotic** drugs available and these provide stability for most people with schizophrenia. Alongside the myth that no treatment exists are the associated myths that the side-effects of drugs are worse than the schizophrenia itself and/or that the drugs reduce those with schizophrenia to 'zombies'. Neither of these associated myths have an iota of truth in them. In some cases the drugs have even led to the symptoms disappearing altogether even when the drugs are stopped.

◁◉▷ Myth 4

If you hear voices you must be a schizophrenic

In truth, this one is only half a myth as people with schizophrenia do often suffer from **auditory hallucinations**. However, schizophrenia is not defined by just one symptom, and hearing voices on its own is experienced by people who do not have schizophrenia. In fact, the prevalence of **auditory hallucinations** in the non-schizophrenic population is large enough for there to be a Hearing Voices Network made up of 180 local groups across the UK.

◁◉▷ Myth 5

Schizophrenia is the result of bad parenting

Whilst we are unsure of the exact causes of schizophrenia, it is highly improbable that it could result from bad parenting alone. If this were the case then we would have a lot more people with schizophrenia in the population. In any case, the label of bad parenting is such a subjective one as to be fairly useless in telling us anything of value in our understanding of this condition.

These are just a few of the many myths that abound where schizophrenia is concerned. Indeed, with so many myths it is easy to see why the public perception of schizophrenia is so wrong. So that's where this book comes in. Hopefully, when you have read it you will appreciate the complexities of this condition and the many theories and debates that surround it. Perhaps we should make a start by looking briefly at the history of schizophrenia and then at the signs and symptoms of schizophrenia, better known as its aetiology.

◁◉▷ A brief history

It is probably the case that schizophrenia was one of the conditions that were simply referred to as 'madness' before the 19th century. References to similar conditions can be traced as far back as the ancient Egyptians, more than one thousand years before Christ. The Ebers Papyrus was an Egyptian medical scroll dating back to around 1550 BC. Within it is a chapter called 'The Book of Hearts' in which there is a detailed description of dementia. Somewhat ironically, this description characterizes dementia as a physical illness as the idea that the mental and physical might be separate was not a concept familiar to them.

During the Middle Ages, all mental illness was considered to be the result of evil spirits and so a common 'cure' was exorcism. If you were lucky then the exorcism would involve you having to listen to certain types of music. However, if you were unlucky then the exorcism would involve drilling holes into your skull to release the evil demons.

Perhaps one of the earliest cases that we might more easily identify as schizophrenia was that of a 14-year-old boy who was treated by the French psychiatrist, Benedict Morel. In 1865, Morel described the boy as suffering from *démence précoce*, which translates to early dementia. In 1899, the German psychiatrist, Emile Kraepelin, converted Morel's term into Latin to give the better known label of *dementia praecox*.

It wasn't until 1911 that a Swiss psychiatrist called Eugen Bleuler coined the term schizophrenia. Bleuler had been unlike both Morel and Kraepelin as he had not been influenced by the medical model but by the **psychodynamic** approach of Freud. Perhaps it was this element that enabled him to add new symptoms to those that Kraepelin had previously characterized. He was the first to describe the positive and **negative symptoms** and he recognized that the label dementia praecox was misleading. The condition Bleuler recognized did not always lead to mental deterioration and could sometimes be seen to develop later in life.

◉ Signs and symptoms of schizophrenia

Schizophrenia is a serious psychotic disorder characterized in the Diagnostic and Statistical Manual of Mental Disorders, better known as the DSM. The latest version, **DSM-5**, was only published in 2013 and has superseded the DSM IV-TR which had been published in 2000. This manual tries to define mental illnesses for clinical purposes. The entry for schizophrenia refers to the disorder as being one involving loss of contact with reality. Schizophrenia is diagnosed when the patient suffers the following key problems (inclusion criteria):

A characteristic symptoms (described more fully below)
B social/occupational dysfunction
C a duration of six months

There are also three further criteria to distinguish schizophrenia from similar disorders. These criteria qualify when a diagnosis of schizophrenia can be made if it accompanies other conditions or if a different diagnosis might be better suited. The criteria for these are:

D the condition better fits a schizoaffective and mood disorder
E the condition is most likely due to drug abuse, medication or a general mood condition
F there is a history of autism spectrum disorder

The characteristic symptoms under criterion A are expanded into five areas. In order to fulfil this criterion, a patient must show at least two of these and one of them must come from categories 1–3. The categories are:

1 delusions
2 hallucinations
3 disorganised speech
4 grossly disorganised or catatonic behavior
5 negative symptoms (i.e. diminished emotional expression or avolition)

You might have noticed that the symptoms fall into two areas defined by the presence or absence of 'unusual' behaviour; items 1–4 are **positive symptoms** and item 5 characterizes **negative symptoms**.

Positive symptoms

These are the behaviours that are obvious because of their presence. The term 'positive' does not mean that they are desirable. They include the delusions, thought disorders and hallucinations that typify the schizophrenic. The delusions can be positive-focused, as in delusions of grandeur, or can be negative-focused, as in a persecution complex. They persist even in the face of overwhelming information to the contrary. So, for example, if a man had the delusion that he was King George VI of England, showing him the king's death certificate from 6th February 1962 would not convince him otherwise.

There are many kinds of disordered thought. The ones of note here centre on speech anomalies. One example would be where a person continually changes the topic of a conversation, seemingly at random. There is no logical sequence to the way in which topics are covered. Other examples might be where the person's speech is illogical, contains neologisms (new, made-up words) or is even completely incomprehensible (typically referred to as a word salad). These speech-oriented disordered thoughts are only part of the set of disorganized symptoms that might be displayed by the schizophrenic. Alongside speech consequences, disorganized symptoms include an inability to take decisions, slowness of movement, forgetfulness and the repetition of gestures or movements.

Hallucinations in schizophrenia are very frequently auditory but can also derive from the other four senses: smell, vision, touch and taste. The voices heard are as if they come from another individual, though no-one is present. This is different from the type of voice that the rest of us might associate with our own inner self; the one that advises, criticizes, and so on but that we know is just our own voice in our own head. For the schizophrenic, the voice is of another person and it usually converses in an information-giving way. Furthermore, it is usually in keeping with any delusion the patient has. As an extension to Myth 4 above, I should add here that these voices are not all necessarily bad and do not just recommend bad deeds, like a devil sitting on one's shoulder.

Negative symptoms

These are symptoms that characterize the absence of healthy behaviours. An example is blunted affect. Here the schizophrenic fails to show an appropriate emotional response to an event. So, for example, if an amusing story is told at a family dinner, the schizophrenic will fail to laugh, smile or show any other indication of amusement. It is important to note that this is not just a one-off. With a blunted affect, the person will virtually never show such emotions.

Another negative symptom is social withdrawal. The schizophrenic will actively attempt to disengage with society as much as possible. Even something simple like a trip to the local shops or to visit a family member can become such an effort that it is preferable to stay at home. Indeed, being around other people may feel uncomfortable. The withdrawal can even be severe enough to lead to the person refraining from washing, cleaning and doing anything positive around the house. They also find it hard to experience any positive emotions, a condition known as **anhedonia**.

It is thought that the **negative symptoms** are more damaging to a schizophrenic's quality of life than the **positive symptoms**. If these **negative symptoms** are more prominent then the person is less likely to respond to available treatments. This ties in with Myth 2 above, in that the least treatable forms of schizophrenia are those in which the result of any violent urges is much more likely to be self-harm than harm to others.

⊙ Subtypes and specifiers of schizophrenia

Prior to **DSM-5**, schizophrenia was also subdivided into various subtypes. These were paranoid, catatonic, disorganised, undifferentiated and residual. These subtypes had little research support, and **DSM-5** concentrates on the way in which schizophrenia changes over time. This has led to the new classification having specifiers of the course of the illness. These are characterized Box 1.1 below.

Box 1.1 Specifiers for the course of illness in schizophrenia in DSM-5 as described by Tandon et al. (2013)

The subtypes of the previous version of DSM have been replaced with a more helpful categorization that tracks the changing nature of schizophrenia over time. These descriptions provide information about both the patient's state (severity of **psychosis**) and the stage of the disorder that the patient is in (**episode** characteristics).

1. First episode, currently in acute episode.
   This applies to the first manifestation of illness that meets all of the diagnostic criteria of schizophrenia. An acute episode is a time period in which characteristic symptoms (criterion A) are present.

2. First episode, currently in partial **remission**.
   Partial remission is a time period during which an improvement after a previous episode is maintained and in which the defining criteria of the disorder are only partially fulfilled.

3. First episode, currently in full remission.
   Full remission is a period of time after a previous episode during which no disorder-specific symptoms are present.

4. Multiple episodes, currently in acute episode.
   Multiple episodes may be determined after a minimum of two episodes, i.e., after a first episode, a remission and minimum one **relapse**. An acute episode is defined as above.

5. Multiple episodes, currently in partial remission.
   Multiple episodes may be determined after a minimum of two episodes, i.e., after a first episode, a remission and minimum one relapse. Partial remission is defined as above.

6. Multiple episodes, currently in full remission.
   Multiple episodes may be determined after a minimum of two episodes, i.e., after a first episode, a remission and minimum one relapse. Complete remission is defined as above.

7. Continuous.

   In order to categorize an individual as having a continuous course, symptoms fulfilling the diagnostic symptom criteria of the disorder must be present for the majority of the illness course with subthreshold symptom periods being brief relative to the overall course.

8. Unspecified.

   Available information is inadequate to characterize course.

How commonplace is schizophrenia?

The term used to describe how frequently something occurs in the population is its prevalence. Schizophrenia is said to be suffered at some point by approximately 1% of the population. That makes a whopping 67.75 million people worldwide, roughly 3 million in the US and 600,000 in the UK. Of these, it is estimated that 15% of these people will attempt suicide (or just over 10 million people). The rates for teenagers with schizophrenia are even worse with estimates placing the figure as high as 50%. These figures are truly staggering and put the disorder into perspective. In fact, in any given year there are approximately 1.5 million people who will be newly diagnosed with schizophrenia. That's about 100,000 Americans and 15,000 new cases each year in the UK. Whilst there are some cultural differences in prevalence, they appear to be quite small. In addition, it is difficult to know how cultural attitudes affect the detection methods and hence the incidence rates across the world.

If we compare these rates for schizophrenia to the rates of other conditions we see that schizophrenia is twice as prevalent as Alzheimer's disease, six times more prevalent that insulin-dependent Diabetes and 60 times more prevalent than Muscular Dystrophy.

According to (Torrey, 1994), the condition of people with schizophrenia after ten years suggests that 25% will have recovered, 25% will have improved enough to be relatively independent and another 25% will have improved but still need extensive network support. Of the final 25%, 15% will still be hospitalized and 10% will have died, mostly from suicide. After 30 years, the figures are pretty much the same, although the number of those who are independent will have risen but so will the number who have died.

⊙ Risks

A number of studies have looked at which types of people are at the most risk from developing schizophrenia. One risk of having schizophrenia is that being unable to look after yourself makes you vulnerable to poor living conditions. It is estimated that 6% of all people with schizophrenia are homeless and that one third of all homeless people in the US are either schizophrenic or manic depressive. Another 6% are in jail and a further 6% are in hospital. Only about 28% live independently, with a further 25% living with a family member.

⊙ Socioeconomic status

Socioeconomic status is related to the prevalence of schizophrenia. Whilst it occurs across all classes, the lower classes seem to be associated with the most cases, being roughly 5 times as likely to exhibit the disorder as those from the highest classes. A number of studies by (B. J. Jones, Gallagher, Pisa & McFalls, 2008) have shown that the those with the lowest socioeconomic status are more likely to be sufferers irrespective of their cultural group or their family history (i.e. whether anyone else in the family suffers from schizophrenia). Of course, as the condition is associated with social withdrawal and this in turn can lead to a greater likelihood of the person ending up in poverty. Hence, these socioeconomic differences might have to be treated with caution.

⊙ Gender effects

You are no more or less likely to get schizophrenia if you are a man or a woman. However, there are some interesting gender differences that are worth noting.

Men

Men seem to get the disorder at a younger age and their symptoms seem to be more severe at this young age. The symptoms do, however, decrease as they get older. Men tend to find the social aspects of schizophrenia harder to deal with. They have a tendency not to accept the disease and are much more likely to show self-neglect, withdrawal and substance abuse. In addition, their inability to cope with relationships, their job or their social obligations only serves to make things worse.

Women

The onset of schizophrenia tends to be later with some women only showing symptoms after their menopause. For women, the more severe symptoms are likely to occur later rather than sooner. It might be that the oestrogen produced by women whilst they are fertile acts as protection. Generally, treatment is better for women, perhaps because they are more likely to comply with it.

At what age does schizophrenia develop?

Most sources show that the most common period of onset for schizophrenia is between 15 and 25 years old, though, as already noted, there is a slight gender difference. The average age of onset for men is 18–30 (depending on the study), whereas the average age for women is 25–35 (again, depending on the study). However, this might be because there is an increase in onset for menopausal women in their late 40s or early 50s increases the overall mean (Lindamer, Lohr, Harris & Jeste, 1997). If we discount the menopausal peak, we see that for both males and females the really critical time is between about 15 and 30.

There are reported cases of childhood onset of schizophrenia. Above the age of seven, children may report that they regularly hear voices that either talk to the child or talk to each other. Other signs can be that the child stares at scary things that are not there and has no interest in forming friendships. Fortunately, these cases are extremely rare, with only about 1 in 40,000 children being affected (compared with 1 in 100 for adults).

What some people with schizophrenia have to say

It is about time we heard from some real people with schizophrenia about what it is like to have this disorder. I've chosen some more interesting analyses to start us off. The first extract is from Kyle Reynolds who describes himself as "a proud schizophrenic artist or a proud artist with schizophrenia." It illustrates his frustration with the fact that so many people completely misinterpret the condition. He says,

> How can one word have so much impact. SCHIZOPHRENIA. It's only a word yet it is packed so tight with ammunition that the mere mutter of it causes such a ripple effect. I never thought I would be

associated with a word that made me a modern day leper. I suppose history has a huge part to play in the way this word has been handled. To some who have the illness it may seem like a life sentence with no chance of parole and for the people on the outside it may cause a lot of fear and misunderstanding. The only word I can think of that might muster up as much impact would be psychopath and, believe it or not, these two words have absolutely nothing in common. This is where a lot of the stigma and misunderstanding stem from misuse of this still so complex word. I remember a short time ago doing a speaking seminar and going out for a smoke with another person attending. This person also had a mental illness. I had mentioned that I had watched a TV show recently that stated the character was dating a schizophrenic and she went on to say that she was only dating one of his personalities. I thought, "wow, in 2009 people still think this." The person's response to my dismay was "isn't that just one form of the illness?" I was floored. Someone with a similar illness needed to be educated. Well, I guess that's how people's perceptions of a word can be changed; one person at a time.

(accessed from http://www.kylereynolds.ca/on 22nd February 2011)

The second extract is Janice Jordan's account of her own schizophrenia (Jordan, 1995)

The schizophrenic experience can be a terrifying journey through a world of madness no one can understand, particularly the person travelling through it. It is a journey through a world that is deranged, empty, and devoid of anchors to reality. You feel very much alone. You find it easier to withdraw than cope with a reality that is incongruent with your fantasy world. You feel tormented by distorted perceptions. You cannot distinguish what is real from what is unreal. Your thoughts race and you feel fragmented and so very alone with your 'craziness'. (p. 501)

This may surprise some of you reading this book in that the account is very lucid and portrays a high level of intelligence. The next paragraph may surprise you even more.

My name is Janice Jordan. I am a person with schizophrenia. I am also a college graduate with 27 hours towards a Master's degree. I have published three articles in national journals and hold a full-time position as a technical editor for a major engineering/technical documentation corporation. (p. 501)

So whilst we have a general conception of a schizophrenic as a jobless, possibly homeless, confused individual unable to look after themselves, this is only one end of the spectrum. Janice represents the other end. It is easy to see, therefore, why this condition presents numerous mysteries as to its origins, symptoms, causes and treatments, which very nicely leads me to the bit where I tell you about the rest of this book.

Biological explanations of schizophrenia

The first part of what follows looks at the evidence to suggest that schizophrenia is no more than a biological disorder. As with any mental illness, the most obvious issue surrounding explanations is the nature–nurture debate. So we will start by looking at the data on the heritability of schizophrenia. We will then move on to look at explanations that suggest schizophrenia is the result of disruptions of one or more neurotransmitter system in the brain. Alongside the exploration of brain chemistry is the question of which parts of the brain are affected. The chapter is called brain correlates rather than brain causes as it is an open question as to whether the data points to brain damage as a cause or as an effect of schizophrenia. The final part of this section asks a rather obvious question. If schizophrenia is a biological consequence with at least a component linked to genetics, why has it survived evolution with a pretty constant prevalence rate? Could it even be argued that it has been advantageous in our evolutionary past?

Non-biological explanations of schizophrenia

Not everyone is convinced that schizophrenia is a purely biological disorder. Indeed, some might even argue that it is predominantly not a biological disorder and that biological changes are only the result of an environmentally caused problem. Two main competing views are serious challenges to the biological perspective. The first is the suggestion that schizophrenia is the result of a combination of cognitive deficits (including attention, memory and problem-solving deficits) and social deficits (such as cognitive bias). Whilst it is relatively easy to show such deficits in a great many people with schizophrenia, it is another matter entirely to show that these are the causes and not the consequences. The second challenge to the biological viewpoint is the **psychodynamic** explanation. Here the suggestion is that schizophrenia is the result of some significant set of events that happen to a person, most likely during childhood and the early teens. One theory, the 'schizophrenogenic mother' theory, would seem to put the blame squarely on one person's shoulders but, as we shall see, it is not quite as simple as that.

Treating schizophrenia

The last part of the book looks at the variety of treatments available to the schizophrenic. A key issue for treatment is whether the aim is to help or to try to cure. As we shall see, the answer is not as straightforward as it may seem. By far the most common form of treatment is to use drugs. However, the history of drug development has been fraught with difficulties as researchers have attempted to develop what is referred to as a 'magic bullet' cure. In addition, not all biological solutions have been drug solutions and a variety of alternative biological approaches have been tried through the ages. Alongside the biological treatments, there are a host of psychological treatments that have reported varying degrees of success. These include cognitive therapies and cognitive behavioural therapies where the intention is to change the person's thinking. Family interventions are based on the belief that it is not just the schizophrenic that must deal with the disorder. Finally, the **psychodynamic** treatments are based around the assumption that schizophrenia has a psychodynamic cause.

Chapter summary

We have seen in this chapter that there are several myths surrounding schizophrenia. The statements from some sufferers near the end of the chapter are, alone, enough to show that people with schizophrenia are far from the 'crazy people' portrayed in much of the popular press. We have also started to explore some of the disorder's characteristics, such as the signs and symptoms and the prevalence of the disorder. In the chapters that follow we will take a look at the variety of perspectives that try to explain how and why the disorder occurs and the best methods by which schizophrenia can be treated.

◉ Further reading

Frith, C. and Johnstone, E.C. (2003) *Schizophrenia: A Very Short Introduction* (*Very Short Introductions*). Oxford: OUP

Jones, B.J., Gallagher, B.J., Pisa, A.M. and McFalls, J.A. (2008) Social class, family history and type of schizophrenia. *Psychiatry Research*, 159: 127–132.

Lindamer, L.A., Lohr, J.B., Harris, M.J. and Jeste, D.V. (1997) Gender, estrogen and schizophrenia. *Psychopharmacology Bulletin*, 33: 221–228.

Torrey, E.F. (1994) *Surviving Schizophrenia: A Manual for Families, Consumers and Providers.* Harper Row.

Chapter 2

Inheriting Schizophrenia

Introduction

The most common debate in nearly all areas of psychology has got to be the nature–nurture debate. For us, this is the question of whether the origins of schizophrenia are genetic (nature) or whether the condition is caused by things that happen within a person's environment (nurture). Like most things psychological, the truth is most often a bit of both and schizophrenia is no exception. So, the interesting questions for us are about how much is caused by genetic inheritance, when do these genetic influences happen and what parts of the brain are affected?

It is one thing to hold the idea that the origins of schizophrenia might be partly inherited; it is another to find the evidence to support such a claim. So the problem for researchers in all aspects of the nature–nurture debate is

In this chapter we will cover:
- Types of heritability study
- Family studies
- Twin studies
- Adoption studies
- Endophenotypes
- Environmental factors
  - Maternal stress
  - Cannabis
  - Socioeconomic status
  - Childhood trauma
- Epigenetics

how to find the evidence. Within some areas, such as the development of perceptual abilities, it is possible to look at lower animals for clues on the basis that if these abilities were inherited, there would be traces of them further down the evolutionary scale. However, we could not make the same assumptions about the inheritance of mental illness and, besides, it would not be easy to demonstrate that an animal had one. This has meant that the entire base for information about inheritance has had to come from the human population.

⊙ Types of heritability study

Three main types of study have been used to try to tease out the degree to which schizophrenia is inherited. The first is the family study. Here the researchers look for trends within whole families to provide evidence that there is at least some genetic component to schizophrenia. If the incidence rate was particularly high in one family compared to the rest of the population, that might indicate a genetic component. It might even indicate more about the genetics if, for example, the disorder were only seen in the male line or in those with brown eyes as this might suggest which gene may carry the inherited trait. However, as we shall see, nothing is quite that simple.

Another kind of study is the twin study, where examination of twins can answer such questions as to how likely it is that if one twin develops schizophrenia then the other twin will also develop it. If identical twins share the same genetic code then any genetic determination of schizophrenia should be apparent in both. However, we have a problem. If the twins are living in the same environment, how will we separate out those influences that are genetic from those that are environmental? Part of the answer lies in being able to identify two types of twin. The first are identical twins as they share 100% of their genetic code because they are both derived from the same gamete (fertilised egg). They are referred to as **monozygotic** twins (or MZ twins). The second, **dizygotic** twins (or DZ twins), are non-identical twins. These have developed in the womb from separate eggs and so do not share all of their genetic material. Nevertheless, we can assume that on average they will have shared 50% of their genetic code as both gametes receive half of the code from each parent (we must remember that this is only an average figure and, in reality, two identical twins could, of course, share virtually no code purely by chance). In terms of the nature/nurture debate we can assume that any differences between monozygotic and dizygotic twins are most likely to be genetic as the two twins will be sharing extremely similar environments.

A third kind of study is the adoption study. This is where twins have been separated and so live in different environments. This provides an opportunity to try to separate out the genetic from the environmental influences. However, it is not as easy as all that. For a start, we would need to consider at what point the separation occurred. If it were at birth then we would have a better dataset than if the separation were some time later when environmental influences could have happened. Even if the separation is at birth we must exercise some caution. If a strong environmental influence were, say, a domineering mother then we couldn't rule out this being present in both environments. Similarly, if the genetic inheritance led to a particular personality trait that was very likely to create a certain type of environment and it was that environment that led to schizophrenia, again we would not so easily be able to separate genetic from environmental influences.

So far we have referred to the environment as something that happens to a person after they are born. However, there is also an environment within the womb and it will be important for us to consider how the foetal environment might influence development and whether any of these influences could play a role in the likelihood of someone becoming schizophrenic.

Finally, before looking at the evidence itself, it is worth mentioning the diathesis-stress model. This suggests not only that the cause of a trait is part genetic and part environmental but also emphasises the importance of the environment. According to this model, the genetic basis only provides the potential internal conditions for the disorder to ensue. However, without the right environmental triggers, the illness will not manifest itself. In the case of schizophrenia that would mean that a person could genetically inherit the potential to become a schizophrenic but the environmental circumstances will determine whether or not the person exhibits schizophrenia. Such a model would explain why not all cases of identical twins with one being schizophrenic automatically determine that the other twin will also be.

Family studies

Family studies were the very first studies of genetic inheritance carried out. Ernst Rüdin, who worked in Kraepelin's clinic, published the first analysis in 1916 of the incidence rates of family members of known people with schizophrenia (though they had been diagnosed with dementia praecox at that time). He and others since then found that the number of schizophrenia cases in relatives was higher than in the general population. The schizophrenic being used for the comparison is referred to as the proband and so we can say that there is a higher incidence of schizophrenia in the relatives of probands. According to Gottesman and Shields (1976), these early studies accepted without question that there was a genetic component to schizophrenia. What seemed to be of more interest was whether the genetic linkage was via a single gene (like eye colour). In the late 1930s, Kallmann (1938) showed that whilst the general incidence levels of schizophrenia are about 1%, the percentage of incidences in all family members of people with schizophrenia was around 15%. The details for each of the family groups are presented in Table 2.1.

In 1976, Gottesman and Shields produced a very comprehensive review of the studies that had taken place up until that point. Concerning family studies, they confirmed Kallmann's findings that a figure of about 10% for siblings of probands had been found in numerous studies. However, these appear to be only European figures. Studies from America appeared to have differing values. Winokur, Morrison, Clancy and Crowe (1974) reported a figure as low as 2.4% whilst Cammer (1970) had made it 27%. Reed, Hartley, Anderson, Phillips and Johnson (1973) reported on a study of 18,000 individuals with psychosis (so not purely schizophrenia). Siblings of psychotics were at 25% and children of psychotics at 26%. What was more interesting was that if the mother was psychotic the risk to children was 20%. However, if the psychotic was the father then the risk was only 8%. As with other research findings, this was not universally found as Bleuler (1972) found no differential maternal effect.

With the wealth of data from family studies pointing to a strong genetic component, researchers were interested in whether the different forms of schizophrenia were genetically separate. It seems here, as with the data on concordance rates, the picture is a mixed one. By examining the forms of schizophrenia seen within family groups, Perris (1974) concluded that different forms were genetically separate, but Larson and Nyman (1974) found no differences between first-degree relatives. However, there does seem to be more schizophrenia in the families of hebephrenic and catatonic subtypes than in the families of those with paranoid schizophrenia.

Since the flurry of activity in the 1970s there has been less interest in family studies as more and more excitement centred on trying to find out the

Relationship Type	Percentage incidence of schizophrenia (number of people)
Stepsiblings	1.8 (74)
marriage partners	2.1 (254)
half-siblings	7.0 (134)
Parents	9.2 (1,191)
full siblings	14.3 (2,741)
dizygotic co-twins	14.7 (517)
monozygotic co-twins	85.8 (174)

Table 2.1 Percentage Co-morbidity Rates Extracted from Kallmann (1938)

genes responsible, more of which later in the book. However, more recently Kendler et al. (1997) did study siblings in Ireland. They examined the concordance rates for 256 pairs where one sibling had schizophrenia and 457 pairs where one sibling had another kind of psychosis. Rather than just say whether the sibling had schizophrenia, they examined the cases for individual symptoms. They found small but significance concordance rates across nearly all symptoms in both groups. This suggests that the family factors that influence schizophrenia are not likely to be different from those affecting other forms of psychosis. When Kendler et al. looked at the types of schizophrenia represented in the sample, they found five separate classes. Through a complicated analysis of their data they concluded that schizophrenia is likely to be heterogeneous. This means that the disorder is likely to stem from more than one genetic focus. It could be that there are two or more genes that predispose a person to schizophrenia or that two or more pathogenic alleles reside at the same locus on one gene.

Twin studies

One of the first twin studies was conducted by Luxenburger (1928). This study was looking at whether there was good evidence of genetic inheritance by comparing the manifestation rates (rate of incidence) of monozygotic (MZ) and dizygotic (DZ) twins. A little later, Kallmann (1946) reported on 174 MZ twin pairs and 517 DZ twin pairs. His concordance rates (the number of cases where both twins were found to be schizophrenic) were higher for MZ twins than that reported by other investigators. Indeed, the incidence in MZ twins (86% after making an age correction) was found to be six times that of DZ twins. As a consequence, he suggested that the genetic component was substantial and far greater than that which could be accounted for by similarities in environmental upbringing. However, this was not accepted by all without criticism. Jackson (1960) stated that the environment for MZ twins was much more similar than that for DZ twins, and so the discounting of any major role for environmental influences might be premature. To counter this, the general incidence levels of schizophrenia were no higher for MZ twins than DZ twins. In other words, it wasn't the number of pairs in which at least one case of schizophrenia was seen that was different, just the number in which both twins were schizophrenic. If environmental factors were key, we might see the general incidence levels to be different.

A second criticism of Kallmann's study was the suggestion that his concordance rates for MZ twins were way higher than seen by other researchers and that this might be a consequence of methodological differences. To give some weight to this criticism, we can consider a study of identical twins by Tienari (1963). He studied 16 pairs of identical male twins born in Finland between 1920 and 1929 in which one of the pair had been diagnosed with schizophrenia. He found absolutely no cases where the other twin was also affected. So where Kallmann had found a **concordance rate** of 85.8%, Tienari found a concordance rate of 0%. Kallmann had not been alone in finding high concordance rates. For example, Essen-Moller (1963) had found a rate of 69% in identical twins and 13% in non-identical twins. So why were Tienari's results so different? It might be in the sampling method. Tienari's sample had been obtained from the register of births whereas the usual route to obtaining participants was hospital populations. It is possible, therefore, that the hospital population were more substantive cases of schizophrenia. Indeed, there is some suggestion that Tienari's population might not have had schizophrenia but some other form of psychosis. Furthermore, 12 of the twins of people with schizophrenia were described as being borderline and were therefore not counted as being concordant.

One of the potential criticisms of twin studies is the assumption that the environment has the same degree of influence for MZ and DZ twins. The concept of the equal environment assumption (EEA) assumes that MZ twins are not treated as more alike than two DZ twins, in which case environmental influences should be identical, leaving only the level of inherited similarity as an independent variable. One way that the EEA has been examined is to compare DZ twins with other siblings. After all, DZ twins are just as likely to share genes as either one of them with another sibling. If a DZ twin and another sibling differ in rates of schizophrenia then this would likely be due to something other than genetics. Kallmann (1946) reports such data and states that DZ twins have a concordance rate of 14,7% whilst sibling concordance is 14.3%. This strongly suggests that the environment is playing little role here. However, there are problems with Kallmann's data in that he reports MZ concordance rates way beyond that reported by anyone else and this must raise some doubt about the accuracy of his figures or of his methodology. This doubt is further strengthened by the fact that he found a difference between the concordance rates for same-sex DZ twins and opposite-sex DZ twins (12% and 6%, respectively).

In an attempt to draw together all that we know about schizophrenia, MacDonald and Schulz (2009) compiled a list of 22 facts that were derived from experts internationally. Concerning twin studies, they agreed that if one MZ twin has schizophrenia there is a 99-fold increase in the likelihood that the other identical twin will also be diagnosed with schizophrenia than a member of the general population. This is more than 20 times more than the odds ratio connected to any environmental marker. They also suggest that the reason the concordance rates are not as high as the odds would suggest is that many twins never fully manifest the disorder.

In summary, then, it would appear that the twin study data is rather inconclusive. On the one hand, the data seem to suggest that MZ twins have higher concordance rates than DZ twins. However, that difference is only valid if we can be sure of the truth of the concept of EEA. This has been questioned by the data comparing DZ twins and siblings. An alternative way of exploring the potential role of the environment was needed, and so we now need to consider the adoption studies.

◉ Adoption studies

Adoption studies involve looking at children who have been adopted and who develop schizophrenia and seeing who else in their biological family also has schizophrenia. The assumption here is that any concordances must be due to genetic factors as the environments in which the individuals would have grown up in would be so different and so would have been unlikely to both lead to schizophrenia developing. The importance of adoption studies should not be underestimated in this regard. Stromgren (1975), in a survey of genetic research in schizophrenia, stated:

> Although family studies and twin-studies tended to show the importance of genetic factors, the only quite unquestionable result of genetic studies, especially the twin-studies, was that environmental factors contribute extensively to the etiology of schizophrenia. Not until large scale studies of adoptees were performed was it possible to demonstrate with certainty the great importance also of genetic factors. [p. 17]

Two criteria for a good adoption study exist. Firstly, the adoption should take place before any diagnosis or suspicion of schizophrenia becomes apparent and not as a result of the discovery of schizophrenia. Secondly, the adoptees and their relatives should be relatively unknown to one another.

One of the main early centres of this work was in Denmark, where Kety and his colleagues examined numerous adoptees. To fulfil the two requirements detailed above, they decided not to carry out the research in the US where they were from. Kety, Rosenthal, Wender and Schulsinger (1968) considered 5,483 adopted children in Copenhagen and examined and interviewed the biological relatives and the adopted relatives of the 33 adoptees that had been diagnosed with schizophrenia. This was to establish whether any of them also had schizophrenia. In addition, Rosenthal et al. (1968) examined adoptees where the biological mother or father had become schizophrenic. Both studies also used matched controls and the examinations were carried out blindly (i.e. by people who did not know who was who). The results of the first study showed that the concordance rates between biological relatives were higher than for controls. This gave a good starting point for arguing that there is a strong genetic component to schizophrenia. The results of the second study gave similar confirmatory results. Where an adoptee was living with a foster parent who developed schizophrenia, there was no greater chance than usual that the adoptee would develop the disorder. However, where a biological parent had been diagnosed with schizophrenia, the adoptee shows more psychopathology even though that person is being raised by unaffected individuals.

Another result that Kety obtained from his adoption study was that there seemed to be a relationship between schizophrenia and other kinds of disorders that we now refer to as schizotypal personality disorder. In addition, latent schizophrenia was seen in the relatives of patients with affective disorders. It would seem, then, that there is a 'schizophrenia spectrum' of disorders that are not full-blown schizophrenia but are related to it (Kety, 1980).

These findings have not been without criticism. It seems that most of the cases reported above refer to incidences among second-degree relatives. If the linkage is genetic, we would expect the greater concordance to be among first-degree relatives, where the degree of genetic similarity would be at its highest (Benjamin, 1976). Similarly, Gottesman and Shields (1976) point out that genetic theory would predict a much higher risk for first-generation siblings.

A further problem for these data is the fact that there were only 33 adoptees found to have schizophrenia out of 5,483 adoptees tested. This is just 0.6% which is below the 1% we would expect in the general population. This begs the question as to whether being brought up in an adoptive family environment is beneficial in preventing someone who may be schizophrenia prone from developing the disorder. If true, that would make the environment significant but in the reverse way to that which was expected and being tested for.

Tienari et al. (1987) conducted the Finnish Adoptive Family Study. The study involved schizophrenic mothers who had offered up their offspring for adoption and these were compared with matched controls where the mother had not been schizophrenic. Of the 112 adoptees from schizophrenic mothers (referred to as index), eight were found to have schizophrenia whereas of the 135 controls, only two of the offspring had schizophrenia. Whilst this might point to a genetic explanation, an analysis of these offspring revealed something more. Of the 10 people with schizophrenia, none was reared in healthy or mildly disturbed adoptive families. All 10 had been reared in disturbed adoptive families. This suggests that the environment may be critical in the expression of schizophrenia where a genetic vulnerability already exists.

To summarise these adoption studies, they do seem to point more clearly to the genetic origins of schizophrenia, or at least to the idea that there is a strong genetic component. However, they also provide us with the need to recognise that there are also environmental triggers, and so the explanation of the cause of schizophrenia is complex.

👁 Endophenotypes

The concept of an **endophenotype** has been borrowed from insect biology and is the idea that there are inherited behaviours that accompany an illness like schizophrenia and that are expressed even if the full-blown illness is not evident. They can be contrasted with exophenotypes which are the external symptoms of a disorder that clinicians detect during an examination. They are less prone to subjective judgment than is the assessment of symptom itself. As Gottesman and Shields (1972) note, the endophenotypes that have been identified for schizophrenia suggest that the disorder is a polygenic condition, that is, it is the result of the combination of a number of different gene effects. One example of an endophenotype that accompanies schizophrenia is the fact that people with schizophrenia typically suffer eye movement dysfunctions. A large number of schizophrenia patients have difficulty following a moving target with their eyes (Lipton, Levy, Holzman, & Levin, 1983). If they are asked to follow a moving spot of light, they do so with irregular eye movements, rather than the smooth eye movements that are typical of the way in which an unaffected person will follow the spot. It is estimated that between 25% and 40% of these patients' first-degree relatives show the same dysfunction. By contrast, only about 5% of the unaffected population shows the same pattern. It has been discovered that the impaired smooth pursuit occurs only when higher cortical centres are recruited, as in following a moving car. A further analysis showed that in schizophrenia patients, the eyes do not move as fast as they should to keep up with the target's speed. That is, those with abnormal smooth pursuit eye movements lag behind the moving target, and compensatory saccadic eye movements (where the eyes make a darting movement) become necessary to keep the target in central view (Levin et al., 1988). The Levin et al. study showed that the eye tracking abnormality occurs about seven times more frequently in the families of schizophrenia patients than does schizophrenia itself. The motor apparatus functions normally in schizophrenia, and it is likely that this dysfunction is located in the middle temporal and the medial superior temporal areas. Studies have shown that lesions to these areas impair motion detection and produce the same kind of eye tracking abnormalities that we see in schizophrenia (Newsome, Wurtz,

Dursteler & Mikami, 1985). Chen, Nakayama, Levy, Matthysse and Holzman (1999) have confirmed that schizophrenic patients and a portion of their relatives do have difficulty in accurately detecting the speed of moving objects, although their other visual capacities, such as detection of colour, contrast or position, are unaffected.

Box 2.1 The Family Study Method (Tienari et al. 1987)

One way of exploring genetic inheritance is to test/study as many people from one family group as possible. Tienari et al. (1987) carried out a nationwide study in Finland to try to find as many families as they could where at least one child had been adopted. They found that a total of 247 families came forward to participate in the study and, of these, 112 were where the biological mother was either suffering from schizophrenia or had been diagnosed with a paranoid psychosis. They then examined the records of all of the adopted children looking to see who had been diagnosed with schizophrenia. They only found ten cases but, remarkably, eight had come from biological mothers with schizophrenia and only two had not.

Despite these quite impressive findings, there are a number of methodological issues that we must consider before getting too excited. Many of the mothers were born as early as 1910 and so we cannot be certain of the accuracy of the original diagnosis. The number of adoptions from people with schizophrenia might be over-represented from low socioeconomic groups. This is because they are more likely to have had adoption forced upon them. The sample will also exclude those who had a very early onset of schizophrenia, those who had severe psychosis and those whose social withdrawal was severe, as they are unlikely to have had children. Finally, a child put up for adoption is likely to have problems that are associated with being an adopted child, particularly if they are placed in a family where there are already children that are biologically related to the adopting parents.

Studies such as these are also inclined to have high attrition rates, that is, where participants do not complete the study. When trying to keep track of the adopted children over a period of years, some may die and some may not wish to be interviewed. Some further children will be found to have been adopted by other families.

Despite these potential shortcomings, family adoption studies provide a useful insight into the possibility that a feature is genetically inherited. Of course, no one methodology can answer the question on its own but, taken together with other lines of enquiry, the family adoption study can ask a genuine question about the relative roles of heritability and environmental control.

Environmental factors

Without denying that the evidence for the heritability of schizophrenia is strong, it is likely that a number of environmental factors can either cause or contribute to the development of schizophrenia. Firstly, we must not rule out the possibility that there are different routes to developing schizophrenia, some that are genetic and some that are environmental. Secondly, any genetic indicators for schizophrenia may well act as propensities rather than absolute causes. In other words, a person may have a genetic vulnerability to developing schizophrenia but it might require certain environmental triggers to occur for full-blown psychosis to be initiated. What, then, have researchers proposed as either environmental causes or triggers for schizophrenia?

A review article by Brown (2011) provides an enormous wealth of detail about possible environmental factors in the development of schizophrenia. Whilst incidence figures are quite varied, there appears to be a difference in incidence rates between developed and developing countries if a broad definition of schizophrenia is used. This might indicate that living in poorer circumstances increases your risk of getting schizophrenia. However, we must not jump to conclusions as it might be that genetic markers are more likely to manifest themselves in conditions that lead to stress and/or poor general health.

It appears that there might be other situational factors too. Being raised in an urban environment increases the risk, although whether or not you are born in an urban or rural environment does not (Pedersen & Mortensen, 2006). Veling et al. (2008) further showed that being an immigrant living in a neighbourhood where there are not many fellow immigrants also increases risk. Perhaps the stress of discrimination is a contributory factor here. Or perhaps these environmental markers lead to physical changes that can elevate the chances of becoming schizophrenic (e.g. lack of vitamin D or increased exposure to microbial pathogens). We will explore the impact of the social environment in much greater detail in Chapter 6.

As well as place of birth, time of birth has been cited as a factor. It appears that you are 5–15% more likely to develop schizophrenia if you are born in the winter or early spring (Bradbury & Miller, 1985). However, the underlying cause of this remains unknown. Nevertheless, taken together with the urban information we might speculate that those born in winter and raised in an urban environment might be more exposed to pathogens early in life and to pollutants throughout their formative years. Suggestions that the development of schizophrenia is caused by the brain failing to develop properly (see Chapter 3) would be consistent with such environmental issues. On a slightly different temporal note, how long ago you were born may also be important. The incidence rates for schizophrenia have declined slightly over the last 50 years or so and this might be due to improvements in obstetric care. We shall see the possible reasons for this shortly.

A number of theories suggest that schizophrenia is the result of complications in the foetus or at birth. We know that foetal exposure to microbes such as rubella, herpes simplex or even syphilis can lead to neuropsychiatric problems such as learning difficulties. A front runner for schizophrenia was the influenza virus. Early studies suggested that exposure to influenza during the second trimester of pregnancy increased the risk of schizophrenia. The link had been deduced from a significant increase in schizophrenia among those who were exposed to the 1957 influenza pandemic. However, subsequent reanalysis of the data have shown that there is some doubt about the accuracy of determining who had and who had not been exposed to the virus so the theory is unreliable. The data concerning exposure to rubella during pregnancy is far more rigorous. It would seem that such exposure confers a 20% increased risk of developing schizophrenia. It would seem that the virus leads to a decrease in development of key intellectual and motor skills during childhood and adolescence.

Nutrition, or lack of it, during pregnancy has also been linked to schizophrenia. There were twice as many people with schizophrenia among those whose mothers were starving during Nazi occupation in the World War II. Similar findings have been obtained for the Chinese famine of 1959–1961. However, the data have been collected retrospectively, so their accuracy may be a little suspect. Given that famine is not seen in hose parts of the world where the diagnosis of schizophrenia is accurate and consistent, we do not have any comparative data to work with. However, we do have animal data. Research in which pregnant animals are food deprived shows that their offspring develop brain abnormalities consistent with those seen in schizophrenia. Furthermore, some of the consequent behavioural impairments are not apparent until after puberty. This is wholly consistent with what we see in humans.

Other nutritional markers include iron deficiency, vitamin D deficiency and prenatal obesity. The latter can be measured using the body mass index (BMI). This is calculated using your height and weight and is standardised for age and gender. An elevated BMI can lead to a number of consequences that could be linked to schizophrenia. These include an inattentiveness to the body's nutritional needs during pregnancy, obstetric complications and diabetes as a direct consequence of being overweight.

One of the more robust correlates of schizophrenia is paternal age. Originally, Johanson, (1958) had suggested that having older parents increased the risk of schizophrenia in their children but was unable to determine if this was mother, father or both. Hare and Moran (1979) were able to confirm that it is older fathers that are the problem. Fathers between 45 and 49 doubled the risk and fathers over 50 tripled the risk. Whilst there have been differences recorded by subsequent studies carried out across the globe, the basic result that older fathers increase the risk has been replicated over and over again. The probable cause of this age-related risk is the fact that the stem cells from which sperm are generated replicate throughout life. With each replication there is a risk that the replication will not be perfect and that mutations will occur. Simple arithmetic dictates that the longer the period over which replication takes place, the more mutations that are likely to have occurred and hence the more likely sperm are to have been produced from maladapted stem cells.

Maternal stress

Many studies have suggested that if a mother gets overly stressed during pregnancy then her offspring can be affected. Some of these studies have proposed a link directly to schizophrenia. For example, Khashan et al. (2008) conducted a study of over 7,000 cases and found that those mothers who had been exposed during their first three months of pregnancy to the death of a relative, or who had a relative who was diagnosed as having cancer, acute heart failure or a stroke, had offspring with a 1.67-fold increased risk of developing schizophrenia and related disorders.

Other studies have suggested a link between the maternal stress during invasions by the Nazis in World War II and from the Six Day War in Israel in 1967. Stress might not just come in the form of external events. In studies of unwanted pregnancy, there has also been a link made to an increased risk of the offspring developing schizophrenia (D. B. Herman et al., 2006).

Whilst we have treated maternal stress here separately from obstetric complications, we must be mindful of the potential links between the two (and, indeed, between several of the environmental issues discussed here).

For example, maternal stress could give rise to poor nutrition which in turn could lead to decreased birth weight. The maturational deficits of the developing foetus' brain could be the trigger for the later manifestation of schizophrenia.

Cannabis

We will now turn to look at some of the links that have been made between cannabis use amongst adolescents and the development of schizophrenia. It is, perhaps, not surprising that this is the recreational drug with the strongest links. On the one hand, we might think of the harder drugs, heroin, LSD and cocaine, as being more dangerous to mental health. However, it is the most widely used drug by this age group and its physiology points to some interesting potential mechanisms.

A study in Sweden looked at 40,000 males who were conscripted into the military and were followed for 15 years. There was found to be a twofold increase in the risk of schizophrenia. These findings persisted when the group was further followed up after 27 years. Amongst heavy cannabis users, the increase was up to six times the risk (Zammit, Allebeck, Andreasson, Lundberg & Lewis, 2002). These findings have been repeated in the Netherlands, Germany and in New Zealand with risk increases all of the order of twofold.

It would seem that the active ingredient in cannabis, tetrahydrocannabinol (THC), enhances the activity of **dopamine** in susceptible individuals. It does this by blocking the inhibitory inputs to dopamine, and so dopamine release is unregulated and allowed to exceed its normal limits. Recent research by Caspi et al. (2005) has found that an alteration to one of the enzymes that breaks down dopamine (catechol-o-methyltransferase – COMT) and is relevant to the development of schizophrenia. Presence of this form of the COMT enzyme was exacerbated by cannabis use and this may account for the increased dopamine activity.

Socioeconomic status

As already mentioned, schizophrenia seems to be more prevalent among the poorer quarters of the population. Two theories have sought to explain this. The first is called social causation and proposes that those individuals from lower socio-economic backgrounds expose themselves to greater risks. The second claims that it is not necessarily the case that people with schizophrenia start off in lower social classes, but because of the nature of the disorder they often end up there. This theory is called social drift. Studies that have tried to distinguish between these two theories have, by and large, failed. However, a recent study by Wicks, Hjern, Gunnell, Lewis and Dalman (2005) does point more towards the social causation theory. They showed in a group of Swedish participants that there was a higher schizophrenia risk if the offspring came from situations where there was parental unemployment, single parenting and the receipt of social welfare.

Childhood trauma

Finally, in this analysis, we will look at the effect of childhood trauma on the risk of getting schizophrenia. There are reports that there is a link between the likelihood of becoming psychotic and having had a childhood traumatic experience. However, unlike elsewhere in this field, the studies have been generally quite small. Bebbington et al. (2004) reported a threefold increase following sexual abuse, and Janssen et al. (2004) claimed a massive sevenfold increase if the abuse occurred before the age of 16. However, another study has not agreed with this and Spataro, Mullen, Burgess, Wells, and Moss (2004) found no link. Whilst it is difficult to draw any firm conclusions, we will revisit this concern when we look at some of the non-biological causes of schizophrenia.

Epigenetics

DNA is the code that exists in every one of our cells to tell them what to be and how to behave. It is the genetic material that makes one cell into a heart muscle cell and another into a neurone. It also controls the way a cell grows, divides and the chemicals that it produces that may be specialist to that type of cell. In short, DNA is the key to how every part of our bodies works. It is the carrier of our genetic code. Whilst it is easy to think of this set of biological processes as set in stone at birth, there is a lot of evidence that these processes can be altered by things that we experience in our environment. At a very basic level, we understand that when we learn something these changes are in some way made permanent within our neuronal system so that we can recall information at a later date. Hence we know that the environment can change our brains. So given what we have covered so far in this chapter about the interplay between inherited charac- teristics and the influence of the environment regarding schizophrenia, it makes sense to ask if we have any understanding of the mechanism by which the environment can influence the development of schizophrenia. **Epigenetics** is the study of the regulatory processes that modify how our DNA works and research in this area has given us clues as to how the environment might have an effect on the expression of our genes.

The epigenome is a further layer of information that mediates these changes to the gene expression.

Epigenetics, as an idea, is not particularly new. Irving I Gottesman, Shields and Hanson (1982) wrote a book called *Scizophrenia: The Epigenetic Puzzle*. However, over the last thirty years our techniques for exploring the molecular mechanisms involved in epigenetics have much improved. After all, thirty years ago we had not yet sequenced the entire human genome. The precise mechanisms of epigenetics are well beyond the scope of this text, so what follows here is the essence of what this field contributes to our understanding of schizophrenia. In brief, the mechanisms of interest are ones that affect DNA transcription, the first part of the protein production factory of a cell. This is the process by which the code on DNA inside the nucleus of the cell gets transferred to RNA which can communicate the commands to the protein factories (ribosomes) in the cytoplasm. Two critical questions are of importance. Does a person's environment influence the way that his/her genes are expressed? Can changes to gene expression be passed on to the next generation? The simple answer to both of these questions appears to be yes. As we will see in the next chapter, both **serotonin** and dopamine are neurotransmitters that are associated with schizophrenia, and there have been indications of epigenetic changes to the receptors for both of these chemicals within the brains of patients. For serotonin, the link first came through the fact that LSD, a recreational drug, can produce a form of psychosis that includes hallucinations and delusions (though not the negative symptoms). This drug is known to work at the same receptor sites that are implicated in epigenetic changes for people with schizophrenia (Williams, McGuffin, Nothen & Owen, 1997). For dopamine, the link seems to be to an alteration of the enzyme COMT (seen previously in relation to cannabis use) such that the enzyme does not function properly. This ties in well with the dopamine theory of schizophrenia that we will explore in the next chapter and we will return to some more of the mechanisms of epigenetics then. For now let us return to the principles of epigenetics to explore further why this is so important to our current thinking about the heritability of schizophrenia.

According to Dempster, Viana, Pidsley and Mill (2013) and others, "Epigenetic processes, which developmentally regulate gene expression via modifications to DNA, histone proteins, and chromatin, have been widely heralded as the 'missing piece' of the aetiological puzzle for a spectrum of complex disease phenotypes including SZ." (p. 11) Epigenetics has been suggested as providing an explanation for why the concordance rate for monozygotic twins is consistently found to be less than 65%. It would appear that the most critical environmental risks for developing schizophrenia occur at around the same time that the epigenome is most responsive to external influences. For example, prenatal exposure to famine has been shown to be linked with schizophrenia and this might be mediated by epigenetic pathways.

Whilst there is a lot of excitement about epigenetics and the fact that this may be the bridge connecting genetic and environmental influences, we must exercise some caution. To date, most of the discoveries have been either via an analysis of the postmortem brain or via experiments using animal models. The former do not allow us to explore the direction of causation and hence leave us not knowing if the schizophrenia is a result of such changes or the cause of them. Nevertheless, some encouraging findings regarding differences between schizophrenic and non-schizophrenic brains are starting to emerge. Whilst animal models can shed some light on this, we must be careful not to simply extrapolate from animals to humans. Future research may be able to use our epigenetic knowledge to produce drugs that are better targeted at relieving the symptoms of schizophrenia.

◉ Chapter summary

It is clear that if schizophrenia is a genetic disorder then the genes involved are complex. Family studies, twin studies and adoption studies all suggest that there is a genetic component to schizophrenia, but there is no clear agreement as to how influential this genetic element is. Whilst a few researchers may deny that it plays any real role at all, most would consider that one can inherit a genetic propensity for schizophrenia but that the manifestation of the disorder is probably via a combination of gene and environmental influences. As far as environmental influences are concerned, many may lead to altered brain functioning. Furthermore, this may be more likely in those individuals who are genetically predisposed, and so the link between environmental and genetic causes becomes very blurred.

◉ Further reading

Bertram, L. (2008) Genetic research in schizophrenia: new tools and future perspectives. *Schizophrenia Bulletin*, 34, 806–812.

Herman, D.B., Brown, A.S., Opler M.G., Desai M., Malaspina, D., Bresnahan, M., Schaefer, C.A. and Susser, E.S. (2006) Does unwantedness of pregnancy predict schizophrenia in the offspring?: Findings from a prospective birth cohort study. *Social Psychiatry and Psychiatric Epidemiology*, 41, 605–610

Khashan, A.S., Abel, K.M., McNamee, R., Pedersen, M.G., Webb, R.T., Baker, P.N., Kenny, L.C. and Mortensen, P.B. (2008) Higher risk of offspring schizophrenia following antenatal maternal exposure to severe adverse life events. *Archives of General Psychiatry*, 65, 146–152.

Morgan, C. and Fisher, H. (2007) Environmental factors in schizophrenia: childhood trauma – A critical review. *Schizophrenia Bulletin*, 33, 3–10.

Zammit, S., Allebeck, P., Andreasson, S., Lundberg, I. and Lewis, G. (2002) Self reported cannabis use as a risk factor for schizophrenia in Swedish conscripts of 1969: Historical cohort study. *British Medical Journal*, 325: 1199.

Chapter 3

Neurotransmitter Explanations

Introduction

We should not be surprised to discover that various researchers have linked schizophrenia to a problem with the functioning of a neurotransmitter (NT) substance within the brain. What might come as more of a surprise is that we still know relatively little about how neurotransmitter function interplays with schizophrenia? Two key questions are at play here.

1   Is the link between schizophrenia and neurotransmitter function one of cause or effect?
2   Which neurotransmitter substances are involved? The first question reminds us that it is not enough to show a correlation between schizophrenia and NT failure. We need to investigate whether the NT failure is enough to cause schizophrenia or whether NT failure is a consequence of having schizophrenia. Even if the NT is believed to be a cause, we can still ask whether it is a primary or secondary cause. A primary cause would imply that the NT failure directly leads to schizophrenia whereas as a secondary cause something else would lead to the NT failure which, in turn, would then lead to schizophrenia. As a consequence of schizophrenia, we would be suggesting that having schizophrenia leads to some form of plasticity changes within the brain that results in the NT not functioning properly. The second question simply reminds us that we must examine carefully the quality of the evidence from neuroscience in determining whether or not a particular NT has either a causal role in, or is a consequential casualty of, schizophrenia.

Rather than treating each of these questions separately, the chapter will examine closely, in turn, each of the NTs that have been suggested to be involved. We begin with the most well-known of the hypotheses, the dopamine hypothesis, and then examine the possible roles of serotonin (5HT) and **glutamate**. However, before looking at the NTs, let's start with a very brief refresher of what a NT is and how it works.

In this chapter we will cover:
- What is a neurotransmitter?
- The dopamine hypothesis
- The glutamate hypothesis of schizophrenia
- The serotonin hypothesis of schizophrenia
- Combining the dopamine, glutamate and serotonin hypotheses

👁 What is a neurotransmitter?

A neurotransmitter (NT) is a chemical substance that is released from the end of the axon of a neuron when the neuron is active and fires an action potential. Once released, it diffuses into the gap between the axon of the first neuron and, let's say for our purposes, the dendrite of the next neuron. If a NT molecule lands on a receptor on the dendrite that is the right kind for that NT, this will have a small effect on whether or not the next neuron in the system will fire its own action potential. Whether this effect is to encourage or discourage that neuron from firing will depend on the NT and the effect it has on the membrane of the receiving neuron.

We do not need to go into further details here. It is enough for you to realize that the NT system is complex, and so there are numerous ways in which it can go wrong. Figure 3.1 shows a few of the key events in neurotransmission at the synapse. For example, not enough NT might be synthesized by the releasing neuron, and so an action potential in that neuron may become totally ineffective. Alternatively, the releasing mechanism can be altered, the receptor may be blocked or a number of other changes to the system may lead to the NT not having the required effect on the receiving neuron. So the net effect of all of this would be that there would be a noticeable reduction of the functioning of the NT. However, we are not finished there. The opposite effect can also occur such that an excess of the NT might be produced and/or released, or the mechanisms that degrade (destroy) the NT after it has had its effect or that scoop it back up into the releasing neuron (called reuptake) might falter and lead to the NT acting for longer

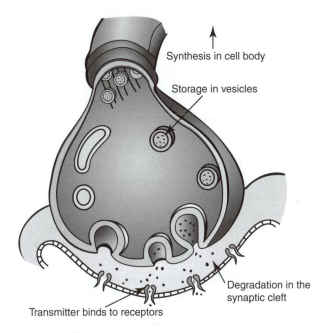

Synthesis in cell body

Storage in vesicles

Degradation in the
synaptic cleft

Transmitter binds to receptors

Figure 3.1 Some Key Neurotransmitter Events

than it should. So the net effect here would be an increase in the functioning
of the NT but one that was, nevertheless, maladaptive.

Given the complexity of healthy NT functioning, we can appreciate how
hard it is for researchers to gather precise information about NT changes
that might be associated with schizophrenia. General ideas, such as the
suggestion that there is too much of a NT present, are relatively easy to
establish but the precise mechanisms that underlie such findings are anything
but simple.

The dopamine hypothesis

This hypothesis suggests that the cause of schizophrenia is the hyperactivity
of dopamine within a system of the brain called the limbic system. The
limbic system is comprised of a number of different brain structures and is
thought to be involved in the control of memory, emotions and our reward
systems. In order to examine this theory in detail, it is useful to first briefly
explain both what dopamine is and what the limbic system does.

Dopamine is a type of chemical molecule called a monoamine. Several monoamines are NTs, others including noradrenalin and serotonin. Dopamine is a catecholamine type of monoamine. Dopamine functions as both an excitatory neurotransmitter substance, making it more likely that the receiving neuron will fire an action potential, and an inhibitory neurotransmitter substance, making it less likely that the receiving neuron will fire an action potential. It is a well-known NT within the brain's reward systems and the actions of recreational drugs like cocaine act to prolong the activity of naturally released dopamine, thereby increasing the pleasure.

The way in which dopamine acts is complicated further by the fact that there are different types of dopamine receptor. These are labelled D_1 to D_5. It is believed the action of dopamine on the D_2 receptor is the critical component in the explanation of schizophrenia.

Dopamine activity is found in a number of brain systems but it is its actions in the mesolimbic pathway that are thought to be associated with schizophrenia. This pathway originates in an area of the brain called the ventral tegmental area (VTA in Figure 3.2) and projects to areas in the limbic system, particularly the nucleus acumbens, hippocampus and amygdala. It also projects to the part of the frontal cortex. These are all major components of the brain's reward system.

Version 1

The dopamine hypothesis has undergone a number of transformations over the years, since it was first constructed from data gathered between 1952 and

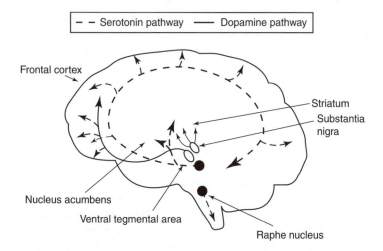

Figure 3.2 Mesolimbic Pathways

the mid-1970s. This very first version of the hypothesis proposed that schizophrenia was simply caused by an excess of dopamine activity. The data that had been gathered which led to this conclusion included three important findings.

1 Delay, Deniker and Harl (1952) had discovered antipsychotic drugs.
2 Carlsson and Lindqvist (1963) had realized that these drugs increased the metabolism of dopamine (i.e. made it degrade more rapidly).
3 A number of studies showed that amphetamine could induce psychotic symptoms and reserpine could treat them. This was significant because amphetamine was known to increase synaptic monoamine levels and reserpine was known to block the reuptake of dopamine.

Then in the 1970s, it was discovered that the effectiveness of psychoactive drugs was directly related to the fact that they blocked the dopamine receptors and so reduced the effectiveness of the dopamine being released by the presynaptic neuron. The first version of the dopamine hypothesis had been born.

There were a couple of important shortfalls to this first version. Firstly, the hypothesis did not explain whether the excess dopamine activity was responsible for the positive symptoms, the negative symptoms, or both. Secondly, there were some known risk factors for schizophrenia but this theory did not address what relationship dopamine might have to these factors.

Version 2

The second, modified version of the dopamine hypothesis was produced by Davis, Kahn, Ko and Davidson (1991). Questions were being asked about the emphasis being placed on the role of the D_2 dopamine receptor since dopamine transmission in the prefrontal cortex is mediated via D_1 receptors. The main evidence for this was the effectiveness of the drug clozapine for those who failed to respond to other drugs, coupled with the knowledge that this drug did not tend to occupy and block the D_2 receptor very effectively. This, along with other information derived from postmortem analyses and PET imaging, implied that schizophrenia was not simply the result of an excess of dopamine neurotransmission.

Davis et al. (1991) proposed that the effects of abnormal dopamine activity could vary by brain region. In the frontal lobe, the indications were that the levels of dopamine activity were low. They suggested that this may account for the negative symptoms of schizophrenia. Furthermore, they argued that the low levels of activity in the frontal regions of the brain gave rise to consequent higher levels of dopamine activity in a region of the brain called the striatum. This increased striatal activity was being suggested as the cause of the positive symptoms.

There was just one drawback to this second version of the dopamine hypothesis. Most of the evidence had been gained from animal studies and it was inferred that the same situation applied to humans. In addition, there was no direct evidence for the suggested low levels of dopamine activity in the frontal lobes and only limited direct evidence for the increased activity in the striatum. Probably most critical of all, there was no explanation of why low frontal levels would lead to the negative symptoms or why high striatal levels would lead to the positive symptoms.

Version 3

So we are now on our third version of the dopamine hypothesis and this is a consequence of the vast interest since 1991. Nearly 7000 articles have been published about the role of dopamine since 1991 and this represents a vast amount of research. So what has this research told us? Firstly, the increased levels of striatal dopamine have been confirmed and the reason for this elevation has been explored (Howes & Kapur, 2009). It would seem that the cause is an increase in its synthesis in the presynaptic neurons and hence an increased release when an action potential travels along that neuron. However, the amount of dopamine synthesized seems to be sensitive to whether or not a person is psychotic at the time. When a schizophrenic patient is having a psychotic episode, it would appear that the amount of synaptic dopamine increases.

Alongside the elevated levels of striatal dopamine, there is also about a 10–20% increase in the number of D_2 receptors in the striatum. This increase appears not to be present outside of this striatal region (Takahashi, Higuchi & Suhara, 2006). However, as we have seen, prefrontal dopamine is mediated by D_1 receptors. Dysfunction in these receptors has been linked to the cognitive impairment and negative symptoms seen in schizophrenia. So we can see that the symptoms of schizophrenia are better accounted for by modifications to the notion that only the D_2 receptor is involved.

The advancement of imaging studies in the last 20 years has allowed researchers to track neurotransmitter function. Such studies have confirmed that striatal dopamine is elevated in patients with schizophrenia and that such elevation is closely linked to the psychotic symptoms. In addition, imaging has also shown that blocking this elevated activity either by blocking dopamine release or by blocking the postsynaptic receptors leads to a reduction of these symptoms for most patients (see Frankle & Laruelle (2002) for a review).

Since the second version of the dopamine hypothesis came out, the Human Genome Project has been undertaken. This project has successfully mapped every gene in human DNA. Of course, that is only the beginning of being able to understand what each of these genes does but that quest is now well underway. So what has this been able to tell us about any genetic origins of schizophrenia? We are now almost certain that no one single gene codes for schizophrenia. There are likely to be a large number of genes that all have a small effect on the overall picture. However, it has been suggested that four of the top ten genes thought to be involved are directly involved with dopamine activity (Talkowski et al., 2008).

One significant advance in the new version of the dopamine hypothesis is that it attempts to take into account environmental risk factors for schizophrenia. We know that a number of these factors cannot be explained by genetics. They include migration, unemployment, urban upbringing, lack of close friends and child abuse. However, there are animal studies that suggest many of these conditions, especially social isolation, can lead to over-activity in dopaminergic systems (Hall, Wilkinson, Humby & Robbins, 1999). We also now know that complications during pregnancy (another suggested environmental risk) can lead to long-term dopamine overactivity (Boksa & El-Khodor, 2003), as can prenatal and neonatal stress, such as maternal separation (Kehoe, Clash, Skipsey & Shoemaker, 1996).

There have been suggestions that psychoactive substance use can also be a risk factor for schizophrenia. Arseneault, Cannon, Witton and Murray (2004) looked at the evidence linking cannabis use to psychosis. It was clearly identified as a risk factor, and the evidence points to the idea that the active component increases striatal dopamine release. Ketamine has also been identified as a drug that can lead to the dopamine levels in people without schizophrenic rising to that seen in people with schizophrenia. There is even a suggestion that psychoactive drugs that do not directly act on dopamine systems may do so indirectly.

So to sum up the interplay between genetic and environmental factors and their relationship to dopamine functioning, these factors do not work in isolation but a lot of them point to changes in the dopamine system. Further-more, these changes are often specific to the region of the brain where the relationship to psychosis is strongest, namely, the striatum. It is even the case that these changes are seen in people who are at risk but who have not yet developed schizophrenia. Some have even suggested that dopamine abnormalities might underlie 'psychosis proneness'.

We can ask whether these dopamine changes are specific to schizophrenia or whether they accompany any form of psychosis. Striatal dopamine eleva-tion is not seen in any psychiatric disorders that do not involve psychosis, but it has been reported in at least one other form of psychosis. In addition, antipsychotic drugs that block dopamine activity are effective in any form of psychosis no matter whether that psychosis accompanies schizophrenia or another disorder, such as mania, depression or Parkinson's Disease.

Our final analysis of the dopamine hypothesis has to ask whether we can link any of these findings to the specific symptoms of psychosis. One suggestion is that the abnormal activity of dopamine leads to the patient attributing too much importance (salience) to innocuous stimuli. This is believed to give rise to the emergence of hallucinations and delusions over time and also accounts for why the manifestations of these delusions and hallucinations can be so different in different individuals and across different cultures. The same problem might account for the negative symptoms. If the change in dopamine activity leads to the heightened salience of all stimuli then the patient may not be able to differentiate rewarding events from other events. If they therefore come to believe that they never receive rewards, then over time that person is likely to socially withdraw and develop negative symptoms.

To summarise all of these pieces of data, it would appear that many of the markers of schizophrenia, both genetic and environmental, have an influence on dopamine functioning so as to elevate levels of striatal dopamine. It would seem that the new focus of this excessive dopamine activity is presynaptic synthesis and release rather than increased D_2 receptor activity. Finally, the altered dopamine activity is linked to psychosis generally and not to schizophrenia specifically and is possibly the result of a misplaced salience being imparted to insignificant stimuli.

👁 The glutamate hypothesis of schizophrenia

You may well be thinking that after such extensive research around the role of dopamine, there could be little room for any other explanations. However, it is clear that, whilst dopamine can explain a lot about schizophrenia, it is by no means a complete hypothesis. Dopamine excess can explain the positive symptoms of schizophrenia, the delusions and the hallucinations, but it cannot explain either the negative symptoms or the cognitive deficits that accompany schizophrenia (we will explore these cognitive deficits in Chapter 6). Furthermore, dopamine antagonists do not alleviate these elements of schizophrenia even after the dopamine system has been stabilised by drugs. One of the other neurotransmitter substances that it has been suggested may play a part in these other elements of schizophrenia is glutamate.

Glutamate is the major excitatory neurotransmitter substance in the central nervous system. Indeed, nearly half of all of the neurons in the brain use glutamate. One of the major places that glutamate acts is the N-methyl-D-aspartate (NMDA) receptor. This is present in areas of the brain that are known to be involved in some of the key functions that are impaired in schizophrenia. These include **working memory**, attention and associative learning. NMDA receptors are also known to be involved in the development of the brain in adolescence. This development involves the reduction of cortical connections in the brain. As adolescence is a key time for the development of schizophrenia, a problem with this developmental process could easily be related to the development of schizophrenia.

It was Kim, Kornhuber, Schmid-Burgk and Holzmüller (1980) who first suggested the relationship between glutamate function and schizophrenia. They discovered that the levels of glutamate were lower in the cerebrospinal fluid of people with schizophrenia than those without schizophrenia. Whilst there was some dispute about this evidence at the time, research since has confirmed the place of glutamate as a significant player in schizophrenia. Two findings, in particular, have reopened the case for glutamate and both come from illicit drug use. The first is the finding that phencyclidine (PCP), also known as angel dust, can induce schizophrenia-like symptoms in unaffected individuals. The second is that ketamine can do the same. In addition, both PCP and ketamine have been shown to reduce NMDA receptor function in the cortical association areas. This would lead to a variety of cognitive deficits of the type seen in people with schizophrenia. Indeed, various authors have noted that these drugs can mimic positive, negative and cognitive symptoms of schizophrenia, including delusions, blunted affect and deficits in attention (Javitt & Zukin, 1991; Lahti, Koffel, LaPorte & Tamminga, 1995).

We can ask whether a glutamate hypothesis can account for the timing of schizophrenia as well as the condition. After all, if a lack of glutamate functioning were present from birth then why would schizophrenia typically emerge around puberty? Also, can glutamate inactivity account for all of the symptoms shown by people with schizophrenia? Olney, Newcomer and Farber (1999) have proposed that a glutamate hypothesis can do exactly that. In the context of the range of conditions associated with schizophrenia, Olney et al. (1999) argue that NMDA receptor hypofunction can not only trigger its own effects but can also trigger knock-on effects downstream of where the glutamate should be working. We know from research using NMDA antagonists (drugs that block the NMDA receptor) that the result is an excessive release of glutamate and acetylcholine in the cerebral cortex. As these are both excitatory neurotransmitters, this could explain the cognitive and behavioural disturbances we observe in schizophrenia. The argument for why this all gets triggered around puberty is that whilst this hypofunctioning of NMDA receptors is present all along, it is only when developmental changes to the brain occur around puberty that the conditions are right for the behaviours to be expressed. In other words, schizophrenia is a neurotransmitter time-bomb waiting to explode.

At the neuronal level, there is now a lot of evidence to confirm that NMDA receptor function is depressed in people with schizophrenia. Some of those genes that we have already considered to be associated with increased risk of schizophrenia have been shown to affect NMDA receptor function (Bita Moghaddam, 2003). Postmortem studies (Clinton & Meador-Woodruff, 2004) and imaging studies (Pilowsky et al., 2006) have confirmed this idea. It would also appear that the decrease in glutamate efficacy has a dopamine effect. Jentsch and Roth (1999) have shown that the decrease in NMDA function as a result of PCP leads to increased activity in subcortical dopamine neurons by removing the inhibition of these neurons. A similar effect has been shown for ketamine (Moghaddam, Adams, Verma & Daly, 1997). All in all, these data suggest that glutamate activity is necessary for a number of cognitive functions, both directly and via its influence on subcortical dopamine activity.

The serotonin hypothesis of schizophrenia

The suggestion that serotonin (5-HT) might be involved in schizophrenia is not particularly new and dates back to a suggestion by Woolley & Shaw (1954) that schizophrenia might be related to a deficiency in serotonin. This suggestion arose from observations surrounding the hallucinogenic properties of lysergic acid diethylamide (LSD). LSD is a serotonin agonist (it increases the activity of serotonin) and was shown to have a number of behavioural consequences that mapped fairly well onto the symptoms of schizophrenia. For example, both can produce paranoid delusions, the negative symptoms and many of the thought disorders. However, there were also distinctive differences. Whereas schizophrenia induces auditory hallucinations and rarely visual ones, LSD induces the opposite. Furthermore, the picture rapidly became confused as the same authors found evidence that these effects might be caused by a serotonin increase (Woolley & Shaw, 1956) rather than the decrease earlier proposed. The difficulty of finding reliable evidence as to the possible role of serotonin meant that interest in its involvement decreased.

A resurgence of interest was initiated by the finding that the postmortem basal ganglia of people with schizophrenia had elevated levels of serotonin but that the number of serotonin receptors in the prefrontal cortex was reduced. The renewed interest was because these regions of the brain are linked to theories of schizophrenia. The role serotonin plays is believed to be one of inhibiting dopamine activity in a particular area of the brain. An overactivity of serotonin here will inhibit dopamine too much and the result will be negative symptoms. Note that this dopamine area is different from the one responsible for the positive symptoms and this explains why LSD results in negative symptoms but visual rather than auditory hallucinations. It is these serotonin regions that are believed to be the sites of action of **neuroleptic** drugs and this discovery added credibility to the serotonin hypothesis. One drug, in particular, made the link between serotonin and schizophrenia very interesting. The drug is clozapine which is considered to be an atypical neuroleptic. It has a superior efficacy to chlorpromazine, a traditional neuroleptic. Furthermore, it has a high affinity for serotonin receptors and so produces a significant reduction in serotonin activity. Moreover, it is this action that is believed to give the drug its neuroleptic properties. Indeed, it will block the behavioural response to LSD (Fink, Morgenstern & Oetssner, 1984).

As has already been mentioned, reduced serotonin function has been implicated in the mediation of negative symptoms of schizophrenia. If this was the case, then drugs that increase serotonin levels should help behaviourally. Two pharmacological mechanisms by which serotonin activity could be increased are to block the reuptake of serotonin into the presynaptic cell or to mimic serotonin and act at the receptor site. Several serotonin reuptake inhibitors have been produced for the treatment of depression, fluoxetine (Prozac) probably being the best known. These drugs have had some success in reducing the negative symptoms of schizophrenia (Breier, 1995).

◉ Combining the dopamine, glutamate and serotonin hypotheses

The three hypotheses that we have considered so far are not competing. They explain different components of the disorder. To give a more complete picture, I will include here some references to pathways in the brain that we will not meet properly until the next chapter. One dopamine pathway is called the mesolimbic pathway, and overactivity of dopamine here is responsible for the hallucinations and delusions experienced by people with schizophrenia. Another dopamine pathway is the mesocortical pathway, and underactivity here is responsible for the negative, cognitive and affective symptoms. Glutamate activity usually has the effect of inhibiting dopamine activity in the mesolimbic pathway. Genetic influences mean that when brain development reaches its maturation stage at puberty, the glutamate brake is not properly applied resulting in positive symptoms. Meanwhile, the knock-on effect of a disruption to glutamate is an upset in the serotonin activity in the mesocortical pathway. This causes an increase in serotonin activity that over-inhibits dopamine in the mesocortical pathway leading to negative symptoms, cognitive deficits and a flattened affect. So it would seem that all three neurotransmitters play a role in the total package of symptoms that make up schizophrenia.

◉ Chapter summary

It is clear that schizophrenia is a complex disorder and that there are many neurotransmitter systems involved in the production of the various symptoms. It is unlikely that any one hypothesis will be shown to be the dominant one and, as we shall see later, the variety of drug treatments available demonstrate that a number of different neuronal systems are involved. What seems to be emerging is that the dopamine system is critically involved in some of the positive symptomology, serotonin is likely to be involved in some of the negative symptomology, and that glutamate is probably important in terms of the effect that disruption to this system has on the dopamine system. However, how these systems fully interact is the subject of current research and we can only speculate at this stage as to the interactions between the three systems.

◉ Further reading

Jentsch, J.D. and Roth, R.H. (1999) The neuropsychopharmacology of phencyclidine: From NMDA receptor hypofunction to the dopamine hypothesis of schizophrenia. *Neuropsychopharmacology*, 20, 201–225.

Moghaddam, B., Adams, B., Verman, A. and Daly, D. (1997) Activation of glutamatergic neurotransmission by ketamine: A novel step in the pathway from NMDA receptor blockade to dopaminergic and cognitive disruptions associated with the prefrontal cortex. *Journal of Neuroscience*. 17, 2921–2927.

Lieberman, J.A., Mailman, R.B., Duncan, G., Sikich, L., Chakos, M., Nichols, D.E., and Kraus, J.E. (1998) Serotonergic basis of antipsychotic drug effects in schizophrenia. *Biological Psychiatry*, 44, 1099–1117.

Chapter 4

Brain Correlates of Schizophrenia

Introduction

Having explored some of the theories concerning which neurotransmitter substances are involved in schizophrenia, we now turn our attention to the areas of the brain that might be affected. We will explore the research evidence that points to a number of different parts of the brain being abnormal in a person with schizophrenia. We will see that these areas of the brain are mostly regions where information is integrated and it is therefore possible to see how

In this chapter we will cover:
- Basic neuroanatomy
- Historical indices of brain damage in schizophrenia
- Neurodevelopment or neurodegeneration
- Enlarged ventricles and other findings
- Cortical asymmetry of the schizophrenic brain
- Damage to brain areas
  - Dorsolateral prefrontal cortex
  - Anterior cingulate cortex
  - Medial temporal cortex
  - Temporal association cortex
  - Primary visual cortex
  - The thalamus and schizophrenia
- Auditory hallucinations
- Neurodevelopment or Neurodegeneration – Can We Decide Between Them?
- Some functional consequences of brain damage

this damage gives rise to the variety of symptoms of schizophrenia. We also consider the root of these changes and two contrasting theories have been suggested. One proposes that the problem lies in the way the brain develops and the other proposes that there is progressive brain degeneration after the disease has started. First, though, a quick orientation to basic neuroanatomy and to the historical beginnings of the relationship between brain damage and schizophrenia.

⊙ Basic neuroanatomy

Before we go through the details of the anatomical changes seen in schizophrenia, it is probably worth considering some very basic elements of neuroanatomy to help you to follow the changes being discussed. The brain is divided into a number of regions and within these regions there are structures and pathways. Structures are composed of collections of neurons (their cell bodies, at least) tightly packed together. Pathways are made from the collection of large numbers of axons coming from a structure and travelling together to another structure. In the peripheral nervous system we commonly refer to these as nerves. The neurons that make up the brain are the basic building blocks. Each neuron has an input side made up of dendrites and an output side made up of an axon. The dendrites often form an extensive tree-like structure so that each neuron receives inputs from a large number of other axons. The importance of this for our purposes is that much of the volume of the brain, particularly in the cortex, is made up of these dendritic processes. This network of synaptic processes is sometimes referred to as the **neuropile**. So supposing we saw that the volume of the brain of a schizophrenic was reduced compared to a healthy brain, this might not necessarily mean that there were fewer neurons but might instead be a consequence of a reduction in the sizes of the dendritic trees. In addition to neurons, there are also support cells called 'glia'. So, once again, a reduction of brain volume might be caused by a reduction in the number of glial cells. With these points in mind, we can now explore the findings concerning how the schizophrenic brain differs from a non–schizophrenic brain.

⊙ Historical indices of brain damage in schizophrenia

When Kraepelin (1899) first described schizophrenia he very much saw it as a progressive brain disease that started with damage to the cerebral cortex. Sometime later, Bleuler (1950) coined the term 'schizophrenia' and saw it as a psychological disorder when he referred to it as a splitting of the mind. Consequently, the disorder was considered not to be an organic one, so the appropriate treatment was seen as psychoanalysis and family therapy. Whilst another influential figure, Jaspers (1923), did think the disorder was organic, he preferred to describe schizophrenia in terms of phenomenology (the study of subjective experience) and so did not really address the issue of whether or not it was a degenerative disease. It wasn't until the introduction of neuroleptic drugs that the organic nature of schizophrenia was taken seriously.

The first finding that indicated that brain damage was definitely involved was the obvious appearance of enlarged cerebral ventricles as seen via Computed Tomography (CT) scans. A CT scan shows a static image of the brain using x-rays. The cerebral ventricles are fluid-filled areas of the brain that supply nutrients and remove waste products. They also provide internal pressure that helps to keep the neurons in place within the brain. If there is brain damage then the pressurised ventricles will enlarge to fill the spaces left by the dead neurons. So it is easy to see that there has been brain damage sustained by the appearance of enlarged ventricles. Note that this does not tell us precisely where the damage has occurred (though it is likely to be close to the enlargement) but only that damage has happened.

👁 Neurodevelopment or neurodegeneration?

One of the interesting debates that does not concern areas of the brain is whether the damage we see in the schizophrenic's brain is stable over time or progressively gets worse. A neurodevelopmental disease is one in which parts of the brain do not develop properly. In this case, then, we would expect to see the damage present right from the beginning of diagnosis, and we would not expect this damage to change much over time. Whether we would expect to see such damage prior to the onset of schizophrenia is unclear as the damage might only become noticeable when developmental brain changes happen around puberty. If, however, the disease was a neurodegenerative one then we might not expect to see much damage prior to the onset of the disease (e.g. in high-risk individuals) but would expect to see a progressive worsening of the brain damage over time. So let's look at some of the evidence to see if we can decide between these two hypotheses.

Some brain abnormalities that can be detected by imaging techniques are visible when schizophrenia first emerges whereas others cannot be seen until sometime later. For example, general ventricular enlargement and damage to the hippocampus is seen at the outset, but damage to the temporal lobes and that to the amygdaloid are not seen when patients first present. To counter this view, a prominent idea in the 1980s was that the changes that trigger schizophrenia happen during a time of massive developmental brain changes that occur naturally during adolescence. Feinberg (1982) suggested that all of the changes seen using imaging techniques could all be explained by the reduction in cortical synaptic density that is a part of the natural brain reorganisation. Hence, the argument from Feinberg is that these are neurodevelopmental changes and not the processes of progressive brain disease. There was other support for this view, and Crow (1997) and Murray, O'Callaghan, Castle and Lewis (1992) also concluded that the data favoured a neurodevelopmental explanation. We can explore this debate further by firstly turning to look at the more recent data concerning ventricular enlargement and other forms of brain damage that are seen in schizophrenia. We will then return to the debate towards the end of the chapter.

👁 Enlarged ventricles and other general findings

The first studies to show that brain damage is suffered in schizophrenia were two studies carried out in quick succession in the 1970s. The first was a small study conducted by Johnstone, Crow, Frith and Husband (1976) and the second was a larger one by Weinberger et al. (1980). Both showed significant ventricular enlargement when their brains were compared to those of controls. Furthermore, it seemed not to matter how long they had suffered from schizophrenia, nor was it related to the type of medication they were taking. Both of these studies used CT scans, so it was difficult to establish anything other than that brain damage had occurred. Once the Magnetic Resonance Imaging (MRI) technique had emerged, it was much easier to see the nature of the damage as indicated by the ventricular enlargement. Firstly, it was clear to see that the enlargement was bigger on the left side than the right side. Alongside this, there was a non-localised reduction in gray matter and a loss of integrity of white matter. There were also regional deficits in the frontal lobes, the temporal lobes and in the superior temporal gyrus and damage to the hippocampus and other limbic structures (Figure 4.1). Interestingly, as we have seen, some of these changes are noticeable when the first episode of schizophrenia occurs whereas others are not seen until sometime later. One suggestion has been that the changes start in the frontal and temporal lobes and only later spread to other areas of the cortex.

There is one finding that doesn't quite fit with the idea of a progressive brain disease. Given the changes seen in patients between schizophrenia onset during adolescence and as patients a relatively short time later, we would be led to believe that older people with schizophrenia would have very little brain tissue left. This is simply not the case and nobody dies of schizophrenia. Furthermore, if there were to be a continual reduction in healthy

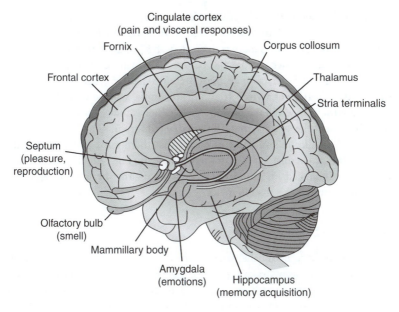

Figure 4.1 The Limbic System

brain volume then we would expect to see those with schizophrenia develop dementia as a result of diminished processing abilities. That this is also not the case suggests that any progression of the disease over time must be sporadic and not continuous (van Haren et al., 2008). We can hypothesise that brain changes occur before the onset of psychosis and that they continue haphazardly throughout the rest of the schizophrenic's life. What changes occur and when are likely to be different from person to person. This scenario would be compatible with both a neurodevelopmental and a neuro–degenerative argument if we presume that the changes that lead to the first psychotic episode are neurodevelopmental (some structures do not develop properly) and that changes continue afterwards (**neurodegeneration** continues to occur).

Cortical asymmetry and the schizophrenic brain

We know that the unaffected brain is far from being symmetrical. Of the four lobes of the brain, the temporal, parietal and occipital are usually larger on the left side of the brain and the frontal lobe is usually larger on the right. A similar set of differences have been shown concerning the cerebral cortex. Many parts of the left-sided cortex show a greater number of folds (fissures) than the right.

As folding is associated with a greater surface area, it seems that there is more cortical space devoted to left-sided rather than right-sided regions of the cortex. Just to make things more complicated, this brain asymmetry does seem to interact with gender so that the patterns for males and females are not quite the same. However, complex this differential patterning is, we can be clear that the usual pattern of asymmetry is not seen in the schizophrenic brain.

Joining the two cerebral hemispheres together is the corpus callosum. We see differences here too from the unaffected brain. The schizophrenic callosum is smaller in size and this means that there must be less cross-talk between the two hemispheres than there usually is. The reduction appears to be less pronounced in the frontal regions of the brain and is more pronounced in females than in males.

Damage to brain areas

Now that we have established that there is brain damage associated with schizophrenia, it seems relevant to ask where, exactly, the damage occurs. Only then could we try to marry up the damage seen with the cognitive and social deficits typical of schizophrenia (discussed in detail in Chapter 6). One common finding from MRI studies is that the ventricular enlargement is always greater on the left than on the right, meaning that more damage has occurred on the left side of the brain. Given that language processes are heavily weighted to the left brain in most individuals, we might have some clue here about language-oriented issues in schizophrenia.

Wright et al. (2000) carried out a meta-analysis that looked at 58 MRI studies that had looked for brain volume changes in people with schizophrenia compared with controls. In total, the analysis covered 1,588 individuals. They found that the frontal lobes are seen to be smaller in volume than in controls and in the region of the temporal lobes, and there were volume reductions in the amygdala, the hippocampus, the parahippocampus and the left anterior superior gyrus. Other areas of the brain have been found to be bigger than usual. These tend to be the motor control structures of the basal ganglia. One of these structures in particular, the globus pallidus, was more than 20% larger than expected. Finally, for this quick excursion around the brain, the thalamus was also reduced in volume.

The first thing to note about these findings is that the extent of the damage is vast and cuts across a large number of different regions. We would therefore expect there to be a number of different functional consequences.

In postmortem studies the anatomical changes appear to be more posterior in the brain; losses or reversal of asymmetry have been detected in fusiform, parahippocampal and superior temporal gyri (McDonald et al., 2000). In frontal regions there was no gross asymmetry in the brains of people with schizophrenia (Highley et al., 2001). There was a lack of asymmetry of the density of cells in the frontal cortex in patients. (Cullen et al., 2006).

Dorsolateral prefrontal cortex

The **dorsolateral prefrontal cortex (DLPC)** is a region of the brain that sits right at the anterior end of the frontal cortex. It is considered by many to be a major site of change in the schizophrenic brain. We will see in Chapter 6 that many of the cognitive deficits seen in schizophrenia are consistent with damage to this part of the brain, and many studies have shown reduced activation of this area when those with schizophrenia perform tasks known to involve the prefrontal cortex (D.R. Weinberger, Berman & Zec, 1986). Studies involving both postmortem analyses and MRI have shown there to be anatomical changes to this area. For example, Gur et al. (2000) have used MRI to show that there is a reduction in the volume of gray matter in this region. Postmortem analyses have further shown that this is not due to a reduction in the number of neurons but to a loss of the neuropile. In addition, there is no evidence that there is any loss or damage to glial cells here (nor anywhere else in the brain, for that matter).

Selemon (2001) has reviewed the types of cells that make up the DLPC. There are two main types of neuron here. One type is called pyramidal cells and these send excitatory signals to other neurons using the neurotransmitter glutamate. The other type is the nonpyramidal cells and these send inhibitory signals using Gamma Amino Butyric Acid (GABA). The nonpyramidal cells have been studied more extensively because they are easier to examine, but there is emerging evidence that there is a disruption to both kinds of cells. This is particularly interesting because of the implications for the glutamate hypothesis that we considered in the last chapter.

Interestingly, this region of the brain has very recently been implicated in the creation of deceptive responses (Ito et al., 2012). If this turned out to also be an area involved in perceiving the lies of others then this might go some way to explaining the social skills deficits we will encounter in Chapter 6.

Anterior cingulate cortex

Some researchers have shown that people with schizophrenia who have a strong level of thought disorder show an increased cerebral blood flow to the right anterior cingulate cortex. However, other researchers have found that cerebral metabolic rates are lower in this region. As increased blood flow is a measure of increased metabolic rate, these findings are totally contradictory. All of the studies agree, though, that the anterior cingulate cortex is dysfunctional. This region of the brain has been linked with many different functions. Of interest to us is the role this region plays in detecting errors (particularly motor errors) and in emotional awareness. Again, we will see later how deficits of these functions feed into the schizophrenic behavior pattern.

Medial temporal cortex

The medial temporal lobe is a part of the temporal lobe that sits between the superior and inferior temporal sulci (a sulcus – plural sulci – is a groove in the surface of the brain created by the brain folding in on itself to increase the total surface area). The structures included in the medial temporal lobe are the perirhinal and parahippocampal (sometimes called entorhinal) regions of the cortex together with some deeper lying structures such as the amygdala, brainstem and hippocampus. These regions of the brain are important for a number of cognitive functions that are known to have gone wrong in schizophrenia, in particular memory. It is therefore no surprise to find a lot of data showing damage to this region of the brain.

These areas have been studied extensively over a long period of time using postmortem analyses, CT scans and MRI. All have shown a reduction in the volume of the hippocampus and the parahippocampal cortex (Weinberger, Wagner & Wyatt, 1983). Further evidence to suggest that this region is damaged in schizophrenia comes for patients who have suffered a temporal lobe injury as they often show some symptoms that resemble those of schizophrenia (Fuller Torrey & Peterson, 1974). In the case of the hippocampus, the volume reduction did appear to include the result of neuron loss which is therefore different to the DLPC. Indeed, the loss of neurons was initially reported to be in the region of 4–36% (Falkai & Bogerts, 1986). Using more modern techniques, it is likely that the loss is nearer the 4% mark if that and the majority of the volume deficit is probably due to loss of neuron density rather than to loss of neurons. This illustrates the importance of having accurate analytical tools in order to determine what is going on at the level of local neurons.

Temporal association cortex

Other regions of the temporal lobe are known to play a role in combining different sorts of information to give a bigger picture. Just above the medial temporal cortex (on the other side of the superior temporal sulcus) is the temporal association cortex in a region called 'the superior temporal gyrus'. This area is involved in memory but, more relevant to schizophrenia, it is involved in two other functions. The first is face recognition and it appears that this area receives information from the primary visual processing areas and can combine it with auditory and emotional information (from the auditory cortex and the limbic system that processes emotion) to give a holistic account of what face, whose face and what emotion the face is expressing. The second function relates to the fact that this region houses two important structures for language processing. One of these structures is the auditory cortex, where sounds are analysed for meaning. Those identified as belonging to language are fed to Wernicke's area and this is a major structure involved in the comprehension of language. Researchers have found the left side of the temporal association cortex to be reduced in volume because of decreased neuronal density. Sun et al. (2009) reviewed 46 studies of the superior temporal gyrus which comprised, in total, 1444 schizophrenic patients and 1327 controls. Thirty-five of the studies showed a volume reduction in this region and fifteen reported this reduction to be specific to the left side of the brain. So this finding is like the finding for the DLPC. Damage here could, again, account for some of the symptoms of schizophrenia. Indeed, Sun et al. reported a number of correlations between the changes to the superior temporal gyrus and positive symptoms such as thought disorder.

Primary visual cortex

This lies at the back of the brain in the occipital lobe. All through the 1970s and 1980s, this region of the brain was believed to be spared in schizophrenia but then data gained from the detailed analysis of the electroencephalogram (EEG) suggested this is not the case (Jibiki et al., 1991). The EEG can be used to capture what happens electrically in the brain in the 500 milliseconds (half a second) after a stimulus has been presented. This is known as an evoked potential. It seems that the part of the visual process that is disrupted in schizophrenia is the capacity to properly detect motion. According to Schwartz, Rosse, Johri & Deutsch (1999), these deficits can lead to a problem with properly recognising objects. This, again, could help to explain some of the misperceptions typical in the schizophrenic. Here, too, we have a similar pattern in that the reason for the changes here are most likely to be exactly the same as those for the DLPC.

The thalamus and schizophrenia

The thalamus lies deep within the brain and is considered to be one of the most important parts of the brain that is not cortex. It is often referred to as the switchboard as it provides the information link between the cortex and the deeper lying structures in the brain. It has the job primarily of directing sensory information to where it needs to go. Damage to this structure has so many implications, and it is therefore no surprise that it is implicated in so many different disorders including amnesia and insomnia. We see a number of changes to the thalamus in the case of schizophrenia. As well as reduced volume, researchers have shown that there is also a reduction in white matter.

Remember that white matter is the collection of axons (outputs) from neurons travelling together as bundles (pathways). Using positron emission tomography (see Box 4.1), Andreasen et al. (1994) have shown that the metabolic rate of the thalamus is lower in people with schizophrenia than controls

Box 4.1 Featured Method – Imaging Techniques

The ability to take images of the living brain has vastly enhanced our understanding of the changes that occur as a result of schizophrenia. There are a number of different imaging techniques and they give a variety of views of the brain. Some, like EEG and MEG record the electrical activity of the brain. CT and MRI scans provide a static image of what the brain looks like at a given moment in time. Finally, PET, fMRI and NIRS scans provide a what parts of the brain are active at any moment in time. All of these methods are non-invasive as they do not involve entering into the brain itself. We will look very briefly at each of these.

EEG

Electroencephalography (EEG) records the activity of the brain from electrodes that are placed on the scalp. These record the electrical activity from vast numbers of neurons so we get a good picture of what is happening but a less good one of precisely where it is happening. The record has millisecond accuracy (called a high temporal resolution) and this is especially useful for detecting things that change quickly (for example, cognitive processes).

MEG

Magnetoencephalography (MEG) measures the magnetic fields that the brain produces as a result of the electrical activity it is engaged in. Like EEG, it has exceptionally good temporal resolution. It can also be used alongside fMRI (described below) to produce an even clearer picture of what is going on in the brain.

CT

Computerised Tomography (CT) scans use x-rays to build up a static picture of the brain. This type of scan can only reveal the general features of the brain and so it is not very good for understanding the fine anatomy of structures in the brain. Nevertheless, the CT scan will pick up large changes associated with schizophrenia, such as the changes to the ventricles.

MRI

Magnetic Resonance Imaging (MRI) is another static technique but this one uses radio waves instead of x-rays and so is a lot safer. The radio waves use magnetic resonance to pinpoint the positions of the atoms in the brain and so can build up a static 3D picture.

PET

Positron Emission Tomography (PET) scanning involves the person ingesting a substance like glucose that has been treated with a low activity, short acting radioactive label. Those parts of the brain that become active will use up more of this glucose and this can be registered by the scanner. This gives a dynamic picture of those parts of the brain that are in use when a person carries out a particular task.

fMRI

Functional Magnetic Resonance Imaging (fMRI) is similar to the PET scan except that it does not involve any radioactive substances. Instead it measures the use of oxygen by the brain. This method contrasts with EEG and MEG in that it is spatially accurate but not temporally accurate. This is why it is often combined with MEG.

NIRS

Near Infrared Spectroscopy (NIRS) is an optical method of measuring oxygen usage in the brain. Infrared light is shone through the skull and sensors measure how much of the light re-emerges. This provides an indirect measure of brain activity.

when performing tasks requiring attention or memory. Metabolic rate is a reflection of the amount of activity happening, so we can see that the thalamus is less active in people with schizophrenia during these kinds of task.

It is evident that damage to the thalamus could result in so much loss of information exchange between the cortex and the other regions of the brain that a number of different symptoms would result. Reports indicate that as much as one third of the total number of cells in the thalamus are destroyed in schizophrenia (Popken, Bunney, Potkin, & Jones, 2000).

👁 Auditory hallucinations

One of the classic features of schizophrenia is the presence of auditory hallucinations. This feature therefore deserves an anatomical analysis of its own. There has been much interest to know which areas of the brain are involved in these, and some recent work by Plaze et al. (2011) has given us a clue as to why these might occur. From a clinical perspective, two different kinds of hallucination are reported. Some experience them as though they are coming from a voice inside the head whereas others experience an external presence. We have already seen that both the left temporal lobe and the right frontal lobe are damaged in schizophrenia and these are the areas concerned with comprehension and production, respectively. Placed right between these two structures, with an equivalent on the opposite side, is the auditory cortex, and the nerve fibres leading from this area seem to divide into two pathways. One of these (the ventral stream) carries information about the content of the sounds and is referred to as the 'what' pathway. The other (the dorsal stream) is concerned with 'where' the sound is coming from. Also playing a role in this 'where' system is the right superior temporal gyrus (the right side seems to be dominant for spatial processing), and we have already seen from the pattern of enlarged ventricles that this area is damaged in people with schizophrenia. Using imaging data, Plaze et al. showed that there were differences in white matter between those experiencing internal and those experiencing external hallucinations. These differences were confined to the right side of the brain where this kind of spatial auditory processing is known to occur. It would seem, then, that the different patterns of brain damage here determine whether the voices are heard coming from inside or outside of the head. Incidentally, this region has also been implicated in out-of-body experiences and this would fit well with the hypothesis concerning auditory hallucinations in schizophrenia.

👁 Neurodevelopment or neurodegeneration – Can we decide between them?

Now that we have considered the specific data concerning the different regions of the brain, we can return to the debate between the neurodevelopmental and neurodegenerative explanations of schizophrenia? Bearing in mind what we now know about changes to individual areas of the brain, we can look at some recent studies that combine these findings in an effort to decide whether one or other theory is more likely to be the case? As we saw earlier, Feinberg (1982) argued that the pattern of damage we see is mainly one of reduced neuronal density. It seems that the neurons do not die but they have fewer connections than would usually be the case. We know that the developmental process of brain development is one in which there are more synaptic connections in the infant brain than are required for adulthood. At around the time of adolescence, large numbers of these excessive synapses are eliminated and this process is referred to as synaptic pruning (keeping the dendritic tree analogy going). It is possible that the synaptic pruning that takes place in the schizophrenic brain is much greater than is required, with the consequence being a decrease in the neuropile. The difficulty for this explanation is that it does not explain why large areas of the cortex are affected but that some areas seem to be spared. Whilst we can accept that the outcome is excessive pruning, it seems that we might need to look elsewhere for the cause. We will first examine three studies that point to a neurodegenerative solution and then consider those that use the same kinds of evidence to point to a neurodevelopmental one.

Chan, Di, McAlonan and Gong (2011) have reviewed studies that include those with a high risk of developing schizophrenia, those who have had their first psychotic episode and those with chronic schizophrenia. They showed that, even before high-risk individuals become psychotic, they have a smaller brain volume and a greater ventricular volume. Those with chronic schizophrenia also show this but with the addition of indications of other damage such as bilaterally smaller hippocampi (the plural of hippocampus). They concluded that the brain abnormalities present in high-risk individuals might well be genetic but that those indicators of damage seen later must be the result of a progressive disorder.

Olabi et al. (2011) have argued that it is difficult to really assess the neurodegenerative hypothesis using data that simply compares one group with another at a particular moment in time (a cross-sectional analysis). They stated that a better indication can only come from longitudinal studies in which individuals are tracked over time. They therefore carried out a meta-analysis of 53 studies where the same individuals had received at least two MRI scans over a period of time. They showed that there is a clear progression in the reduction of volume of grey matter in general, in frontal lobe volume decreases and in reductions of frontal, temporal and parietal white matter volume. This would point to clear support for neurodegeneration. However, they warned that there are at least two reasons why we should not be too hasty in jumping to conclusions about these two hypotheses and that they might not be mutually exclusive. The first is that other degenerative diseases show gliosis but none is found in schizophrenia (gliosis is where the glia cells locally increase in volume as a response to the death of neurons). The second is that it is unclear whether there are cognitive deficits in the aging schizophrenic (post 65 years old) that are over and above what would be expected due to healthy ageing. If schizophrenia were a progressive disorder then we might expect that to be the case.

Ziermans et al. (2012) have examined brain changes as they occur during the development of psychosis. They achieved this by monitoring adolescents that were deemed at ultra-high risk (UHR) for psychosis and comparing their brain development with that of a typically developing adolescent. It is usually the case that 30-40% of UHR individuals go on to develop schizophrenia, so there is a fair chance of being able to see changes that are specific to this disease. Forty-three UHR individuals and 30 typically developing adolescents were given two MRI scans with a time interval of two years between scans. Those who went on to develop psychosis had significantly greater reductions in the amount of gray matter and white matter than either those UHR individuals who did not develop psychosis or the controls. This loss of gray and white matter resulted in a loss of cortical thickness in specific places across the surface of the brain but was noticeably pronounced in the region of the speech areas in the left temporal lobe. Ziermans et al. argue that these data point to brain changes that start to occur very early in psychosis and then progress as the disease becomes more established.

Researchers who favour the neurodevelopmental explanation can hardly disagree with the research findings. However, their interpretation of those findings is very different. The problem for this hypothesis is that we might expect to see all of the developmental changes to occur prenatally or, at least, in the first few months after birth. So any neurodevelopmental account would need to explain two potential problems. Firstly, why are there further changes that occur around adolescence and, secondly, why are the signs of schizophrenia not so obvious before its emergence (usually around adolescence)? The neurodevelopmental answer centres around the idea that there are two key time periods but that beyond these there are no further significant changes to the brain (hence the disorder is not progressive). Keshavan (1999) termed this a '2-hit' model, with the hits happening in early brain development and during adolescence. Fatemi and Folsom (2009) argue that there is good evidence for these two hits. They state that there is abundant evidence for the first hit. This combines a genetic propensity for schizophrenia with one or more environmental events that act as a trigger (obstetric complications, maternal infection, maternal stress and so on – see Chapters 2 and 5). This initial developmental brain insult then leads to abnormal changes during adolescence when synaptic pruning is naturally taking place. The changes that happened developmentally prenatally or perinatally lead to an excessive amount of pruning and this gives rise to the emergence of psychosis.

Pantelis et al. (2005) have argued that a combination of the two hypotheses might give us a more accurate picture of the brain abnormalities associated with schizophrenia. They suggest that there are significant changes that occur in early development and that these result in further significant changes that occur at adolescence (both compatible with the neurodevelopmental hypothesis). However, they suggest that the neurodegeneration occurs between these two time periods and that after the onset of psychosis there are no further significant changes. They propose that there are a number of possible reasons that the progressive degeneration might occur between early development and adolescence and they include among them both physiological (e.g. hormonal dysregulation) and environmental (e.g. substance abuse) triggers.

◉ Some functional consequences of brain damage

To finish this chapter, it is useful to consider the relationship between brain abnormalities and functional deficits. We will look at the cognitive and social deficits in detail in Chapter 6, but there we will concentrate on the psychological processes rather than their anatomical underpinnings. Here, then the details of the psychological relevance of cognitive and social failings will be glossed over. There is not room here to go through each type of cognitive and social deficit and explore what parts of the brain are associated with a deficit in schizophrenia. What follows are a selection of studies to give you a feel for the kinds of relationships that are being explored and also to give you some insight into how the combination of imaging techniques and cognitive tasks can combine to provide a coherent picture linking brain abnormalities with their functional consequences.

Most of the areas of the brain that we have considered in this chapter are regions where information is integrated so that some higher order function can be carried out. One such function is the recognition of emotions in others and those with schizophrenia are known to perform poorly on tasks that require this capability (e.g. Schneider et al., 2006). We have already seen in this chapter that areas of the temporal lobe (superior temporal gyrus, hippocampus, amygdala and others) are involved in the processing of speech, and another area of the temporal lobe (the fusiform gyrus) is involved in the perception of faces. We also know that these areas are affected in people with schizophrenia. It makes sense, then, to ask if damage to this region is responsible for those facial emotion recognition deficits. Goghari, Macdonald and Sponheim (2011) have looked at how damage to temporal lobe structures might be responsible. They tested schizophrenic patients, their first-degree relatives and controls on their ability to recognise the facial expressions of fear, anger, happiness and sadness. They also collected brain images from these participants to establish the volume of specific regions. They found that there was a reduction in fusiform volume in both the brains of those with schizophrenia and their relatives, but that emotion recognition was only impaired in the people with schizophrenia. They did, however, find that a reduction of gray matter volume in the hippocampus was only evident for people with schizophrenia. Firstly, these data give a clear indication of a relationship between temporal lobe abnormalities and facial recognition deficits in people with schizophrenia. The puzzle is why relatives showed a temporal lobe abnormality but no deficit in facial emotion processing. It might be that the test used in the study was not subtle enough to show any impairment in the relatives.

Schobel et al. (2009) have investigated the relationship between the abnormalities of the hippocampus and dorsolateral prefrontal cortex (DLPC) and cognitive deficits in schizophrenia. Data on this relationship have been confusing as reductions of brain volume in frontal regions have been linked with deficits in working memory (a known frontal lobe function) but also with long term memory (usually attributed to the temporal lobes). Similar confusion exists concerning reductions in temporal lobe volume. There are known to be links between the temporal lobe and the frontal lobe and this represented a possible explanation. Schobel et al. found a link between decreased volume of the left anterior hippocampus and areas of the frontal lobe with various cognitive deficits, including verbal performance. However, their data did not compare those with schizophrenia with controls and they were not able to account for any effects that the psychotic medication might have had on cognitive performance. This latter point is something we will have to bear in mind when we look at cognitive deficits in more detail in Chapter 6.

One final study that we will look at here is interesting because it combines functional MRI (fMRI is a technique that allows the MRI to be explored over a continuous period of time) with a complex and emotive attentional task. Dichter, Bellion, Casp and Belger (2010) used an attentional task that involved participants looking at shapes and scenes presented for 500 milliseconds (half a second) each. There were circles and squares and there were aversive and neutral scenes. Participants were instructed to press one button for circles and another button for everything else. The aversive scenes were quite strong and included human violence, mutilation and disease. Schizophrenic patients and controls were used in the study. Different patterns of brain activation were apparent in the two groups. It would appear that whilst the controls were able to separate their processing of task relevant information (circle or not) from emotional processing (response to aversive scenes), people with schizophrenia were less able to do this. These differences were most apparent in parts of the frontal lobes where the function of focusing on a specific task seems to reside.

⊙ Chapter summary

In this chapter we have looked at some of the main brain areas that are affected by schizophrenia. In every case it has been possible to see how the damaged contributes to a functional deficit that is displayed by patients, be it a lowered emotional perception because of limbic system abnormalities or a lack of being able to see the bigger picture because of damage to parts of the temporal association cortex. We have also tried to address the bigger question of whether these brain abnormalities are the result of developmental changes or are due to degeneration of the brain after the onset of the disorder. In the end, it is possible to explain the same data from both perspectives, and a plausible explanation would be that both **neurodevelopment** and neurode-generation are involved.

⊙ Further reading

Crossman, A.R. and Neary, D. (2010) *Neuroanatomy: An Illustrated Colour Text*. Churchill Livingstone.

Fullerton, M. (2013) *Schizophrenia, Brain Damage and Recovery: From case histories and scientific studies*. CreateSpace Independent Publishing Platform.

Pantelis, C., Yücel, M., Wood, S.J., Velakoulis, D., Sun, D., Berger, G., ... McGorry, P.D. (2005). Structural brain imaging evidence for multiple pathological processes at different stages of brain development in schizophrenia. *Schizophrenia bulletin*, 31 (3), 672–696.

Chapter 5

Alternative Biological and Evolutionary Explanations

👁 Introduction

Whilst much of the research into schizophrenia has concentrated on genetics as a cause and alterations to brain structure and chemistry as consequences, not all theories fall into these categories. A number of theories suggest that traumas in the womb or during the process of birth can induce brain changes that give rise to, or the potential for, the development of schizophrenia. The chapter concludes with some evolutionary explanations that may seem a little strange until you think about it. So we will explore why it might either be an advantage to be schizophrenic or not disadvantageous enough for it to have been selected out.

In this chapter we will cover:
- Alternative biological explanations
  - Obstetric complications
  - Maternal infection
- Schizophrenia and birth order
- Evolutionary explanations
  - The principles of Darwinian evolution
  - The speciation hypothesis
  - Group splitting
- Schizophrenia as a by-product of social cognition

👁 Alternative biological explanations

In this section we consider a number of alternative biological explanations that are not directly linked to either disruptions of neurotransmitter systems or to direct links with the dysfunction of various parts of the brain (though, of course, these might be linked to the topics here).

Obstetric complications

The suggestion that complications related to pregnancy and birth might be linked to schizophrenia goes back at least to the 1930s. However, up until the late 1960s only a handful of articles reported investigations of this link. One of the earliest links between pregnancy and psychosis was preeclampsia. This is characterised by high blood pressure and excessive amounts of protein in the urine. It often leads to the necessity of a caesarean birth or early induction of labour. Because preeclampsia involves problems with the functioning of the placenta, the possible association with schizophrenia could be as a result of too little oxygen getting to the foetus or too little nutrition getting to it, both of which could lead to brain damage.

Another pregnancy link is between diabetes in the mother and schizophrenia. Diabetes can cause an abnormally high pregnancy body mass as a result of altered glucose metabolism. This is known to lead to impaired intellectual and psychomotor development and has been linked to schizophrenia as well. A further link in pregnancy is abnormal foetal growth (as evidenced by a low birth weight). There appears to be a strong inverse correlation between birth weight and propensity towards schizophrenia. That is, the higher the birth weight the less likely it is that the person will develop schizophrenia.

There have been several other links to events during pregnancy, especially regarding exposure to noxious substances (including lead). In addition, it is not just pregnancy that can be causal, as there are also reported links due to complications in delivery. These are probably as a result of hypoxia (lack of sufficient oxygen) or asphyxia (choking). Individuals with such complications can be up to five times more likely to develop schizophrenia and, in particular, early-onset schizophrenia.

We have already seen in the previous chapter that the schizophrenic brain is abnormal in many regards. One hypothesis suggests that the development of schizophrenia is the result of faulty development of the brain during pregnancy and/or damage caused during birth. This neurodevelopmental hypothesis begs the question of what might be happening during pregnancy or birth to cause the lack of healthy brain development. A number of links to pregnancy and birth have been noticed. Cannon, Jones and

Murray (2002) have suggested that obstetric complications increase the risk of schizophrenia by about a factor of 2.0. Hultman, Ohman, Cnattingius, Wiselgren and Lindstrom (1997) confirmed in a study of 107 Swedish schizophrenic patients that their birth size was significantly lower compared to the rest of the population. In a later study (C. M. Hultman, Sparén, Takei, Murray & Cnattingius, 1999) they looked at maternal age, a number of pregnancy and delivery factors (e.g. bleeding during pregnancy), child characteristics (e.g. birth weight, birth length) and season of birth. Their results showed that any of the factors that seemed to be linked to schizophrenia were only linked for males. Among the factors associated with increased risk were bleeding during pregnancy and size at birth (relative to gestational age, that is, taking into account whether the baby was full term or premature). Whilst not showing as a significant risk, the authors also identified maternal diabetes, weak contractions during birth and a late winter birth as factors that could also play a part. We can hypothesise as to why many of these factors might be important. We know that bleeding during the latter stages of pregnancy can retard intrauterine growth and this could have an effect on brain growth. Retarded intrauterine growth results from problems with the functioning of the placenta (due to bleeding) and this results in a lack of oxygen (asphyxia) to the brain.

It is not only the details of the uterine environment during pregnancy that are important. These changes could, themselves, be the result of behaviours of the mother. One suggested explanation for the low birth weight of infants that go on to develop schizophrenia is that the mother was more likely to smoke and we know that this can lead to reduced birth weight. Another suggestion is maternal malnutrition. Hoek, Brown and Susser (1998) have investigated data from the Dutch Hunger Winter that occurred at the end of World War II (see Box 5.1). They have shown that prenatal famine was significantly associated with the incidence of schizophrenia. Another possibility is that the mothers whose children developed schizophrenia were less inclined to follow the antenatal care routines that were in place for Swedish women. The data for these peripheral causes are not overly reliable but they do underline the difficulty of pinpointing the exact causes of schizophrenia amongst a multitude of possibilities.

One excellent set of studies concerning the effects of maternal malnutrition has been labelled the Dutch Famine Study. At the end of World War II, there was a severe food shortage across Holland. Due to the fact that the Dutch maintained extremely comprehensive health records, the conditions were in place for a natural experiment. A natural experiment is where the variables are not under the control of the experimenter but are determined entirely by the prevailing natural conditions. As such, they provide a perfect way to study phenomena outside of the laboratory setting and outside of the problems of self-selecting groups who volunteer for particular studies. In this particular study, Hoek et al. (1998) looked at events in Holland towards the end of World War II. Due to a failed attempt by the Allies to capture bridges over the River Rhine in September of 1944, the Germans imposed a total embargo on occupied Holland. The west of the region suffered a devastating food shortage, and by the time the Germans agreed to partially lift the embargo so that food could be brought in from the north, the relief barges could not get through as the canals had already frozen over. The food shortages reached their peak between February and May 1945. The daily ration was now below 1000 calories and consisted exclusively of bread, potatoes and sugar beet. When the famine ended in May 1945, 200,000 people were ill from starvation. The children examined in the study were those born between 15th October and 31st December 1945 as these were thought to be the worst affected by the famine conditions of the mother. It was found that males were 1.9 times more likely to have schizophrenia and females were 2.2 times more likely. These are very significant increases, and whilst we cannot be sure that other factors were not also in play at this time, the link to malnutrition is fairly convincing.

Box 5.1 The Meta-analytic Method (Cannon, Jones and Murray, 2002)

A meta-analysis is an effective way of reviewing the vast body of literature that exists on a particular topic. In the case of Cannon, Jones and Murray (2002), they were interested in finding out what research had been carried out into the possible links between problems associated with pregnancy and birth and the likelihood of becoming a person with schizophrenia. They carried out an online database search. A database such as MEDLINE (the one they used) houses thousands upon thousands of articles from an enormous range of academic journals and going back a very long way. In any meta-analysis the authors will set criteria for whether or not articles should be included (inclusion criteria). For this study there were four inclusion criteria.

1. A well-defined sample of cases

2. Use of standardised, objectively collected obstetric information from birth records or registers

3. Inclusion of comparison subjects drawn from the general population with information on obstetric complications collected from the same source

4. Use of a standardized format for presentation of data, allowing for comparisons between studies.

The results of this search yielded just 13 articles that met at least the first three criteria. Had the authors used less strict criteria they would have had more articles but they would have the difficulty of making direct comparisons between them. This is always a judgement that researchers have to make to try to get the balance right between the tightness of the criteria and the number of studies the search yields.

In a study conducted in Denmark, Byrne, Agerbo, Bennedsen, Eaton and Mortensen (2007) looked at a number of different obstetric factors that could be linked to the development of schizophrenia. What is interesting about the sample in this study is that it was possible to capture the data across the entire population of people with schizophrenia in Denmark as there are no private psychiatric facilities and all treatment is free, so everyone with a psychiatric problem comes through the Danish Psychiatric Central Register. The factors that they found were linked to an increased risk of schizophrenia included haemorrhage during delivery, premature birth, lower birth weight and a lack of antenatal visits to the hospital. One further factor they referred to was maternal influenza which we will look at in more detail in the next section.

Before we leave the topic of obstetric complications, we should note that alongside the findings of risks for unaffected mothers, there is a literature that suggests a risk of obstetric complications in mothers who have schizophrenia. Bennedsen, Mortensen, Olesen and Henriksen (1999) reviewed the literature and examined several of the factors known to be linked to intrauterine growth retardation and premature birth. These included smoking, alcohol consumption, caffeine consumption and the use of illicit drugs. Pregnant schizophrenic women were shown to be more likely to be smokers, were more likely to be substance abusers (particularly cannabis) and were more likely to have alcohol-related problems. There were too few studies looking at caffeine for any conclusions to be drawn. As a result, schizophrenic women did have an increased risk of giving birth to babies with a low birth weight and/or delivering prematurely.

Cannon et al. (2002) have also suggested that there might be a further familial link in that the schizophrenic mother's mother might have had a predisposition to schizophrenia that was never manifested. This would increase the likelihood that she would have obstetric complications and that this propensity would then be passed on to her schizophrenic daughter. If this were the case then it might not be that obstetric complications are a marker of schizophrenic risk but the other way around. In other words, the possession of a schizophrenic disposition, whether expressed or not, might be the cause of obstetric complications. We are not currently in a position to be able to decide between these two possibilities.

☉ Maternal infection

It is quite astonishing to think that a simple infection like influenza during pregnancy can have the devastating effect of leading to schizophrenia in the unborn child. However, there are well-documented links between a number of infections during pregnancy and the future development of schizophrenia. Brown and Patterson (2011) argue that we should not be too surprised at these findings as we know that microbial pathogens can cause several kinds of brain abnormalities including a number of childhood disorders. One of the first links between infection and schizophrenia occurred in the 1980s when Mednick, Machon, Huttunen and Bonett (1988) showed that prenatal exposure to the influenza virus during an epidemic was the cause of schizophrenia that later developed in their offspring. However, at that point there were question marks as to how accurately the diagnosis of influenza had been made. Since then, a number of better studies have emerged linking schizophrenia not just to the influenza virus but to a range of infections.

A number of birth cohort studies have been undertaken to examine the relationship between infection and schizophrenia. Cohort studies usually include data that have been routinely collected during pregnancy from a large number of mothers over a long period of time. Often the serum and other specimens that were taken at the time of pregnancy have been stored and can be used for fresh analyses. This means that the latest technology can be applied at the time of the investigation. Brown and Derkits (2010) have reviewed a number of such studies and have shown that the influenza virus leads to a threefold increase in risk if contracted in the first half of pregnancy and a sevenfold increase if contracted in the first trimester. No additional risk was associated with contraction of the virus in the second half of pregnancy.

It is not just influenza that has been linked to schizophrenia. Toxoplasma gondii is a parasite that can be contracted from contaminated soil or water or from undercooked meat. Simply gardening can lead to infection if gloves are not worn, and microwaving meat does not guarantee that the parasites will be killed. The likelihood associated with this disease is a twofold increase in risk. An added worry here is that Brown and Patterson think it likely that for most cases the parasite was probably acquired before the onset of pregnancy.

Another set of infections that are linked to schizophrenia are genital or reproductive infections. Most are sexually transmitted infections (STIs) and one of these is Herpes Simplex Virus Type 2 (HSV-2). The infection gets passed to the offspring in the birth canal, and the resultant risk ratio for schizophrenia has been reported to be as high as 4.4 (Buka et al., 2001). Another STI that has been implicated is Human papillomavirus (HPV). This is the most frequent STI in the world and has been linked to numerous diseases from genital warts to cancer as well as being linked to schizophrenia.

One of the general markers that an infection is present is an increase in chemicals called cytokines. These are proteins that are released in response to an infection and their job is to regulate the immune response. We know that some cause inflammation and some are anti-inflammatory. We also know that their over-secretion can be dangerous. In the context of schizophrenia, probably the worst attribute is that they cross the placenta and can enter the foetal brain. Brown and Patterson have suggested that it might be the activity of cytokines that is responsible for the changes to neurodevelopment in response to infection that lead to schizophrenia emerging in later life.

◉ Schizophrenia and birth order

About 40 years ago, whether or not schizophrenia was more likely to occur in a first-born child or in one born further along the birth order was a hot topic. There were data that claimed a birth order effect just about anywhere in the sequence. Goodman (1957) claimed that the last-born male was most at risk, Schooler (1964) said it was later born females, Weller and Miller (1978) argued that it was middle and later born females and Wild, Shapiro and Abelin (1974) put the risk on first-born males. The ambiguity in the data made many believe that there was probably no relationship between birth order and the risk of developing schizophrenia. However, interest has been regenerated. Kemppainen et al. (2001) carried out a 31-year follow-up of 96% of the people born in Northern Finland in 1966. The sample amounted to over 12,000 people and they analysed the relationship between the development of schizophrenia and birth order. They found that the risk of schizophrenia was significantly greater among first-born males and last-born females. It was lower among last-born males and all of the females who were not born last. They found that this was true just for schizophrenia and not for other kinds of psychosis. They suggest that this is of importance only in as much as it adds to the suggestion that schizophrenia is a complex and multifactorial disorder. However, even now, the available evidence is contradictory. In a recent study by Ansari, Rahman, Siddiqui and Zaidi (2010), using a sample of patients from southern India, no birth order effects were found. The authors do, though, point out that there may be cultural differences here in that Indian families tend to have a much greater family cohesiveness than most Western families.

👁 Evolutionary explanations

In some ways, this is probably the strangest topic in the book. It is difficult to see how on earth there could be an evolutionary explanation for schizophrenia. What is nature playing at if it lets something like schizophrenia have a survival value? Surely, it can't make any sense to suggest that schizophrenia continues to exist because it confers some adaptive advantage on those individuals afflicted with it? If we believe schizophrenia to be genetically derived and expressed when the necessary environmental conditions ensue, then we must consider whether or not schizophrenia has an evolutionary purpose. If this turns out not to be the case then we might need to ask the question why it has not died out according to Darwinian principles. As we have seen, the prevalence continues to be about 1% of the population so it would seem, on the face of it, that schizophrenia does have a purpose.

In this section we will concentrate on two major theories concerning the evolutionary survival of schizophrenia. One suggests that schizophrenia is the price that homosapiens has to pay for having the ability to use language. The second suggests that schizophrenia is necessary for the successful growth of the population size. However, it is probably useful to start with a brief reminder of the Darwinian principles against which these theories must be judged.

👁 The principles of Darwinian evolution

Before we explore the evolutionary theories of schizophrenia, it is prudent to make sure that Charles Darwin's idea of evolution is properly understood. In his *Origin of Species*, Darwin set out the theory that new species evolve because they possess some survival advantage over the other species in the environment. We must remember that Darwin knew nothing of genetics and it was not Darwin who coined the term 'survival of the fittest' but Herbert Spencer. Darwin gave us the concept of natural selection but he didn't really comment upon the fate of evolutionary changes that were neither advantageous nor disadvantageous, and one might question whether he considered such a possibility. However, we need to consider just that possibility in what follows. We can agree that anything that confers an advantage is likely to be reproduced and emerge as a species characteristic. We can easily imagine that a change that is neutral would continue if it were linked to another change that had an advantage. We might even accept that a change that is neutral might continue if it makes no difference whatsoever. We will see in what follows that another possibility exists, that is that something that is a disadvantage might continue if it is the price to be paid for something else that is hugely advantageous.

Before we consider the main contenders for the theory of the evolution of schizophrenia, we should recognise some of the earlier ideas that paved the way for today's leading contenders. Given our more recent understanding of Darwinian mechanisms, it became reasonable to suggest that schizophrenia could only continue to exist within the population if it was tagged onto an advantageous trait. So the search for an evolutionary explanation started with a consideration of what advantages might be obtained from the schizophrenic gene (or genes). Huxley, Mayr, Osmond and Hoffer (1964) suggested that the reason schizophrenia has survived is that it gives the individual a resistance to endocrine and physiological stress factors. They also suggested that the mothers of people with schizophrenia are more protective than unaffected mothers (an idea we will meet in Chapter 6 when we consider the idea of a **schizophrenogenic** mother). The problem with Huxley's hypothesis is that the changes he describes are ones that take a long time to emerge in the population. As such, it is difficult to see how the small first steps in resistance to stress would produce an evolved change. Such small changes usually continue only as variances within normal limits (such as the variation in height).

Kuttner, Lorincz and Swan (1967) came up with an alternative view. They recognised that what they were looking for must be a uniquely human trait as schizophrenia is not found in other species. They suggested that intelligence and complex social ability were good candidates for the link between evolutionary change and schizophrenia. They did also consider language as another possibility but rejected it as a primary cause because they believed language to be derived from intelligence and social capabilities. They also reasoned that the lack of communication in deaf people does not increase the incidence of schizophrenia in that group. It would have been tempting to suggest that social evolution was the key as several authors had suggested a link between schizophrenia and leadership, especially political leadership. However many of the accounts (e.g. Karlsson, 1966)) were anecdotal rather than based in research. Kuttner et al favoured social evolution for a different reason. They discounted intelligence as a likely source as they claimed that differences in intelligence amongst the members of society have always been reasonably tolerated. Even the least intelligent have been found work to do and a place to belong (at least, throughout most of history). However, society has been far less tolerant of those who go against social expectations. So Kuttner et al. suggest that the schizophrenic has survived because of the ability to withdraw from society when things 'get bad'. The withdrawal from the ever-increasing pressures of society can, therefore, be seen as some kind of immunity to the stresses of everyday social interactions and offers an advantage in coping with normal life. However, as we shall see, Crow (2004a) argues that all three are linked but that the lynch pin is language.

There have been lots of other attempts to explain why schizophrenia might be advantageous. Mayer-Gross, Roth and Slater (1969) suggested that the **schizotypal** personality was ideally suited to isolated habitats. The person is happy with their isolated existence and Slater and Roth even suggested that the auditory hallucinations might in some way be comforting to the isolated individual. Erlenmyer-Kimling and Paradowski (1966) have explored, and rejected, the idea that in history, people with schizophrenia were revered for their mystical status and enjoyed privileges in much the same way as a shaman. However, we should not dismiss this idea so hastily. After all, we know that many schizophrenic delusions are mystical or religious in nature and that such a person could become a cult leader. I discuss this further in the analysis of the group splitting hypothesis.

The speciation hypothesis

One of the most puzzling features of schizophrenia is the fact that the incidence rates are uniform across cultures. No matter how cultures differ in their geography, climate or social structure, the incidence rate is about the same. This naturally makes one think that schizophrenia must be a consequence of being human and must have first developed when the species first came into existence. This is referred to as **speciation**. Even more puzzling is that the disease persists even though it presents the worst possible case for its continued reproductive success. We have already seen that the onset of schizophrenia coincides with the reproductive phase of life and that it decreases the fecundity of the individual (the likelihood of reproductive success) by 30% in females and by a massive 70% in males. How, then, does it manage to persist? If we consider Darwin's principle of evolution then we have to conclude that it is inextricably linked with a genetic advantage that balances out the disadvantage of schizophrenia. According to some, the phenomenon that best fits the bill of being a defining characteristic of being human, and one that we know to be linked to significant changes in neural structure, is language. Just to make clear that language is uniquely human,

I am defining it as a form of communication in which there is a formal use of symbols with grammatical structure and which provides a virtually infinite combination of words into sentences that can be understood by any competent speaker on first hearing. This definition separates language from the forms of communication in other species, including other primates. According to Berlim, Mattevi, Belmonte-de-Abreu and Crow (2003), what is unusual about the emergence of language in humans is that it could not have developed gradually in the way that you would expect new, complex features to evolve. It must have happened quite abruptly as the components of language can only function as a whole rather than as a set of features that gradually emerged. So what has the emergence of language got to do with schizophrenia?

Circumstantially, we note that wherever in the world schizophrenia presents itself, its features are identical. That means it must have emerged before the species got geographically separated (about 10,000 to 50,000 years ago). The earliest findings of human language date back about 60,000 years, so this timing would fit with the emergence of schizophrenia at about the same time as the emergence of language. It is therefore a feasible hypothesis that the genetic change that gave us language also gave us schizophrenia. The key to the argument is the hemispheric lateralisation that was required for language to emerge. Language in most people is a function of the left side of the brain (the left hemisphere), and the reason for its specialisation on one side is to minimise the delay caused by information travelling from one side of the brain to the other (across the connecting bridge called the corpus callosum). So the development of language brought with it cerebral asymmetry (different functions being controlled by the two different cerebral hemispheres). The link to schizophrenia is that these people tend not to show such asymmetry. This is evidenced, in part, from their lack of manual preference, that is, their tendency to be ambidextrous (Sommer, Ramsey, Kahn, Aleman & Bouma, 2001). We can explore this lack of symmetry a little further.

If language needs to be lateralised in order to function properly then anyone with a lack of symmetry should show a deficit in language. Crow (1997, 2004a) has argued that in people with schizophrenia this deficit of language manifests itself as auditory hallucinations. We need to examine the component parts of an auditory hallucination in order to see how this arises from a lack of lateralisation. Wing, Cooper and Sartorius (1974) have provided an easy-to-follow account (Table 5.1).

What we have here is a disruption to the links between four elements of language. These are thought, meaning, speech input and speech output. Crow argues that these four elements are handled in what he calls the four quadrants of the association cortex of the brain. This gives an anterior left

Component	Description
Thought echo	the person experiences thoughts as echoed internally with very little time between the original and the echo
Voices commenting	the person hears a voice speaking about him and referring to him in the third person
Passivity	the person feels as though his will is being replaced by that of another agency
Thought insertion	the person experiences thoughts intruding into his mind from another source
Thought withdrawal	it feels as though the person's own thoughts have been removed
Thought broadcast	the person experiences his personal thoughts being shared with others
Primary delusions	the person believes that sensory experiences have special meaning

Table 5.1 Component Parts of an Auditory Hallucination (Wing et al., 1974)

and right and a posterior left and right. The anterior region is mostly motor and the posterior region is mostly sensory. However, the asymmetry is not the same anteriorly and posteriorly. On the anterior half of the brain the left side is dominant so the information flow tends to be from right to left. In the posterior half, dominance is reversed so the flow tends to be from left to right. The sensory half on the left handles speech input and it has a special relationship with the more abstract and dominant sensory equivalent on the right side that extracts 'meaning'. Conversely, the speech output quadrant on the left is the dominant side and it has a special relationship with the more abstract equivalent on the non-dominant side which mediates 'thought'. This crossover between the anterior and posterior parts of the brain is referred to as torque.

That the human brain has evolved this way is unique and gives us our special relationship with language. Why, then, is language so important here? The function of language is to mediate the person's relationship with the outside world, particularly with another person. Each linguistic utterance is the interplay between a speaker and a hearer. So for the individual, some utterances are self-generated and some are other-generated. The self-generated stems from the anterior, motor half whilst the other-generated stems from the posterior, sensory half. Imagine, now, that the thoughts generated in the anterior right quadrant pass to the motor output, anterior left quadrant but lose their marker which defines them as self-generated. Those words will be spoken and will be heard by the sensory part of the system. Usually they would be identified as things the person has said because they will have the 'self-generated' marker. If they have now lost that they will be interpreted as other-generated, in other words, as coming from someone else. It is relatively easy now to make the leap to auditory hallucinations which are a trademark characteristic of schizophrenia. If the schizophrenic makes an out-loud utterance when no-one else is present and that utterance does not have a self-generated tag then the conclusion must be that the voice came from someone else inside their own head. It is not necessary for the utterance to actually be made as long as the thought is transferred to the left hemisphere.

So we can see how it is plausible that schizophrenia is an unhappy consequence of the development of language and how its incidence persists because of a genetic predisposition to a brain that develops without the usual asymmetry. In terms of the evolution of the maladaptation in people with schizophrenia, many have suggested that the critical genetic change happens on the sex chromosomes. It is believed that the gene for asymmetry lies on the sex chromosomes as those who are lacking an X chromosome (Turner's syndrome) and those with an extra X chromosome (Klinefelter's syndrome) both have deficits in just one hemisphere. Whilst the details are complicated, the basic principle is that there is an asymmetry gene on the X chromosome and a copy of the gene on the Y chromosome. This arrangement can quite easily explain why the incidence rates in males and females differ. Berlim et al. (2003) sum the whole argument up nicely. They say that, "… a single genetic change on the Y chromosome (e.g. the one that originated the 'asymmetry gene') could be propagated within the population, and by the mechanism of sexual selection, will lead to a gradual transformation of the population as a whole. According to this concept, age at procreation may be seen as representing the point at which linguistic competence is maximized and brain growth reaches a plateau. Moreover, some individuals with extreme genetic variants of hemispheric specialization may be predisposed to develop the deviations of psychological function that we describe as schizophrenia." (p. 12)

Group splitting

The group splitting hypothesis is not as obvious as the speciation hypothesis but it is every bit as interesting as a theory of how schizophrenia confers a species advantage and thereby maintains its incidence rate within the population. The principle of group splitting is that for any species there is an optimal size for a group of individuals. That size is determined by the availability of food, shelter and mating opportunities, to name just a few. If the group size starts to become too big then the optimal strategy is for a breakaway group to go off and find a new habitat to colonise. Stevens and Price

(1996) have argued that schizophrenia can play a pivotal role in group splitting in humans. They argue that a certain type of characteristic is needed for a group to split. Price and Stevens (1998) describe two different types of dispersal strategy. In the first type, the dispersal group fully adopts all of the norms of the parent group. This is seen as a colonisation as the new group are an identical copy of their parent group. This is very much the sort of behaviour we have witnessed through history in places like America and Australia. The other kind of dispersal is when the daughter group adopts new norms and beliefs. This is the type of behaviour we see in the formation of a cult. Here the cult leader offers something new and different to potential followers. Price and Stevens argue that if the conditions are right this second form of dispersal produces a leader who is hailed a prophet (or some such title), but if the conditions are not favourable then the person is labelled psychotic.

Price and Stevens explain how group splitting comes to occur. They suggest that when a new group forms there is an initial growth phase where the group norms are established and the group takes on its own identity. Once the group size has become large enough, there will naturally be competition between the group and other neighbouring groups. Whilst there are other groups to blame for events, the group has a level of cohesiveness. Once all of the competing other groups have been eliminated, any further competition has to happen from within the group. Subgroups will emerge, some of which become dominant and some of which become suppressed. It is here that group splitting is most likely. However, splitting from the parent group is not an easy thing to do. After all, the members of the suppressed groups still buy in to the principles and norms of the oppressors. It will take something special, like a cult, to drive the wedge between the parent group and the new splinter group.

Wallace (1970) described the way in which a prophet creates a new cult and populates it with disciples. He called this the mazeway resynthesis. The basic principle is that after a stressful situation, such as depression, a person's cultural beliefs and values (the mazeway) can be reorganised. The prophet has the desire to preach the newfound belief system and collects converts. The converts undergo a hysterical conversion rather than a mazeway resynthesis and so have to be continually fed the new doctrine, or they will return to their previous beliefs. If successful, though, the cult leader will have the power to control reproduction. If the cult leader is female then this power is likely to be conferred to any sons. Stevens and Price (2000) have suggested that characters like David Koresh and Jim Jones fit the mould of the schizotypal 'guru' who has led a cult and achieved reproductive success. There are also suggestions that other strong leaders, like Hitler and Joan of Arc, were schizophrenic, but these suggestions are wholly anecdotal.

This mazeway resynthesis hypothesis suggests that this description is fairly close to the changes that are undergone by the person who fails to become a cult leader and becomes a schizophrenic. The schizophrenic undergoes a mazeway resynthesis and has the urge to preach it to everyone within earshot. If this preaching is successful then a new cult will form. If it is not successful then the schizophrenic feels the need to leave the group, at least socially if not physically. The schizophrenic now becomes socially isolated because he cannot communicate with those who do not share his new beliefs.

What, if any, are the problems with the group splitting hypothesis? It proposes that there is an advantage to being schizophrenic in times when the group needs a leader to initiate a split. However, there is no good evidence that this is the case and, as we have seen, the examples put forward are all anecdotal. Other, similar, claims like greater creativity or genius are equally unfounded. Furthermore, there is no good evidence that being a genius or creative confers some reproductive advantage. Indeed, historically we might even argue the reverse. So, whilst this theory is a fascinating idea, it is difficult to verify because it is almost impossible to gather evidence that indicates it is the real reason for the emergence of schizophrenia.

Schizophrenia as a by-product of social cognition

It might be argued that whilst the speciation hypothesis described above could explain the auditory hallucinations that people with schizophrenia experience and whilst the group splitting hypothesis might explain some of the behavioural traits of the schizophrenic, neither theory explains how and why the whole picture of schizophrenia emerged. We have already encountered in Chapter 4 the areas of the brain that are said to make up the social brain. Burns (2004) proposes that the root of schizophrenia can be traced to the emergence, in humans, of the social brain. The suggestion is an alternative form of the speciation hypothesis in that it too argues that schizophrenia is a costly trade-off for an evolutionary advantage. As with Crow (2004b) version of speciation, you cannot have one (in this case, social evolution) without the potential for the other (a spectrum of social behaviours that includes, at one extreme, schizophrenia).

Burns argues that prior to the emergence of humans, the various functions of the brain were not very connected to each other. Whilst their brains functioned harmoniously, there was not much cross-talk between the various processes. By way of analogy, imagine the production of a car. In one area of the factory, people are assembling the engine. They are responding to local things like "are there enough of part x to complete the current job?" and so on, but they are oblivious to what is going on in the part of the factory that makes car seats. If everything runs smoothly in all parts of the factory, the result is that somewhere all of the parts get combined and the result is a finished car. Imagine, though, what happens if the seat makers have a problem making their seats and the engine folk know nothing about it. We end up with lots of engines not enough seats and, most importantly, not enough cars. How much better it would be if the areas of the factory communicated with each other! The integration of information from various parts of the whole factory system is critical to the improved functioning of that system. And so it is with brains.

Burns argues that prior to human evolution there was some, but not much, cortical connectivity, so the various functions of the brain did not communicate very much with each other. Most importantly, the result was that there was little capability for the animals to work collectively in a social environment. That is not to say they could not do this at all. We know that many lower animals function in social groups. The important difference was the lack of what we refer to as **social cognition**. Social cognition guides us in understanding how we should behave in situations. This information doesn't just come from the environment. Imagine you are at a family gathering. Your immediate family, mum, dad and siblings, know why Uncle Tommy is not at the gathering but your cousins do not. Uncle Tommy is not there because he is at his workshop building a surprise gift for one of the cousins. You, however, know he is at his workshop but not why. You innocently start to say where Uncle Tommy is and mum instantly shoots you a glare that says "stop talking right now!" This is social cognition in action. A lot of connected things happened in your head during this simple event. You perceived not only the obvious elements of the situation but also the hidden ones that enabled you to appreciate what mum was thinking. We call this having a **Theory of Mind** (further discussion of this appears in Chapter 6) and it is critical to higher order **social functioning**. That one glare is instantaneously interpreted as:

- Mum is angry.
- Mum is conveying a message that I should not continue saying where Uncle Tommy is.
- Mum believes that it would be bad for me to say where Uncle Tommy is.
- Mum probably has information about Uncle Tommy that I do not have and this is why she is responding this way.

Without social cognition, you could only derive the first of these points and possibly the second. You would not be able to derive the third and fourth points.

What we have in these stories is the idea that an increase in cortical connectivity allowed an increase in social competence through social cognition. However, it also created an opportunity for aberrant connectivity. In other words, in some individuals, genetic changes caused the connectivity to be faulty. The development of social cognition might have been critically important to this new species' survival. Whiten (1999) comments that the development of what he called a deep social mind would have allowed early humans to compete for food with monkeys, who were better adapted to climb trees, and other carnivores who were stronger and faster across the savannah plains of Africa.

So how did schizophrenia emerge according to this theory and why has it persisted in the population? The increased cortical connectivity brought with it huge leaps and bounds in the social co-operation amongst the members of this new human species. This change is therefore highly adaptive but comes with a risk. The risk is the possibility of these adaptive genes also carrying the small possibility of the cortical connections being wired in wrongly. There are lots of different mechanisms by which the details of this can occur that are beyond the scope of this book. However, they each point to a plausible argument for the development and the incidence rate of schizophrenia. This would also explain why we do not see schizophrenia in any other species. Furthermore, this theory can account for the language proposal of Crow. The emergence of higher thought and especially language could also be accounted for by the increase in cortical connectivity.

To summarise what we have explored with the evolutionary theories of schizophrenia, all of the theories agree that the emergence of schizophrenia was the result of the increase in brain size and, especially, the neocortex as a result of social living. They also agree that this probably happened between 40 and 16 million years ago (mya). They also all agree that cerebral reorganisation and increased connectivity would have taken place from 16 mya onwards. What then caused the internal environment for schizophrenia to be possible is then under debate. Crow argues it is the emergence of language, Price and Stevens suggest it is the need for leaders who can split the group when resources are stretched to the limit and Burns believes it to be the emergence of the social brain and the development of a theory of mind. All three perspectives are plausible and all may have a grain of truth. They are not necessarily mutually exclusive and, given that we cannot recreate the exact conditions of evolution all that time ago, we will never properly be able to decide between them. One thing, though, is certain. Schizophrenia is a uniquely human disorder and must have remained in existence because its damaging effect was outweighed by the advantages that led to its possibility.

◉ Chapter summary

The first half of this chapter has explored some of the causes of schizophrenia from a bio-evolutionary perspective. We have explored whether there are any events that occur during pregnancy that might lead to the changes we learned about in the previous two chapters. We have seen that there are, indeed, increased risks from obstetric complications and from maternal infection. We can be less clear about the possible effect of birth order on the risk of developing schizophrenia. That obstetric complications or maternal infection might be the critical events can be understood in the context of the potential damage these can do to the brain development of the foetus.

The second half of this chapter has asked why schizophrenia still exists in the population if it is so disadvantageous to the point of limiting the reproductive chances of the sufferer. We have looked at some very different ideas as to why schizophrenia evolved and why it has remained. Speciation considered that it is the price we pay for having the capability of language whereas the group splitting hypothesis proposes that such characters are needed periodically to maintain an optimal resource management. The social brain hypothesis suggests that it is the result of our increased social competence due to flexibility in our cortical wiring. All three are both fantastic and plausible at the same time. That language and the social environment have been so prominent in the evolutionary theories leads us nicely to the next chapter where we consider the cognitive and social psychological changes that accompany schizophrenia.

◉ Further reading

Crow, Timothy J. (2004) *The Speciation of Modern Homo Sapiens*. Oxford: Oxford University Press.

Dalén, P. (1975) *Season of Birth A Study of Schizophrenia and Other Mental Disorders*. North Holland.

Polimeni, J. and Price, J. (2013) *Shamans among Us: Schizophrenia, Shamanism and the Evolutionary Origins of Religion*. Evobooks.

Chapter 6

Social and Cognitive Explanations

👁 Introduction

In this chapter we take a look at the theories about schizophrenia that try to explain the role of social and cognitive factors. These ideas span the influence of these factors on the functioning of the individual as well as the possible contributions of these factors to the development of

In this chapter we will cover:
- Cognitive explanations of schizophrenia
  - The general nature of the deficits
  - Perceptual deficits
  - Attentional deficits
  - Working memory deficits
  - Other forms of memory deficit
  - Language deficits
  - Reasoning deficits
- Social psychological explanations of schizophrenia
  - Schizophrenia and social cognition
  - Does the impairment in social cognition contribute to the development of schizophrenia?
  - Theory of mind
  - How schizophrenia affects social functioning
  - People with schizophrenia and their local environment
  - How Cognitive and Social Deficits Affect the Quality of Life of the Schizophrenic

schizophrenia. It should be noted at the outset that these theories do not necessarily deny an underlying biological underpinning, but what they seek to do is explain how and why people with schizophrenia display abnormal social and cognitive behaviours. From a purely cognitive perspective, schizophrenia can be associated with problems at all stages of cognition, including attentional processes, memory and problem-solving skills. From a social perspective, these predominantly involve problems with what is called social cognition and how this impacts on a person's ability to interact normally within a social world. Social cognition includes the processing of emotion and social cues, the Theory of Mind and attributional biases. In addition, we will look at the possibility that a poor social environment could be the cause of schizophrenia rather than simply the consequence.

Cognitive explanations of schizophrenia

The degree of cognitive impairment seen in people with schizophrenia can vary greatly, especially if the schizophrenia is controlled with medication. Nevertheless, most of them exhibit some form of cognitive deficit. Much of the research into these deficits has concentrated on key areas such as perception, attention, working memory, language and problem solving and reasoning. More recently, the recognition that there are brain correlates of these impairments has led to the term 'neurocognition' being routinely used to describe these deficits. A lot of research in this area has not only looked at those with full-blown schizophrenia but has also examined first-episode patients and a number of at risk groups such as relatives of sufferers. The intention of the research is threefold, firstly to examine the extent of deficits in schizophrenia sufferers, secondly to determine which, if any, of these deficits have genetic or environmental markers and thirdly to use the information to inform treatment regimes.

The general nature of the deficits

Before going into details about each type of deficit that is seen, it is useful to have an overview of the types of cognitive problems people with schizophrenia face. The first thing to note is that they cover virtually all areas of cognitive activity. This poses an interesting question about the nature of the cognitive impairment. We can ask if all areas of cognition are affected because there is a generalised cognitive deficit or whether each deficit is specific to its own domain. If the former were true then we might be looking for a single feature that is deficient and which leads to all areas of cognition being affected. For example, the problem may be, for example, the reduced motivation in these individuals or it might be a side effect of the medication they are taking. If the latter were true then we should see patterns in those with schizophrenia where some functions are spared in some individuals. Finally, before we review the evidence, we should note that to take the viewpoint of a generalised deficit would be to see cognition from a systems approach, whereas to take the viewpoint from a components perspective would be reductionist and would suggest a more modular system for cognition.

Researchers such as Dickinson and Harvey (2009) argue that the deficits are global and a general cognitive impairment. They point out that the data continually show that people with schizophrenia have reduced cognitive performance across all of the sub-areas compared to controls. What is the evidence to support this view? Their argument comes from a number of strands of biological research, two of which are useful here. The first is the data on the structure of the central nervous system where it is seen that there is a reduction in the amount of grey matter (Honea et al., 2005) and, in particular, dendritic arborisation (the extent of the neuron's dendritic tree). This would reduce the number of synapses that a cell could make which would lower its functionality. In addition, Bartzokis and Altshuler (2005) have found reduced myelination of the axons. This would slow down processing speed and so, again, lead to a generalised impairment. The second strand is the fact that NMDA receptors for glutamate (see Chapter 3) are impaired across the whole neocortex (Coyle, 1996) and so has widespread cognitive implications. Glutamate is an important cortical neurotransmitter in its own right and it is also important in the functioning of GABA, another neurotransmitter. Again, disruptions to these systems would point to a generalised deficit rather than specific and separate impairments.

We must, before leaving this idea of a global deficit, point out one methodological issue that you should bear in mind for the rest of this section. It is at least partly true that many of the cognitive tests employed to tease out particular features of cognition are, indeed, multifactorial and tap into multiple areas of the cognitive system. If this is the case then it would be no surprise to see deficits in all domains, despite the widespread and generalised nature of the biological deficits. On the other hand, the multifactorial nature of tests could reflect the integrated nature of the entire cognitive system. For example, a perceptual deficit would have knock-on effects throughout the system and, as we know that cognition is a top-down as well as a bottom-up process, a reasoning deficit could have implications for the expectations of our perceptual system. Here, then, a specific deficit in one component of cognition would, nevertheless, show up as consequential deficits in other components.

Perceptual deficits

The work on perception in the field of schizophrenia has not really dealt with the typical cognitive elements of visual perception such as depth, colour and so on. Researchers, here, have been much more interested in how more complex elements of perception impact on a schizophrenic's functionality. So there has been an emphasis on face perception, the role of top-down processing and perceptual sensitivity to things lime criticism. As we will see later in the chapter, these cognitive skills all have important implications for the social judgements made by people with schizophrenia.

Shin et al. (2008) carried out a study to investigate the type of face processing problems people with schizophrenia have. They identified that in order to recognise a face you have to combine knowledge of the general features of a face (eyes, nose, and so on), the specific features of a face (which nose, which eyes, etc.) and also the configuration of the face (how far apart are the eyes, how far above the mouth is the nose, and so on). Shin et al. tested these last two elements using a paradigm where participants had to judge whether two presented faces were the same or different. Pairs of faces that were presented either did or did not differ in feature or in configuration. Face pairs were also presented either the right way up or upside down as it is known that faces are harder to judge when they are upside down. A control task involving chairs presented the right way up or upside down was also used. Twenty patients and 20 matched controls were tested, and the results showed that people with schizophrenia were much poorer on the configurational task than on the features task. Their performance was so poor that the usual difference between upright and inverted pictures was not seen. For the featural faces, the usual inversion effect was seen showing that there is a specific deficit in detecting the configurations of faces. This could explain why people with schizophrenia have difficulty in interpreting facial expressions as these involve configurational rather than featural changes to a face.

Another, related study was carried out by Chen, Norton, Ongur and Heckers (2008). They showed patients' line drawings in which there was either an embedded face or an embedded tree. As with the previous study, faces and trees were sometimes upright and sometimes inverted. They found that patients showed little inversion effect for faces compared with trees and the reason for this was their poor performance with upright faces. Chen et al. suggested that these results indicate a failure of face recognition at the initial visual detection phase. The authors suggest that there may be a link between the inability to recognise a face quickly and the inability to properly process facial information such as emotional expression. However, as they point out, their study does not directly shed light on that issue. So is there any evidence of altered perception of facial emotional expression in people with schizophrenia?

Kohler, Walker, Martin, Healey and Moberg (2010) undertook a meta-analytic review of research linking facial emotion perception and schizophrenia. They discovered that almost all of the studies conducted between 1970 and 2007 showed that people with schizophrenia perform poorly on facial emotion perception tasks. The tasks generally fall into two categories. Identification tasks require the patient to look at a picture of a face and use one of a limited set of emotional labels to describe that face. The labels are often drawn from Ekman and Friesen's (1978) list of six key emotions (happiness, sadness, anger, disgust, fear and surprise). The other task used is a differentiation task that simply asks the patient to judge whether or not two presented faces have the same or different emotional expressions. It does not seem to matter which task is used; emotion perception is poor. Whether this is something separate to the generally poor face perception is difficult to say from these kinds of studies. We do know, though, that people with schizophrenia tend to scan faces more globally and do not concentrate on the expressive facial components like those without schizophrenia do (Loughland, Williams & Gordon, 2002; Phillips & David, 1998). Interestingly, there is an age related element to the emotion processing deficit but no gender effect. Things get worse with age and this shows that facial emotion processing declines gradually. However, schizophrenic males and females perform equally badly whereas there is a female advantage for controls. It might be that once the deficit has reached the level it does in schizophrenia, any gender differences are masked by the poor performance.

One final perception study is included in this section. This study (Tschacher & Kupper, 2006) looked at the reasons behind patients' inability to perceive cause, in particular, the nature of who is the cause of events in their lives. They were interested in how patients perceive external events that have one or more causal explanation. They displayed on a computer screen two discs horizontally separated by a distance. The two discs slowly moved towards the centre of the screen until they reached each other. They then moved apart again until they were in their starting positions. The discs can be seen either as passing through and beyond each other or as bouncing off each other. Accompanying the visual display is a click that is made either before the discs meet, as they meet, or after they have met. This can lead a person to believe that the discs bounced off each other rather than passed through each other. In unaffected people this interpretation is not favoured unless the click is close to the point of contact. The proportion of trials on which a participant says the discs bounced off of one another is used as a measure of 'perceived causality'. Tschacher and Kupper found that the degree of perceived causality was associated with the degree of positive symptoms shown by the patient. This indicates that people with schizophrenia who suffer hallucinations and delusions may have dysfunctional perceptual processes regarding the causes of events in their lives.

Attentional deficits

The inability to properly attend to incoming stimuli has the potential to go some way to explaining the irrational thinking typical in schizophrenia. There are, though, different kinds of attentional process and different ways in which the processes can be measured. One form of attention is selective attention, through which we are able to discriminate between stimuli. This is particularly important in our ability to distinguish between important stimuli that have some predictive value and unimportant stimuli that have no predictive value. One good test of this is the Kamin Blocking effect. Here the participant is given a cue (stimulus A) which is a good predictor of some outcome. Having learned this, the participant is introduced to stimulus B which is also a good predictor of the same outcome. As stimulus B is effectively redundant, participants selectively attend to only stimulus A and so learning about stimulus B is blocked. People with schizophrenia do not show this block and, whilst they generally tend to learn less than controls, they learn as much about stimulus B as they do about stimulus A (Jones, Hemsley, Ball & Serra, 1997). So it would seem that people with schizophrenia have a tendency to pay too much attention to irrelevant cues. In a similar experiment by (Morris, Griffiths, Le Pelley & Weickert, 2012) a measure of positive symptoms of schizophrenia was obtained using the Positive and Negative Syndrome Scale. Using this measure they could divide their schizophrenia sample into low and high positive symptoms and they found that those performing worst on the Kamin blocking task were those with the highest positive symptom scores. Hence, it seems plausible to suggest that the inability to distinguish between important and unimportant social cues is a contributing factor to the development of positive symptoms. In other words, not being able to distinguish important elements of a social situation from non-important ones can, over time, lead to feelings of persecution or grandeur and/or to errors in thinking about the meaning of a social interaction.

Braff (1993) reviewed the literature on attention processing and concluded that the deficit in attention shown by people with schizophrenia was for conditions that needed conscious, effortful attentional processing rather than those situations where automatic attentional processes were sufficient. Automatic attention seems to utilise parallel processing (processing several pieces of information simultaneously), whereas effortful attention seems to occur via serial processing (where items are processed one at a time). For example, the Span of Apprehension (SOA) task is one where a person is presented with a very brief exposure to a large array of items. Part way through the display the person is informed which elements are to be recalled (a particular line, where a particular item is, and so on). Asarnow, Granholm and Sherman (1991) showed that those with schizophrenia are poor at this task. However, so are children at high risk of schizophrenia, first-degree relatives and even unaffected people who score towards the schizophrenia end of the Minnesota Multiphasic Personality Inventory (MMPI). It would seem, therefore, that this might indicate attentional problems to be a primary cognitive deficit in schizophrenia. Cornblatt, Lenzenweger, Dworkin and Erlenmeyer-Kimling (1992) suggested that these attentional problems are present in children with a susceptibility for schizophrenia and can affect personality development. They proposed a model for how attentional deficits can lead to the classic symptoms of schizophrenia. In essence, their model proposes that the attentional deficit particularly affects the person's ability to process social information. This makes interactions with others stressful. Unsuccessful attempts to maintain relationships make the situation worse and can act as an environmental trigger for the full-blown manifestation of symptoms. To counter the affects the schizophrenic may avoid contact with other people and in this way try to control their symptoms.

The lack of attentional processing has also been used to account for the lack of emotion processing in people with schizophrenia that we saw in the last section. Indeed, it is not too difficult to make this link given that Bruce and Young's (1986) model of face perception included a visual attentional component. Phillips and David (1998) have shown that people who are deluded tend to spend more time scanning irrelevant areas of a face than do non-deluded controls. Combs and Gouvier (2004) examined the relationship between attention and emotion processing in 65 people with chronic schizophrenia. Four components of attention were considered. These were focus-execute, encode, sustain and shift. For focus-execute, the participant must show that they can focus their attention and then execute an action on the basis of the attended information. The encode element uses digit span to test how many items can be attended to and encoded into short-term memory. The sustain element indicates how well a person can keep their attention focused by asking them to press a key whenever a zero (25% of trials) appears in a long sequence of single digits. Finally, the shift element uses the Wisconsin Card Sorting Task. Here participants are asked to sort a pack of cards into piles according to some feature, say, red or black. They are then asked to change to sorting by another feature, say, into suits. An ability to do this indicates an ability to shift attention. Emotion processing was tested using the Bell-Lysaker Emotion Recognition Test and the Face Emotion Identification Test. Both tests involve showing faces with one of six emotions or no emotion. Participants must correctly identify the emotion being displayed. Combs and Gouvier found that all four measures of attention were positively correlated with emotion perception. The shift and encode elements showed the strongest correlations, and this could explain the lack of emotion perception. An inability to shift attention could mean that the person fails to register a shift in emotional expression from one emotion to another. This would make following a social dialogue difficult. A failure to properly encode could mean that whilst one part of the body or face was indicating one emotion, another part might be giving a different signal. For example, a body position of being fed up might be accompanied with a smile. By only encoding one part of the total emotional presentation, a misperception could easily arise. Unfortunately, Combs and Gouvier did not include a control group in their study, so judgement about just how bad their participants' attentional abilities were is difficult to ascertain. However, Kohler, Bilker, Hagendoorn, Gur and Gur (2000) have indicated that in unaffected people there is no relationship between attentional capabilities and emotion perception. Combs and Gouvier have provided a model of how each attentional element might be associated with a particular element of emotion perception (Figure 6.1).

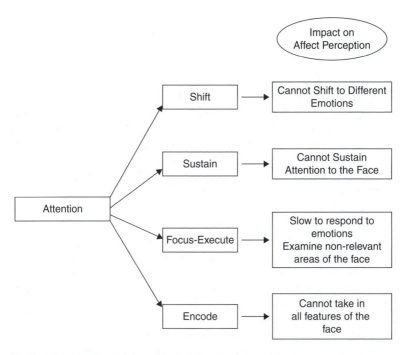

Figure 6.1 Theoretical Model of the Relationship between Attention and Affect Perception (taken from Combs and Gouvier, 2004, p. 735)

Working memory deficits

Working memory was first described by Baddeley and Hitch (1974) as a limited capacity working space for information processing. The system of a central executive and slave sub-systems provides "temporary storage and manipulation of the information necessary for such complex cognitive tasks as language comprehension, learning, and reasoning" (Baddeley, 1992, p. 556). Working memory deficits are seen as a core feature of schizophrenia (Cohen & Servan-Schreiber, 1992) and were first demonstrated by Park & Holzman (1992). Working memory has to function by encoding a representation of the information, maintaining that mental representation for as long as it is needed and updating it when new information requires it. If a person fails to properly encode the information then an incomplete mental representation will be formed and this will lead to performance errors. The maintenance part, which is seen by many as the primary element, is the direct link to attention. A failure to maintain the mental representation in the presence of distractors, whether they are internally or externally sourced, will mean that the information is not available when needed by other cognitive systems. It is possible, therefore, that tasks that require a delay in responding, and therefore a longer maintenance period, will be more impaired than tasks requiring no delay. Lee and Park (2005) carried out a review of 124 working memory and schizophrenia studies. They found several studies that pointed to poor encoding as the reason for the poor performance on working memory tasks, with impaired perceptual processing being the possible cause of the poor encoding. It might be that people with schizophrenia find it hard to choose the appropriate elements of the perceived world to focus on, and so their encoding of information into working memory is inefficient. However, Braver, Barch and Cohen (1999) have suggested that whilst the encoding problem might account for some of the working memory deficit, it cannot explain the whole story. Tek et al. (2002) have illustrated that even if techniques are used to maximise encoding, some spatial memory deficits still persist.

It is worth considering a methodological issue at this point. Most of the patients in these studies are taking medication to control their psychosis. We can ask if the medication masks the findings concerning working memory. Of course, this might skew the findings either way. It could be that the medication, in decreasing the cognitive systems that give rise to disordered thinking, somehow also decreases the ability to encode or maintain information in working memory. On the other hand, in that the medication is designed to raise mood and thereby reduce the negative symptoms of schizophrenia, it might be that the medication improves the patient's ability to focus attention and select more accurately the salient information to be encoded. If this is the case then we might expect that the working memory performance in an unmedicated patient would be even more impaired. Carter et al. (1996) carried out a study in which patients were taken off their medication for a period of 10 days prior to testing. Fortunately, this had no effect on the degree of impairment in spatial working memory, so we can rule out medication as being a factor.

Another finding from the Carter et al. (1996) study just referred to was that the degree of spatial working memory deficit was correlated with the level of negative symptoms. This finding has been confirmed very recently in a study by Manglam, Ram, Praharaj and Sarkhel (2010). They tested 78 medication-free patients on two components of the Wechsler Memory Scale. These were the Letter-Number Sequence and Spatial Span. The former involves the presentation of a sequence containing a mixture of letters and numbers. Participants must recall all of one type (letters or numbers) before recalling all of the other type. This task, therefore, involves not only the holding of information in working memory but also the added task of sorting the information into the correct category. The Spatial Span task is similar to the digit span task but uses the positions of blocks. In the computer version, you are presented with an array of blocks. On each trial blocks light up one at a time and you have to then recall which ones lit up in their correct sequence. Each time you are correct, one more block is added to the length of the sequence. Your span is the maximum number you can correctly recall. Schizophrenia patients performed worse than controls on both of these tasks compared to controls. They also tested patients and controls on the Scale for Assessment of Positive Symptoms and the Scale for Assessment of Negative Symptoms. Carter et al. found that patients with more severe negative symptoms performed worse on the spatial memory tasks but did not find a similar correlation for positive symptoms.

We have seen, then, that there is good evidence that the spatial part of the working memory system is impaired in schizophrenia. Lee and Park (2005) and others have all found that auditory working memory is equally impaired. Perry et al. (2001) have explored whether or not the central executive is also impaired. They have argued that we can define two types of use of the working memory system, one that involves simply the transient online storage and recall of information and one which involves the central executive in manipulating the information prior to recall. To illustrate the difference, the digit span forward task (hear a sequence of digits and repeat it back) only involves the holding and then recalling of information and so is a transient online storage task. The digit span backwards task (as the forward task but the digits must be recalled in reverse order) involves manipulation as well as straightforward storage and so is a central executive task. Other commonly used central executive tasks include the Wisconsin Card Sorting

Task (WCST: in which a set of cards must be sorted according to a named category – e.g. black cards and red cards, after which the category is changed – e.g. sort by number). When comparing forward and backward span performance, Perry et al. showed that people with schizophrenia were worse than controls by the same amount on both tasks. Like controls, they performed slightly better on the forward task than on the backward task. When tested on a number of central executive tasks, the pattern of performance was mixed, with those with schizophrenia performing worse than controls on some tasks but as well as them on others. The authors conluded that even though these patients have a significantly impaired working memory, the deficit is not particularly dramatic and does not appear to be specific to a certain aspect of working memory.

In Chapter 2 we looked at the heritability of schizophrenia. There we considered the concept of an endophenotype, and Saperstein et al. (2006) have argued that spatial working memory deficits might be one such endophenotype. They carried out a study which looked at the relative impairment of spatial working memory in sets of participants with decreasing risks of expressing schizotypical symptoms. These were people with schizophrenia, first–degree relatives with **schizophrenia spectrum personality disorders (SSPD)**, first–degree relatives without SSPD, individuals with SSPD traits but who had no family history of psychotic illness and, finally, individuals without SSPD and without a family history of psychotic illness. They used a task in which participants looked at a screen and were presented with three dots that were arranged so as to clearly indicate that there were places on a circle. Usually the circle would be complete with 12 dots, so on any trial a third of the circle placements were shown. After a short gap of 300ms, they were then shown a single dot that was either in the same place as one of the original three (hit) or in a different place (lure). Their results showed the greatest errors to be made by the schizophrenia group and the least errors to be made by the individuals without SSPD and without a family history of psychotic illness. Although each group's performance was not significantly different from each other group's performance, the order of group performance was as predicted and the performance of the people with schizophrenia was significantly poorer than the performance of the no SSPD and no family history group. Despite the fact that the sample size was fairly small, this study demonstrates that spatial working memory is a good candidate for a cognitive endophenotype of schizophrenia.

Other forms of memory deficit

Whilst there has been a lot of focus on working memory because of its link to executive functioning, we also need to explore how people with schizophrenia manage in terms of long-term memory. The picture here is not good either. Their recall and recognition scores are poor, though recall performance is usually the poorer. Many studies have shown that long-term memory is impaired beyond what one would expect from the level of intellectual impairment and, McKenna et al. (1990) even suggested that there was evidence for a schizophrenic amnesia. However, not everyone has found the impairment of memory to be that large and some have argued that it is a secondary consequence of the impairment in attention (Culver, Kunen & Zinkgraf, 1986). A meta-analysis by Aleman, Hijman, Haan and Kahn (1999) confirmed that the bulk of the literature points to long-term memory impairment, but this is not as severe as the impairment in working memory. Their findings do not, therefore, support the notion of schizophrenic amnesia. Indeed, Barch, Csernansky, Conturo and Snyder (2002) have indicated that the pattern of memory deficits resembles that we would expect from prefrontal cortex damage than that we would expect from medial temporal lobe and hippocampal damage, the latter being more usual in people suffering from amnesic syndromes.

It seems to make little difference if the information is presented visually or verbally (Paulsen et al., 2009), performance is about equally as poor. Leeson et al. (2010) reported that on tests of verbal learning and visual recognition memory patients showed impaired performance even when the scores were controlled for general IQ. The verbal memory task required patients to repeat a list of 15 nouns immediately, after a distractor task and then again after a 25-minute delay. Leeson et al. suggested that the poor performance on this task was due to the patients having a poor information processing speed. The visual recognition task required patients to identify which of two abstract patterns had been presented earlier.

Episodic memory is particularly impaired (Reichenberg & Harvey, 2007). Episodic memory is a person's ability to recall specific events that have happened in their lives, and it has been argued that this kind of memory is separate and distinct from semantic memory, our knowledge about the world. A confusion around this episodic–semantic distinction is where auto-biographical memory sits. This is personal memory that you hold about yourself. It is often labelled as episodic, but my knowledge of what school I went to when I was five years old is different to any particular memories of episodes whilst I was there. The episodic memory impairment shown by people with schizophrenia is present before the onset of the illness (Brewer et al., 2005) and remains quite stable at least until the person is 65 years old (Toulopoulou & Murray, 2004). The episodic impairment appears to arise because of problems with encoding rather than with storage or retrieval (Bonner-Jackson, Haut, Csernansky & Barch, 2005). Their impairment appears to follow a similar pattern to amnesics with an episodic memory deficit in that they fail to encode context information and so have trouble remembering when, where or how information was presented. If we look specifically at autobiographical memory, we see that schizophrenic patients recall fewer details than age-matched controls (Wood, Brewin & McLeod, 2006). The deficit is particularly acute in late adolescence and early adulthood, suggesting that disruptions in encoding and/or retrieval processes are particularly marked during this period.

People with schizophrenia also have poor semantic memory (Chen, Wilkins & McKenna, 1994). This has been confirmed using a number of different semantic memory tasks. For example, McKay et al., 1996 administered five separate tests of semantic memory to 46 schizophrenic patients. These were category fluency (generating as many items as possible in a category for one minute), naming (naming line drawings), sorting (sorting 48 pictures into semantic categories), word–to–picture matching (asked to point to the picture depicting a named item) and definitions (required to generate the defining features of named items). The patients performed poorly on all aspects of semantic memory.

All of the studies we have looked at so far in this section are concerned with the ability to remember past events. In some ways, a more interesting use of memory is as a prospective device. This prospective memory is the memory we use to remember to do something at some time in the future. The memory can be time–based, whereby we need to remember to do something at a particular time, event–based, whereby we have to remember to do something when a particular event presents itself, and activity–based, whereby we have to remember to carry out a task that follows on from and is part of a previous task. An example of time–based prospective memory would be to remember to go to the dentist at 3 o'clock. An example of an event–based task would be to remember to ask a question of someone when you next see them. An example of an activity–based memory task would be to remember to turn off the cooker when you have finished cooking. We might expect the activity–based task to be the easiest to remember as you are already in the middle of the relevant task whereas for the other two tasks you have to associate behaviours that are not necessarily of the same set. Shum, Ungvari, Tang and Leung (2004) gave people with schizophrenia and controls examples of all three task types and found that for both groups the activity–based task was the easiest and the time–based task was the hardest. The difference between the people with schizophrenia and controls was not that large for the activity–based and event–based tasks but was very large for the time–based task. Shum et al. claim that the difference is in the fact that whilst the event–based task requires an interruption of an ongoing activity in response to a cue, the time–based activity requires the person to initiate the interrupting activity using only their recall ability. The cue must be generated internally and this adds an additional difficulty for the schizophrenic. Shum et al. have proposed that the time-based task adds an additional processing load to the prefrontal cortex and this is an area of the brain we know from Chapter 4 to be impaired in schizophrenia.

Language deficits

One of the central features of schizophrenia is the interplay between disordered thought and the language used to express that thought. A lowered level of functioning has been seen in fluency, the complexity of language used and use of grammar, to name just some (for a review, see DeLisi, 2001). However, some aspects of language seem to be spared, such as knowledge of sentence rules (Miller & Phelan, 1980). Some have suggested that it is the importance of language to the condition of schizophrenia that defines it as a uniquely human phenomenon. Indeed, we have already encountered the evolutionary perspective of Crow (1997) in Chapter 5. However, not all agree with this position and some have put the language deficits down to a consequence of the problems with working or semantic memory. Furthermore, all of these aspects have been tested individually, so it is not clear if any given schizophrenic would possess all of these deficits or just a selection of them.

There does seem to be some selectivity regarding language deficits. Thomas, King, Fraser, & Kendell (1990) showed that there were no impairments in written language, only in spoken language. They suggested that this might be due to the quick retrieval needed for speech. Writing slowly does not expose a lack of linguistic fluency whereas speaking slowly does. To avoid this, people with schizophrenia tend to use simplistic rather than complex forms of speech but their writing shows the levels of complexity you would expect to find in those without schizophrenia. This difference, along with many of the other linguistic problems can be understood in the context of the working memory problems we encountered earlier.

As well as deficits in language output, there are well-documented studies showing deficits in language comprehension. Studies have shown deficiencies in comprehension levels and in semantic processing (Condray, Steinhauer, van Kammen & Kasparek, 1996; Hoffman, Hogben, Smith & Calhoun, 1985). Condray, Steinhauer, van Kammen and Kasparek (2002) looked at the comprehension of syntax in people with schizophrenia. Syntax is the system of rules used by a language. In English, the order of words is usually subject, verb object so presenting the object before the subject would increase the demands on the comprehension system. Similarly, the use of clauses can be manipulated, particularly what are called relative clauses. For example, if I said, "the boy, *who liked to play chess*, was good at problem solving," then the section in italics would be classed as a subject-relative clause. If, however, I said, "the woman, *whom the children liked a lot*, was good at making up stories," then the section in italics would be classed as the object-relative clause. Condray et al. gave people with schizophrenia and controls sentences in which an actor (either the subject or the object of the sentence) was defined in the main clause or in the relative clause. Whilst everyone does worse when the actor is denoted in the subordinate clause, those with schizophrenia show a bigger drop in performance.

It is possible that the language deficits are evident long before the signs of schizophrenia emerge. For example, Jones, Rodgers, Murray and Marmot (1994) showed that children who later went onto develop schizophrenia have language abnormalities earlier in childhood. Given that these problems precede the onset of the disease, they can act as indicators of high risk in those who are biologically predisposed towards schizophrenia. Bearden et al. (2000) have conducted a longitudinal study looking at language development (along with measures of behavioural problems) at ages 8 months, 4 years and 7 years. They found that whilst behavioural problems were evident as early as four years old, there were distinct signs of language problems by the age of seven years. They also found that there were qualitatively similar problems at a sub-clinical level in siblings of these children even though the siblings did not go on to develop schizophrenia.

Overall, then, it would seem that language difficulties are prominent in people with schizophrenia and that such difficulties develop early in childhood. That these may be of clinical significance as early as age seven could provide useful evidence that these deficits are a part of the genetic profile of schizophrenia. Such information could also prove useful in enabling clinicians to work with such children and their families before the onset of the disorder.

Reasoning deficits

One of the fascinating features of schizophrenia is **delusional thinking**. A number of researchers have been interested to know what goes wrong with the cognitive processes that allow most of us to reject fanciful ideas as not being real. Why is it that the delusional schizophrenic has such ideas in the first place and then fails to reject them as having any basis in reality, even when the available and obvious evidence points to the idea or belief being untrue? A two-factor theory has been proposed to answer this question. The first factor tries to explain why the deluded person has the delusional belief in the first place and the second factor tries to explain why it is not rejected. Suggestions for why some delusions come to mind at all include explanations from Capgras syndrome (when a family member is believed to be an imposter) to being controlled by an alien. The former is explained as a mismatch between the visual processing of the person's image and the lack of autonomic responding that should indicate familiarity. The latter is explained by a lack of internal monitoring of a person's actions leading to a feeling that they are not controlled by that person. It is possible that these cognitive disruptions are the kinds of event that might explain the delusions of the schizophrenic. The other factor, accepting the belief to be true without question, has been researched fairly extensively over recent years. Three explanations have been proposed for this second factor: jumping-to-conclusions (JTC), an extreme causal attribution bias and a theory-of-mind deficit. The tendency to jump to conclusions can be tested using a 2-jar task. Two jars are presented, both containing two colours of beads. In one jar, there are twice as many beads of one colour as the other and in the other jar the ratio is reversed. Unseen by the patient, beads are drawn from only one jar and shown to the participant. They simply have to say when they think they know which jar the beads are being drawn from. Garety et al. (2005) showed that deluded individuals take significantly fewer trials before they decide they know which jar the beads are being drawn from. In other words, they jump to conclusions. The extreme attributional bias has been shown by Kinderman and Bentall (1997). They showed that deluded individuals are much more likely to attribute negative events to external causes and that those causes are likely to be other people rather than situations. Theory of Mind is the ability to understand that others may hold different thoughts and beliefs to you and the ability to interpret those alternative thoughts and beliefs from the behaviours others display. Frith (1992) has shown that deluded individuals lack this ability and has claimed that this might contribute to the belief that delusional thoughts are true. Langdon, Ward and Coltheart (2010) have shown all three processes, JTC, attributional bias and a lack of theory of mind, to contribute to the maintenance of delusional beliefs in people with schizophrenia.

There is further evidence regarding why the delusional thoughts come to mind at all. Lincoln, Lange, Burau, Exner and Moritz (2010) have suggested that paranoia is related to state anxiety. State anxiety is a response to a situation rather than a permanent personality attribute (that would be trait anxiety). State anxiety provides a good background to the development of delusional thoughts because it narrows a person's attention to emotionally relevant cues. However, this is moderated by the person's general level of vulnerability and mediated by their tendency to jump to conclusions. So if a person has high state anxiety, is vulnerable and has a tendency to jump to conclusions then under certain circumstances they will find it difficult to simultaneously maintain cognitive and emotional control over the information coming in and this can lead to paranoid delusional thinking.

A final aspect to consider in this section is the role played by semantic memory in the ability to make reasoned judgements. In formal logic, conditional reasoning is often used as a test of reasoned thinking. Take, for example, a situation in which you are told, "if Jenny presses the power button on the remote then the TV will come on." There are two logical conclusions and two fallacies that can be drawn by knowing one piece of information. These are the two logical conclusions. If Jenny pressed the button then the TV came on. If the TV did not come on then Jenny did not press the button. The two fallacies are as follows. Jenny did not press the button so the TV did not come on. The TV came on so Jenny must have pressed the button. In both cases, someone else might have pressed the button. Whilst these are the logical answers, humans do not merely apply logic to the situation but also use what are called 'disabling conditions' and 'alternative causes' to help them make a decision. A disabling condition in our example might be that there are no batteries in the remote so that even if Jenny does press the button, the TV will not come on. An alternative cause refers to the fallacies above, that is, someone else presses the button. Both disabling conditions and alternative causes require our semantic memory, that is, our implicit memory of how the world works. People with schizophrenia are known to have poor semantic memory (Chen et al., 1994), so we can see how this might lead to them not exploring alternative explanations for events and jumping to conclusions as we have seen previously.

◉ Summing up the cognitive effects

We have seen in the first part of this chapter that people with schizophrenia suffer from quite severe cognitive deficits. These go some way to explaining positive symptoms such as delusions and thought disorders and also explain the development of negative symptoms. We will now turn to the social psychological explanations of schizophrenia, and you will see that a number of these build on what we have learnt from the cognitive deficits. This is especially true when it comes to how people with schizophrenia interact with other people.

◉ Social psychological explanations of schizophrenia

There are three dimensions to the relationship between social factors and schizophrenia. Firstly, we have the degree to which the social environment contributes to the development of schizophrenia, secondly we have the effect that schizophrenia has on an individual's ability to function within a social environment and finally we have the influence those people with schizophrenia have on their local social environment.

Schizophrenia and social cognition

Our awareness of the meaning of our social environment and hence our ability to function within our social environment is known as social cognition. This incorporates a large number of different processes, including emotion perception, social perception, Theory of Mind and attributional style. Emotion perception is our ability to use the information contained in facial expressions and voice intonation (known as prosody) to build up an appreciation of the emotional state of the person we are interacting with. Social perception is the ability to use the various cues in the social environment to derive knowledge of the social context. Such cues provide vital information about social conventions and social rules. If we misread these cues then we are likely to produce an inappropriate behaviour for the social situation (e.g. being over-familiar at a formal social gathering). Theory of Mind refers to our understanding that others have mental states that are different from our own. For example, I might believe that I am a good footballer but not everyone will share that mental state. Finally, our attributional style is how we tend to explain the things that happen to us. For example, if we fail at something we could blame ourselves, blame others or blame the situation. People with delusions or paranoias have a tendency to blame others.

We know that people with schizophrenia are not very socially adept and that they show marked impairments in all kinds of social situations. They have difficulty in communicating with others, they are poor at developing and maintaining relationships (whether these are friendships or sexual partnerships) and they have difficulty in maintaining a job. Given what we also know about the positive and negative symptoms of schizophrenia, it seems pertinent to examine the processes of social cognition to see if any of these are the root cause of the lack of social functioning, especially since a number of aspects of social cognition have been investigated in people with schizophrenia.

Couture, Penn and Roberts (2006) reviewed the degree to which the difficulties that people with schizophrenia have in their everyday social functioning are a consequence of deficits in social cognition. They examined 22 studies looking at four areas of social cognition: emotion perception, social perception, Theory of Mind and attributional style. The greatest variety of measures used was found with social perception where four separate measures were used across the studies. For emotion perception, the Facial Emotion Identification Task was most used. This provides participants with a number of photographs of facial expressions and for each photograph the participant must name one of six emotions that applies to that photograph. The only Theory of Mind task used was the Hinting Task in which participants listen to a story presented verbally and must interpret the hint made by one of the characters. For example, if one person said to another in a domestic situation, "I would love to wear that shirt but it is very wrinkled," you would be right to interpret that as a hint for the receiver of the information to offer to iron the shirt (irrespective of whether or not they did iron the shirt). Attributional style was most often measured using a questionnaire that used various situations (e.g. a friend forgot to drop off a DVD at your house), and asked the participant to explain why this might have occurred. In order to determine as precisely as possible the links between social cognition and social functioning, the latter was divided into four domains: social behaviour, community functioning, social skills and social problem solving. A standard battery of tests was used to assess these along with assessments obtained from the nursing staff looking after the patients. The outcome of this review was that emotion perception and social perception are negatively related to all of the social functioning markers, but the lack of studies measuring Theory of Mind and attributional style makes it difficult to draw any firm conclusions. We can, perhaps, start to see a pattern of cascading causes if we combine these results with some we considered earlier. For example, the lack of attentional processing might cause a lack of emotion processing which might, in turn, lead to a lack of social functioning. We will draw out these links more clearly later.

Does the impairment in social cognition contribute to the development of schizophrenia?

We heard in the cognitive section of this chapter that researchers have proposed endophenotypic models of schizophrenia with cognitive impairments as a core component. To remind you, endophenotypic models are ones that suggest that there are inherited behaviours that accompany an illness. Eack et al. (2010) were interested in whether the same might be true of social cognitive impairments. In other words, could social cognitive deficits also function as endophenotypic markers of schizophrenia? Clues to the link have come from studies showing that siblings of schizophrenia sufferers are impaired on emotion perception tasks relative to controls but are not as impaired as the people with schizophrenia themselves (Kee, Horan, Mintz & Green, 2004; Leppänen et al., 2008). From these findings it is possible that deficits in social cognition, especially emotion perception, could increase the liability that a person at risk of developing schizophrenia is more likely to develop it. In their study, Eack et al. tested 50 first-degree relatives and

20 second-degree relatives of people with schizophrenia who were the first in their family to present with the disorder (referred to as probands) together with 63 controls on a series of tests that included emotion cognition, neurocognition and prodromal psychopathology (prodromal refers to the early onset stage of a disease). The results of the emotion processing task were interesting. The task consisted of viewing a number of photographs of faces, some of which displayed an emotion and some of which were neutral. Participants merely had to say which emotion (one of six or neutral) was displayed. Whilst there was no difference between these at risk relatives and controls for the emotional faces, the relatives were more likely to attribute an emotion to the neutral faces. Furthermore, that emotion was far more likely to be negative (e.g. sad). When looking at the neurocognitive performance, the relatives did have a lower performance than the controls. However, a further analysis ruled out these neurocognitive deficits as the cause of the reduced emotion perception capability. Eack et al. concluded that a deficit in emotion perception can be used as an endophenotypic risk marker. The interpretation of neutral facial emotions as negative emotions could indicate the beginning of the information processing biases that ultimately lead to the development of some of the positive symptoms of schizophrenia (e.g. paranoia).

If the last piece of research gave us an idea of how social cognitive deficits might relate to the positive symptoms of schizophrenia, it is sensible to as whether there is a similar relationship between social cognition and the negative symptoms. A recent study by Bell, Corbera, Johannesen, Fiszdon and Wexler (2013) looked at this relationship. In addition, they wanted to know whether either of these factors might contribute to their ability to function within the community. To do this, Bell et al. adopted a factor analytic approach. They looked at 77 outpatients and measured them on a number of social cognitive and schizophrenia symptomology measures. A couple of these social cognitive measure are worth outlining here. The Social Attribution Task – Multiple Choice Version is a task in which participants watch a small animation of some geometric shapes enacting a drama. The participant is then asked a series of multiple choice questions designed to tap into his/her understanding of the scenario. The Hinting Task is the test of Theory of Mind that was described earlier. Using these and a few other tests of social cognition, together with a battery of tests that explore the participant's positive and negative symptoms, Bell et al. were able to show that the social cognitive deficits and the negative symptoms were two distinctive factors for all but the Hinting Task measures. Using a further analysis, it appeared that three distinctive groups emerged. One group were high on negative symptoms (HN) and these people tended not to show any particular pattern with respect to social cognition. However, two distinctive social cognition groups emerged for those with low levels of negative symptoms.

One group had high levels of social cognitive (HSC) abilities whilst the other group had low levels of social cognitive abilities (LSC). Furthermore, when the social histories of these two latter groups were examined, distinctive patterns emerged. For example, the HSC group were more likely to have been married whilst the LSC group were much more likely to have been arrested. Bell et al. state that, "a picture familiar to clinicians begins to emerge for the prototypical member of each group. There is the withdrawn, HN patient who avoids social interactions and also avoids getting into trouble; the low negative symptom patient with poor social judgement who is active but accomplishes little and gets into lots of trouble; and the low negative symptom patient with better social judgement who has generally better community functioning and may seek help more readily." (p. 194). The ability to separate these groups may have clinical significance in terms of the treatment schedules one might adopt.

Of all of the elements of social cognition, attributional style is probably the one that has been studied the least. It is this element, though, that might best explain the processes that lead to paranoia and delusions of persecution. Whilst we saw earlier that dysfunctional emotion processing can lead to paranoia with respect to facial expressions, attributional style might explain a more widespread negativity to the interpretation of social situations. Martin and Penn (2002) conducted a study using people with schizophrenia who were both with and without persecutory delusions. They used a battery of attribution measures including the attributional style questionnaire (ASQ), where participants have to explain the cause of 12 scenarios (six positive and six negative), the pragmatic inference task (PIT), where participants have to answer both factual and attributional questions about scenarios, and the internal, personal and situational attributions questionnaire (IPSAQ), where participants are given scenarios to tease out whether they make internal, external-personal or external-situational judgements about the cause of the situation.

We can see that deficits in social cognition are clearly indicated in schizophrenia. These deficits may, in part, account for symptom elements such as paranoia, but they do not account for all of the symptoms and appear to be separate from at least some of the negative symptom elements. We can now turn our attention to the way in which these social cognitive deficits impact on the schizophrenic's ability to function within the social world.

Theory of mind

It might be more expected for a section about Theory of Mind (ToM) to appear within a consideration of cognitive factors rather than a section about social factors. However, I wish to use the ToM literature to illustrate just how important it is to normal social functioning. ToM is the ability to internally represent mental states. It not only permits a person to do that for their own mental states but also to estimate the mental states of others. Take, for example, having a belief about whether or not psychology is the best topic on the planet. We can instantly appreciate that we each have our own belief about that (that it is or that it isn't) and we can also appreciate that someone else may hold a different belief. This is having a ToM and it is crucially important for our social and cognitive well-being. You may or may not be surprised to learn that before the age of about four years old, humans do not possess a ToM. This has been demonstrated using the Sally and Anne test (Wimmer & Perner, 1983) described in Box 6.1.

Box 6.1 What Develops When? The Sally-Anne Test

One of the issues we have been exploring in this book is whether the deficits seen in people with schizophrenia are visible in very early childhood (even from birth) or whether these only come to light when the schizophrenic episodes of psychosis begin to emerge. In addressing this question we need to be aware that not all human functions are either present at birth or develop early in infancy. One such feature is Theory of Mind (ToM) and the following is a version of the simple test that can be used to see if a person possesses a ToM.

One version of this test involves a person being shown drawings that depict a scenario where Sally and Anne are both in a room. Sally has a bar of chocolate and she puts it into a cupboard. Sally then leaves the room and, whilst Sally is out, Anne moves the chocolate from the cupboard to a draw. We can ask two simple questions. Where does Sally believe the chocolate to be? Where does Anne believe the chocolate to be? It is obvious to us (because we have a ToM) that the two beliefs will be different. However, if you ask a 3-year-old, they are likely to say that Sally believes the chocolate to be in the drawer because that is where they, themselves, believe (or know) it to be. In other words, 3-year-olds have not yet developed the ToM that enables them to understand that not everyone holds the same beliefs that they do. Higher order elements of ToM develop even later in childhood. For example, the knowledge that someone else thinks that a third person has a different belief does not develop until about 6–7 years of age. The skill of understanding a faux pas comes even later (at about 10 years of age).

ToM is important in all manner of social situations. As well as being important in everyday scenarios (Fred likes me), it is important for the detection of lying (Fred says he hasn't seen my wallet but I can tell he knows where it is) and even humour (Fred just said I was ugly but I know he was kidding). Could it be, then, that any or all of the symptoms of schizophrenia are a consequence of patients having a deficient or non-existent ToM? There is a lot of research that suggests that ToM is impaired in people with schizophrenia. Frith (1992) has suggested that these patients may not be able to distinguish between their subjective representations of reality, in other words, their beliefs, and what is actually real. Everyone is capable of making this error at times. Take, for example, the person who goes on X Factor but who clearly cannot sing. They have a mismatch between their subjective representation of their ability to sing and the reality. Imagine, though, if you did that all the time for everything. It is possible to see how that might lead to delusional thinking of the kind displayed by the schizophrenic. Frith suggests that if we add the inability to understand their own behaviours as a result of their own intentions we can derive most of the major components of schizophrenia from a lack of ToM. This would include disorganised thinking, delusions of alien control, auditory hallucinations and delusions of persecution.

Some researchers have explored the characteristics of the ToM deficit in people with schizophrenia. We know that a lack of ToM is a major factor in disorders like autism. Langdon, Coltheart, Ward and Catts (2001) have demonstrated that the ToM deficit in schizophrenia is not the same as that shown by autistics as people with schizophrenia are usually able to understand that beliefs can be false (as in Anne's belief about where the chocolate is). They also showed that the ToM deficit is independent of any other cognitive deficits such as intelligence or executive planning. So if ToM is independent of other cognitive abilities, we can ask if the deficit is a trait characteristic or a state characteristic. In other words, is it shown by all patients (trait) or just by some (state) and is it seen in people who display schizotypical behaviours without being schizophrenic (trait)? It seems that not all patients show the same level of deficit (Frith, 1992) which would point to it being a state phenomenon. However, the more schizotypical a person's behaviour is, the more ToM deficits they display (Langdon & Coltheart, 1999) and that points to a trait phenomenon. The deciding piece of evidence came from Janssen, Krabbendam, Jolles & van Os (2003) who showed that first-degree relatives showed some impairment of ToM to a level greater than controls but not as much as people with schizophrenia. This clearly indicates that the ToM deficit is a trait characteristic in schizophrenia. Whether or not the lack of ToM is the result of it never properly developing in infancy or a change that is the result of a neuropathological process occurring just after puberty is unknown. It might be that those who develop schizophrenia have a genetic predisposition to an impaired ToM.

The reason for placing the section on ToM within the consideration of social factors rather than cognitive ones and for placing it after the section on social cognition is the importance of ToM to social competence. Sullivan and Allen (1999) have shown that without a fully functioning ToM it would be difficult to apply strategic social rules in social situations (e.g. being sensitive to another person's feelings). This has recently been supported by Mazza, De Risio, Tozzini, Roncone and Casacchia (2003) who has suggested that the degree of ToM impairment might be a good predictor of the level of social functioning displayed by a schizophrenic. We should now explore social functioning in more detail.

How schizophrenia affects social functioning

Now that we have explored the elements of social cognition and the role of Theory of Mind, we can try to piece it all together to get a picture of how these deficits affect the social functioning of the schizophrenic. In other words, we want to examine the impact of these problems on the way in which the schizophrenic views the social environment. A good place to start is a model proposed by Couture et al. (2006). They have tried to outline how they think social cognition and social functioning interact and the model, with their explanatory example, is reproduced below (Figure 6.2).

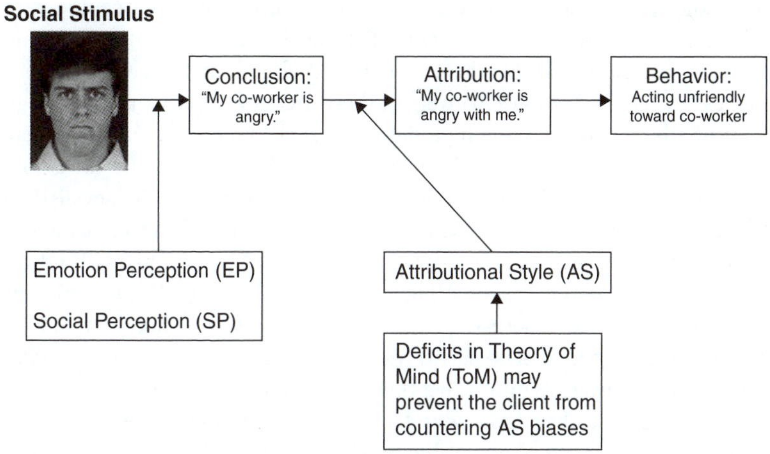

Social Stimulus

Conclusion: "My co-worker is angry." → Attribution: "My co-worker is angry with me." → Behavior: Acting unfriendly toward co-worker

Emotion Perception (EP)
Social Perception (SP)

Attributional Style (AS)

Deficits in Theory of Mind (ToM) may prevent the client from countering AS biases

Figure 6.2 Conceptual Framework for Understanding the Interplay between Social Cognition and Social Functioning (from Couture et al., 2006, S46)

The model describes how a schizophrenic might misinterpret the intentions behind a co-worker who rushes past him without saying hello. The expression on the co-worker's face might be socially and emotionally misperceived as angry when, in fact, the co-worker was stressed at being late for an appointment. Having come to this conclusion, the schizophrenic tries to explain the anger but because of the personalising bias in attributional style, together with an inability to put themselves in the co-worker's position, the attribution made is mistakenly that the co-worker is angry at them. This results in future behaviour towards the co-worker that is unfriendly, untrusting and may even be tinged with anger and hostility. If this repeats with other co-workers then the schizophrenic will find it difficult to carry out their own job (because of anger at co-workers) and will likely become isolated from the rest of the group.

Bora, Eryavuz, Kayahan, Sungu and Veznedaroglu (2006) also proposed a link between social cognition and social functioning. They measured social functioning, theory of mind and neurocognition in 50 schizophrenic patients. Those patients with a better level of social functioning scored higher on the Theory of Mind tasks and on the battery of neurocognitive tasks.

People with schizophrenia and their local environment

It is fairly obvious that people with schizophrenia have problems existing in the social world at least some of the time. Before we look at suggestions for the relationship between the social environment and schizophrenia, we need to understand some of the baseline data that we are trying to explain. It has been known for a long time that there are significantly more people with schizophrenia in urban areas of cities than in the rural areas that surround them. Even Faris and Dunham (1939) had found that, in Chicago, the highest levels of schizophrenia were in those areas of the city that had a high level of ethnic conflict and a high degree of social mobility (i.e. areas where people came and went with a high frequency). At that time and for a long time since then, the reason for this has been assumed to be social drift (Dohrenwend et al., 1992). This is where a particular social group comes to congregate in a particular area of a city, and we often see this with ethnic minorities and religious groups. The case for people with schizophrenia was presumed to be one of necessity rather than choice. It was thought that they congregated in the more socially deprived areas of cities because their personal circumstances meant that they failed to fit in elsewhere.

Two recent studies have found a similar relationship between being schizophrenic and the demographics of the area in which they live. In Maastricht, van Os, Driessen, Gunther and Delespaul (2000) found more single people with schizophrenia in areas with fewer single people. They examined a number of individual and neighbourhood factors from 220 cases of schizophrenia during the period 1986–1997. They discovered that from all the cases from different parts of Maastricht, only one neighbourhood had a significantly larger number of people with schizophrenia than that found in the standard population. This tied in with their finding that a person was more likely to be schizophrenic if they were foreign-born, unemployed or dependent on welfare benefits. They also found that schizophrenia was more likely in single males living alone, irrespective of whether these were never married or divorced individuals. It would appear that the commonality of these indicators might be social isolation. However, van Os and others (Faris and Dunham, 1939; Hare, 1956) have pointed out that the social isolation is likely to be linked to schizophrenia if many of the neighbours are not single, not foreign-born, not unemployed, etc. In other words, these indicators are not, in themselves, such an issue unless an individual finds that they stand out within the neighbourhood for such indicators. So being a single male in the neighbourhood is only problematic if most of those surrounding you are in relationships. Similarly, Silver, Mulvey and Swanson (2002) found in a US study that there were more people with schizophrenia in areas where there was high social mobility and Boydell, van Os, McKenzie and Murray (2004) found that there were more cases of schizophrenia among migrant groups when they formed a small proportion of the local community. However, as we shall now see, what is not clear from these studies of the relationship between incidence and social deprivation is which factor is the cause and which is the effect.

So why do we find this demographic distinction in the levels of schizophrenia? Could the apparent finding that there are larger numbers of people with schizophrenia in deprived areas be an artefact or a consequence of misdiagnosis? Could, for example, the behaviour of a migrant be totally consistent with their culture but misdiagnosed by the clinician as aberrant behaviour? Hickling, McKenzie, Mullen and Murray (1999) compared diagnoses made independently of 66 patients by a British and a Jamaican psychiatrist. They found no evidence that there was any bias in diagnosis or a misdiagnosis of black patients. Other studies have confirmed these results (e.g. Minnis, McMillan, Gillies & Smith, 2001). If it is not due to misdiagnosis, could it be that those with schizophrenia are more likely to migrate to another country and, once there, find that they are unable to live anywhere but the deprived areas of cities? Again, this seems unlikely. Morgan, Charalambides, Hutchinson and Murray (2010) have turned the question on its head. They have noted that there are differences in incidence rates in the UK between Asian and black Caribbean populations. They have suggested that the strong family and social structure within the Asian community can act as a buffer against developing schizophrenia. Furthermore, they claim that the deprived social environment can actually act as a catalyst for schizophrenia to develop because it contains a greater tendency towards exposure to threat and adversity. These could have the effect of inducing paranoia and persecutory delusions. We are left, then, with the idea that it is not so much that people with schizophrenia end up in socially deprived areas of cities but that the social deprivation increases the chances that a genetic predisposition to schizophrenia will develop into the full-blown disorder.

The evidence suggesting that the social environment plays a key role in determining whether or not schizophrenia emerges has recently been summed up by Stilo et al. (2013). They collected data from 278 patients and found that their childhood environment might be important. People with schizophrenia were three times more likely to have had a parent die before they were 17 years old and were twice as likely to have had parents who separated before that age. When other markers were included, such as living in more than one family home (because of separation), living in a socially deprived area and so on, the schizophrenic group were nine times more likely to have been exposed to two or more of those markers. It is quite possible that the disadvantages reported for adults with schizophrenia actually started when these people were very young and prior to the onset of their schizophrenia. If this is true then it would suggest that the social environment can trigger the onset of schizophrenia in someone who has a predisposition for the disorder but who might not otherwise developed the full-blown condition.

How cognitive and social deficits affect the quality of life of the schizophrenic

Before we leave this topic, we should consider, by way of a summary, how all of the factors we have discussed here impact on the schizophrenia sufferer's quality of life (QoL). The idea of QoL as a measure emerged in the 1960s and was equated to a sense of general well-being. However, in the 1980s the term also became used as a measure of functioning in everyday life and QoL scales emerged to measure it. It also became clear that, in the context of psychiatric patients, it was not just important to ask the patients but the family too. We also need to consider what the benchmark is against which we should judge QoL in people with schizophrenia. Myers, David G. and Diener (1996) reported that in surveys of over one million ordinary people, the modal QoL on a scale of 1–10 was around 7 or 8.

It might be reasonable to assume that economic status would be an important marker for QoL, and we have seen that people with schizophrenia often end up living in poor economic conditions. However, this aspect of social life does not determine QoL in this group (or in others for that matter). From the results of questionnaire studies, the things that are important seem to be things like lower education, being female and a sense of personal control, all of which improve QoL. Negative symptoms, motor control side effects from medication and the stigma of being schizophrenic all seem to lower QoL. However, there is a danger that the questionnaires are not suitable as they may be misinterpreted due to the cognitive and social deficits suffered by patients. When we look at the data from more qualitative approaches, we tend to see that the perceived QoL is not so good (Barham & Hayward, 1991).

If we take a 'hierarchy of needs' approach to this question based on the work of Maslow (1954), we can easily see that some of the lowest level requirements for needs satisfaction cannot easily be met by those with schizophrenia. The lowest two levels of the hierarchy are physiological needs (e.g. food) and safety needs. The social and cognitive deficits suffered by people with schizophrenia make the fulfilment of those needs difficult. According to Maslow, these need to be achieved before self-esteem and self-actualisation are possible, so we can assume that people with schizophrenia are not able to achieve these levels of need satisfaction.

From a more recent meta-analysis, Eack and Newhill (2007) found that positive and negative symptoms both had an effect on quality of life. Positive symptoms were more strongly related to health-related QoL measures such that the worse the positive symptoms, the poorer the health-related QoL. Positive symptoms seemed not to be related to subjective QoL measures or to QoL measures of general well-being. Negative symptoms, however, were related to poor objective QoL. This measures things that can be objectively assessed like the number of close friends and a person's monthly income. Overall, it seems that the symptoms of schizophrenia themselves do not contribute as much to a poor quality of life as one might imagine. What seems to be more important are the things that would apply to anyone with a general psychopathology and they are often associated with the difficulties that psychiatric patients have with community living.

◉ Chapter summary

This chapter has covered a lot of ground. We have taken a look at the myriad of cognitive problems faced by those with schizophrenia and we have seen that they cover just about every aspect of cognitive mental life from perceptual processing to reasoning skills. We have also seen that the person suffering from schizophrenia has just as many social problems. These problems are clearly related to each other and have a combined effect on the person's quality of life. We have also explored the role that a lack of Theory of Mind might play in contributing to the person's difficulties with social situations.

In the latter part of the chapter we looked at the relationship between the social shortcomings of the person with schizophrenia and the environment. It was long believed that the demographic pattern of schizophrenia was simply a reflection of the difficulty sufferers have in coping with the social world. However, we have explored some compelling evidence that has suggested the environment might play a key role in the manifestation of schizophrenia in vulnerable individuals.

⊙ Further reading

Beck, A.T., Rector, N.A., Stolar, N. and Grant, P. (2008) *Schizophrenia: Cognitive Theory, Research, and Therapy*. New York: The Guildford Press.

Penn, D.L., Sanna, L.J. and Roberts, D.L. (2008) Social cognition in schizophrenia: An overview. *Schizophrenia Bulletin*, 34 (3), 408–411

Read, J. and Dillon, J. (Eds) (2013) *Models of Madness*. 2nd edition (The International Society for Psychological and Social Approaches to Psychosis Book Series). London and New York: Routledge.

Chapter 7

Psychodynamic Explanations and Family Functioning

👁 Introduction

Our last look at ways of explaining schizophrenia involves some of the oldest ideas about the development of psychosis. We shall see that they had their day as credible explanations before the discovery of antipsychotic drugs and their establishment as a mainstream treatment. However, their inclusion is important, not just for completeness but to enable us to consider whether there is still some contributory explanatory power to these ideas. Although Freud did not have an awful lot to say about the development of psychosis, many of the psychodynamic explanations derive from his principles of the ego, the id and the superego so we will start our analysis there. We will then concentrate on five main ideas that derive from the psychodynamic approach in psychology. The first is referred to as the Schizophrenogenic mother and suggests that certain types of significant family member (usually the mother) can induce schizophrenia. The second is called the **double bind** and involves a family situation where the child is exposed repeatedly to mixed messages. The third looks at whether communication between the parents and the offspring plays a role in the development of schizophrenia. The fourth section looks at another focus point regarding parents and this is the way they interact among themselves. Does this, perhaps, have a damaging effect on the high risk child? The final idea analyses the quality of interactions within families more generally and suggests that whilst schizophrenia develops as a result of genetic and biological markers, its maintenance is contributed to by the type of expressed emotions being displayed to a child.

You might already have spotted that these explanations are mostly concerned with family dynamics, and so we shall look at the degree to which this might contribute to the development of schizophrenia where there is an individual whose genetic profile puts them at risk. As we shall see in a later chapter, the psychodynamic principles we discuss here are the root of the psychoanalytic treatments we will discuss in Chapter 9.

> **In this chapter we will cover:**
> - Freud's analysis of psychosis
> - The case of Daniel Paul Schreber
> - Does the family contribute to the aetiology of schizophrenia?
> - The schizophrenogenic mother
> - The double bind theory
> - Communication disorders
> - Skewed and schismatic families
> - Expressed emotion

Freud's analysis of psychosis

According to Freud, disturbances of the psyche were derived from an imbalance of the id, ego and superego. To remind you, the id is the element of the psyche that wants to carry out every desire that comes to mind, however unsavoury that desire might be. The superego provides our moral compass, considering the moral implications of any action and adopting an overly cautious approach. The superego would deprive us of many of our normal activities for fear that they might be deemed immoral in some way. The ego provides the reasoned judgement between the desires of the id and the cautions of the superego. If the ego is in any way damaged then a number of potential mental instabilities would ensue, among them the instability of psychosis.

In addition to the id, ego and superego, Freud postulated a number of other concepts that might be helpful in the context of schizophrenia. One of these was the libido and another is the concept of cathexis. Libido refers to the instinctual energies that are derived from the id. Cathexis simply means the investment of mental or emotional energy in a person, object or idea. If we put these concepts together we get what is called 'libidinal cathexis'. So libidinal cathexis is an attachment to people or objects that are the focus of the id and it is this that Freud saw as a key causal element in the development of psychosis. Libidinal cathexis changes throughout our lives. As infants, the focus is on basic needs like food and care. In childhood they centre on physically growing and on the importance of family. During puberty the focus changes to sexual maturation and as an adult they are mainly to do with procreation and various vocational drives. According to Freud, as each stage is reached, the attachments of the previous stage are discarded or subdued. If earlier attachments are, for some reason, not subdued then Freud referred to this as a fixation.

It is worth noting at this point that the term 'schizophrenia' did not exist for Freud. In his time mental disorders were divided into three types that had been characterised by Kraepelin. Kraepelin called the psychotic disorders dementia praecox (DP). The other types of mental illness were dementia paranoides (paranoia) and manic depressive insanity. Freud considered cases of psychosis to be DP (Freud, 1911). Whilst he saw these cases in his role as a neurologist, he did not see them in the context of psychoanalysis as he did not believe they were able to establish the necessary relationship with the therapist for treatment to be effective. Nevertheless, that did not stop him from having a view on how the psychoses develop, and his interests were particularly aroused by the case of Daniel Schreber (see Box 7.1).

Box 7.1 The Case of Daniel Paul Schreber

Schreber was born in Leipzig in 1842. In 1884 he had his first psychotic episode whilst working as a judge. He was hospitalised for about six months but then returned to his job in 1886. He was readmitted in 1893 and spent the next eight years in two different asylums. It was during the last two of these years that he put together a legal case for why he should be released. In 1902 he won his case and was discharged. Whilst fighting his case, Schreber wrote his memoirs and these included detailed descriptions of his thoughts and feelings during that two year period. Unfortunately, by 1907 he was back in an asylum again. This had probably been triggered by the death of his mother and by his wife having a stroke. He spent a further four years in the asylum and died there in 1911.

Freud's interest in Schreber was because of his ability to continue to work whilst simultaneously suffering from his psychosis and because of the insight into his condition that his memoirs afforded. It seemed as though he was able to separate the two modes of mental working, a phenomenon referred to as compartmentalism. Schreber's psychosis took the form of hypochondriasis together with religious delusions. His apparent illnesses extended from a softening of the brain to a belief that he was dead and decomposing. His religious delusions led him to believe that he was in direct communication with God. Its manifestation was that he was on a mission to restore mankind to a previous state of blissful existence. To do so, he was under the impression that he had to become a woman and to give birth to a new breed of humanity.

As is typical of those suffering from schizophrenia, Schreber was distrustful of other people, not least his clinician Fleschig, whom he hated. Freud considered this to be a consequence of two libidinal cathectic fixations. The first fixation he proposed was one of homosexual attraction in which Schreber went through the stages of denial (I don't love him) followed by reversal (I hate him). The second fixation was centred on omnipotence and gave rise to his religious delusions. You would imagine that these symptoms would add up to a pretty cut and dried diagnosis of a psychosis. However, due to the periods of apparent remission, Freud classified Schreber as a sufferer of dementia paranoides who had a tendency to exhibit an hallucinatory psychosis typical of DP.

Freud's account of the sequence of a developing psychosis, particularly Schreber's, did not focus on the positive symptoms (i.e. the delusions and hallucinations) but was rather modelled on a deficit hypothesis. As already mentioned, cathexes comprise a mixture of attentions, some on the self, some on others and some on objects. Freud believed that the development of psychosis starts with a withdrawal of all cathexes other than those focused on the self. This leads to the development of self-obsessed ideas like hypochondriasis. Being disengaged with the outside world but still being in possession of an active mind then leads to the creation of alternative realities that are not part of the real world. As this is still tied in with a self-obsession, these hallucinatory realities take the form of delusions of either grandeur or persecution. In other words, the libidinal cathexes have been removed from real objects in the world (other real people and things) and have been reinvested in the fabricated existence. For Freud, this last step was the patient's attempt to recover a sort of 'normality' from this withdrawn existence. Having the need to interact with something external to oneself combined with a distrust of everyone out there who is real leads to the necessity to create an alternative set of non-self, referential objects.

McGlashan (2009) suggests that psychosis is similar to the possession of a phantom limb. He says,

> As in the phantom limb syndrome, where the brain creates in mind what has been severed from the body, in psychosis the brain creates persons and relationships in mind to fill the blankness created by the brain's diminished capacity to gather and process daily social experiences and relationships.

So what might trigger this sequence that leads to the development of schizophrenia? The remainder of this chapter explores the psychodynamic explanations of what these triggers might entail. They all involve the idea that people with schizophrenia are made within the family home by way of the interactions between family members. They don't deny that there may well need to be some underlying biological or genetic propensity for the disease, but they all suggest that the family provides the catalytic trigger for its manifestation.

⊙ Does the family contribute to the aetiology of schizophrenia?

In general terms, between the late 1940s and the late 1970s there was much interest in the contributions of family life to the development of schizophrenia. Early suggestions were that the mother was to blame for her child's manifestation of the disease. Later, the whole family came under scrutiny. The research has mostly attempted to look at elements of communication between family members from numerous perspectives, all designed to establish whether or not schizophrenic families engage in deviant patterns of communication. Some (the group) have argued that the total system of family communications is disturbed (Lidz, Cornelison, Fleck & Terry, 1957). The models of how these family variables contribute to the development of schizophrenia make a number of assumptions such as the idea that schizophrenic families are different to families with other psychological disorders or that these disordered family conditions are a necessary but not a sufficient condition for the development of schizophrenia.

The ways in which family interactions can be divided up are many and varied. Many of these were explored in a series of studies by Wynne and Singer (1963a, 1963b), Singer and Wynne (1965a, 1965b) or by Singer alone (1968). For example, if parents reinforce each others' deviant communication styles then the likelihood of schizophrenia developing is increased.

If, on the other hand, one parent acts to correct the deviant communication style of the other then that is likely to lessen the probability that schizophrenia will develop. As we will see presently, the methodological requirements of studies such as these leads to a simplification of the operationalised measures used to test theories, so we are always left with inadequate tests of the theory. Furthermore, some variables that are believed to be important have been ignored because of the difficulties of sampling. One such variable is the gender of the patient which has been shown to be important when analysing the types of family interaction that take place (Lidz, Fleck, Alanen & Cornelison, 1963).

In the following sections of this chapter we will examine three specific elements of family interactions: dominance, contradictory communications, marital schisms and the expression of emotion. A few other dimensions of family interactions are worth a brief mention here for completeness. One of these is conflict, where researchers (e.g. Mishler & Waxler-Morrison, 1968) have used activities such as interruptions and speaking at the same time as someone else to judge conflict. They have mostly found less conflict in families with a schizophrenic than families without. Affect is another aspect of family interaction that has received some attention. Again, according to Mishler and Waxler-Morrison, unaffected families expressed more laughter and positive affect than families of good premorbid people with schizophrenia. One consistent finding across a number of studies is that schizophrenic families manifest a poorer clarity of communication than unaffected families (Friedman & Friedman, 1970). However, Reiss (1981) has suggested that the communication style used in a conversation is very much dependent on whether family members are talking amongst themselves or talking to others from outside of the family circle. So we can see that there are many factors that have been considered in the search for family markers that might be triggers to the development of schizophrenia.

The schizophrenogenic mother

This theory was the brainchild of Fromm-Reichmann (1948). She suggested that the trigger for schizophrenia came from mothers who were overly dominant within the home, particularly with respect to the potentially schizophrenic child. During the late 1940s and the early 1950s a number of studies suggested that the mother–child relationship was disordered where the child was schizophrenic (Lidz & Lidz, 1949; Arieti, 1955). Then in the 1960s and 1970s there were numerous studies that tried to establish whether or not parental dominance, generally, was a trigger factor for schizophrenia.

The focus seemed to be moving away from the mother in particular and towards a dysfunctional family in its entirety. Wild, Shapiro and Goldenberg (1975) looked at families in which there was a father, mother and one schizophrenic son. They used the game 20 questions and had the family group construct the questions to be asked. They noted how many of each person's questions made it onto the final list and used this as a measure of dominance within the group. As controls, they used families with a non-schizophrenic psychiatric son and families in which the son was unaffected. In their study they found that it was the fathers of schizophrenic children rather than the mothers that played the more dominant role. No particular pattern was observed in the control families. Wild et al. suggested that the father might have learned to fill in for the schizophrenic son to hide the son's lack of participation. However, the story is not that simple. Whilst the authors found length of hospitalisation to have no effect on dominance, they did find that there was less dominance within the family if the son had a job. Furthermore, it seemed that the dominance is more prominent in lower class families than in higher class families.

Herman and Jones (1976) examined the dominance roles in families at risk of having a schizophrenic child. When low- and high-risk families were examined for their communication deviance using the Thematic Apperception Test, it seemed that it was, once again, the mothers who were dominant in families with high-risk adolescents. So we can see that there is enormous inconsistency in the findings relating to parental dominance. Incidentally, the same pattern of inconsistent results was obtained when researchers looked at coalitions within the family. These are defined as sequences of talking between family members (e.g. mother–father, mother–son and father–son).

There are numerous inadequacies with this type of approach. Firstly, the situations in which the family members are asked to interact are very contrived and unnatural. When was the last time your family all sat down together to create a set of questions for the 20 Questions game? Secondly, we can debate whether or not the measures of verbal interactions used in these studies are a true reflection of parental dominance. After all, dominance can be expressed equally through non-verbal communication as through verbal communication. Lastly, the examples used in these studies all involve situations in which all (three) members of the family are present together. I would suggest that many, if not most, interactions between family members involve only two people at a time. Under these circumstances the dominance exerted by one family member over another can be much greater. Needless to say, the concept of the schizophrenogenic mother and its counterparts did not gain much support and by the end of the 1970s it had pretty much run its course as a credible theory for the development of schizophrenia.

◉ The double bind theory

The double bind theory was first proposed by Bateson, Jackson, Haley and Weakland (1956). Basically, the double bind is described by them as, "a situation in which no matter what a person does, he 'can't win'" (p.251). The theory centres around the different types of communication mode that humans can adopt and the degree to which these modes are correctly interpreted. It is necessary to consider these so that we can comprehend what the double bind is. The elements of the modes described by Bateson et al. can be identified along a series of parameters. These are: the mode itself (play, fantasy, etc.), the use of humour (often incorporating an unexpected change in mode as in, for example, a man walks into a bar – ouch), the false portrayal of a mode (an artificial laugh, kidding, etc.), learning (we have to learn how to act on the signals being presented – either verbally or physically) and learning about the signals (we have to first learn about modes, humour, false portrayals and learning itself). Being able to distinguish different communication modes is considered to be the domain of the ego and, as we have already explored, the ego of the schizophrenic is weak. Accordingly, the schizophrenic finds it hard to ascribe the correct communication mode to utterances made by others, utterances and non-verbal signals exhibited by him/herself and his/her own thoughts and perceptions. In particular, the schizophrenic uses metaphor but struggles to use or understand metaphor appropriately.

So now we have the elements we need to consider, we can explore how Bateson et al. argue that it is the role of the family environment that triggers the development of schizophrenia through the double bind situation. They define the process as one that occurs over time by virtue of this double bind situation being repeated. This reinforces for the schizophrenic the faulty interpretations that have been created. The requirements for the double bind situation are as follows.

- Two or more people are needed, one of whom is the 'victim' and the others of whom are family members. (Bateson et al. specifically point out that this does not have to include the mother, and so this is a break away from the schizophrenogenic mother theory.)
- The experience is repeated on numerous occasions.
- A negative injunction (this may take the form of a threat of punishment – if you do X then I will punish you). The principle here is that the focus for the individual is to avoid punishment rather than seek reward. The punishment can be the withholding of something pleasant (e.g. love) as well as an expression of negativity (e.g. anger).

- A second injunction that directly conflicts with the first. This is the critical part of the double bind. It is often delivered as a gesture rather than as a conflicting statement but can also be the latter. For example, a scolding comment might be accompanied by a non-verbal posture that implies love for the child.
- A third negative injunction that prevents the victim from escaping the situation. In younger children this is not usually necessary as escape is not an option, so this part of the situation is usually only seen with teenagers and adolescents.
- The double bind is complete when these behaviours are no longer necessary in an explicit way as the whole sequence can be triggered in the victim's head by just initiating part of the situation. Indeed, the whole situation could be played out as a hallucination.

Bateson provides a clinical example to illustrate the double bind and it is useful to reproduce that here in full.

An analysis of an incident occurring between a schizophrenic patient and his mother illustrates the "double bind" situations. A young man who had fairly well recovered from an acute schizophrenic episode was visited in the hospital by his Roman mother. He was glad to see her and impulsively put his arm around her shoulders, whereupon she stiffened. He withdrew his arm and she asked, "Don't you love me any more?" He then blushed and she said, "Dear, you must not be so easily embarrassed and afraid of your feelings." The patient was able to stay with her only a few minutes more and following her departure he assaulted an aide and was put in the tubs.

Obviously, this result could have been avoided if the young man had been able to say, "Mother, it is obvious that you become un comfortable when I put my arm around you, and that you have difficulty accepting a gesture of affection from me." However, the schizophrenic patient doesn't have this possibility open to him. His intense dependency and training prevents him from commenting upon his mother's communicative behavior, though she comments on his fold forces him to accept and to attempt to deal with the complicated sequence. The complications for the patient, include the following:

The mother's reaction of not accepting her son's affectionate gesture is masterfully covered up by her condemnation of him for withdrawing, and the patient denies his perception of the situation by accepting her condemnation.

The statement "don't you love me any more" in this context seems to imply:

"I am loveable"

"You should love me and if you don't you are bad or at fault."

(p. 253)

More generally, the schizophrenic in the double bind situation has learnt that s/he has no idea how to respond to most of what is said in conversations. The person is likely, therefore, to adopt a unitary mode of thinking to everything that is said. This could be the stance that all statements contain hidden meanings that are potentially harmful. Or it could be that all statements are taken literally. Another alternative is that the person could adopt a mode of trying to avoid interacting with anyone for fear of misinterpreting what they say. Finally, the person might interpret statements as being derogatory and so might become defensive. These would lead to an external person interpreting their demeanour as suspicious, childish, aloof or paranoid, all elements we would recognise as part of the repertoire of a schizophrenic.

The double bind theory implies that the development of schizophrenia is a consequence of some inadequacies (usually emotional) on the part of a parent (usually the mother). For example, the parent may have an anxiety about not liking the child. This may then lead to a scenario where they do not want to be around the child. So the statement "I think you should go to bed as you are looking tired" appears to be loving whilst the underlying feeling in the parent and, hence, the unconscious expression through body language is "get out of my sight, I cannot stand to look at you any longer." An accurate comprehension of the situation on the part of the child would necessitate a confrontation with the realisation that s/he was not wanted by the mother. Under these circumstances it is easier for the child to buy in to the belief that s/he is tired. We can now consider whether he should approach to give her a kiss goodnight. Should s/he do so there is a certainty that the approach will be rejected (possibly veiled under a comment like "don't be soft"). If no approach is made the child will be punished for not showing the parent how loving they are. Either way, the child loses because s/he is in a double bind. As this relationship is with someone who is a role model for the child, the child will believe that this is how normal relationships proceed and so will have future problems in establishing what we might call normal relationships.

You may be wondering why, in a family where there is more than one child, this treatment isn't meted out to all of the children in the same fashion. The fact that it might affect only one of many siblings is accounted for by suggesting that this particular child has some specific significance for that parent (is the same birth order as they are, has the same birth month as an important sibling of their own, and so on).

In evaluating the double bind theory, Gibney (2006) suggests that it is still of value to the modern practitioner as it still provides ongoing insights and proposes interventions. He reminds us also that the theory does not blame parents for the interactions that are described, but it might be accused of being somewhat sexist in its emphasis that it is most frequently the mother that is the source of the double bind. Not all commentaries are as positive about the theory, though. Schuham (1967) made a number of criticisms of the double bind theory. Among them was an evaluation that there had been no research findings that supported the theory. He cited the five pieces of research that had directly assessed the theory in the ten years since the original paper and demonstrated that none had found supporting evidence. One study by Ringuette and Kennedy (1966) had a particularly negative result. They used judges who were experts at the double bind theory (having formulated the hypothesis) along with non-experts and got them to make judgements about letters written by parents to either their schizophrenic or non-schizophrenic offspring or by hospital staff as if they were writing to these people as their parents. The data did not show that those who were experts were any better at determining the double bind than the non-experts. Shuham concluded that:

> There is little agreement about what elements are necessary to produce double-bind situations. (b) There is little agreement about what communicational phenomena are unique to double-bind interaction, (c) The confusion surrounding the definition of the double bind has impeded research, (d) The result is that little research has been carried out at all and those studies which have been done provide no support for the theory.

Hoffman (1981) questions whether the double bind theory has the causal relationship between the system and the symptom the wrong way around. According to the theory, the system (double bind) causes the symptom (schizophrenia). Hoffman suggests that maybe the schizophrenic is so confusing in their communicative attempts that the family finds itself saying contradictory things that are interpreted as double binds. In other words, Hoffman argues that the symptom causes the system.

◉ Communication disorders

In both of the two previous sections we have seen reference being made to the way in which parents are communicating with their schizophrenic offspring. Indeed, many researchers (Reiss, 1976) have suggested that poor communication is the best of all of the family variables at predicting the development of schizophrenia. In this section we will examine more closely the relationship, if any, between these communication problems (called communication deviance) and the aetiology of schizophrenia. First we should try to define what we mean by communication deviance. According to Wynne and Singer (1963a, 1963b), it is when the conversation style of one or both parents has a poor focus of attention, either because the communication is vague or because it is fragmented and easily disrupted, that schizophrenia is most likely to follow. A well-used test of communication deviance is the Rorschach test (Figure 7.1). The family is tasked with coming up with a consensual view of what the ambiguous figure represents and the conversational dynamics can be analysed. According to Singer, Wynne and Toohey (1978) this test is the closest approximation we can get to the everyday conversations that occur naturally in the home. In one large study involving 114 families (228 parents, 114 offspring ranging from unaffected, through neurotic, to schizophrenic and 141 siblings of those offspring), the communications in the families with a schizophrenic stood out compared to the others. Furthermore, the schizophrenic offspring tended to have both parents with high communication deviance scores, whereas the other groups had parents with low scores. Where only one parent had high scores, the child tended to be a borderline schizophrenic (Wynne, Singer, Bartko & Toohey, 1977).

Figure 7.1 A Roscharch Inkblot

We need to be a little cautious about these results. These are families where there is already a schizophrenic present, so we cannot clearly determine if the communication deviance is a cause or an effect. To do this we might want to look at studies where we can establish the risk of an individual (a teenager or adolescent) becoming schizophrenic but where any illness has not yet manifested itself. Lieber (1977) looked at lack of attentional focus (one of Wynne and Singer's markers) in parents with low, moderate and high risk of schizophrenia in one of their offspring. She found no relationship between the degree of attentional focus and risk. This would suggest that what is seen in families where the schizophrenia has already become expressed might be a consequence rather than a cause. However, Jones (1977) found that parents of male adolescents from the high-risk symptom groups exhibited significantly more communication deviance than parents of low-risk males. For females, only offspring that were withdrawn and isolated (a high-risk marker) had parents exhibited higher levels of communication deviance. So we can see that the picture is, somewhat, unclear.

Probably the best kind of study would be one that adopted a longitudinal approach. That way we could identify the risk associated with each child before any schizophrenia did or did not develop, monitor the parental communication styles and see whether this has any predictive value later on. Such a longitudinal study was started by Goldstein and Rodnick (1975). Doane, West, Goldstein, Rodnick, H. and Jones (1981) conducted a five-year follow-up on 39 families and found that seven out of eight where the child had developed schizophrenia spectrum symptoms had parents with high communication deviance at the start of the study. By contrast, 19 of 26 children diagnosed as not having schizophrenia spectrum symptoms had parents with low communication deviance at the start of the study. Furthermore, those parents with schizophrenia spectrum children were more critical, intrusive or guilt-inducing than other parents. Similarly, Lewis (1979) found that the parents of at-risk adolescents adopted a negative tone of voice when addressing them. This was also seen to be the critical factor involved in the few families where schizophrenia later developed even though the communication deviance of parents was low. We will look at this aspect of family life in more detail again when we consider high expressed emotion.

⊙ Skewed and schismatic families

In contrast to the theories that had placed communication deviance at the heart of the development of schizophrenia, a group led by Lidz suggested that the root cause was the whole system of family relationships and did not just centre around communication. They termed these structural disorders 'marital schism' and 'skew', and they argued that this affected the personality development of all children within the family and not just the person who developed schizophrenia. However, the other members of the family were affected to a much lesser degree.

Expressed emotion

Whereas all of the previous discussion has focused on whether psychodynamic considerations can predict differences between schizophrenic and those without schizophrenia and/or between schizophrenic families and non-schizophrenic families, the concept of expressed emotion has been used to look at the possible causes of relapse in someone who has had one or more previous psychotic episodes. Indeed, it is this area of the whole field of psychodynamic interpretations of schizophrenia that has persisted into the modern era. The other theories have all but died out in more recent times.

Expressed emotion (EE) was first defined by G. W. Brown, Birley and Wing (1972) as a measure of the quality of the social interaction between a patient and a carer. There are a number of components to EE and these are derived from the Camberwell Family Interview (Brown & Rutter, 1966). The main components that have been linked to schizophrenia are:

1 Critical comments (CC) which are unfavourable remarks about a person's behaviour or personality
2 Hostility (H) which is defined either as a generalisation or a rejecting remark
3 Emotional over-involvement (EOI) which comprises elements of over-protection, self-sacrifice and past exaggerated emotional responses, together with behaviour during the interview (such as crying, and dramatisation indicated by extravagant praise, or the tone and tempo of speech)

More recently, hostility has been dropped as being a sub-component of critical comments, so that leaves us with just CC and EOI as measures in the majority of studies.

Early studies laid the claim that high-EE was a major contributing factor to people with schizophrenia going into relapse (Brown & Rutter, 1966; Vaughn & Leff, 1976). Vaughn and Leff even suggested that a low-EE environment could have some protective value against relapse over and above that provided by medication – even to the point where medication was no longer needed. However, what followed these early reports was a mixed set of results that cast some doubt on this latter claim. It was also established early on that whilst high-EE was a good predictor of relapse it was not a good predictor of first admission (Birchwood & Smith, 1987).

Bebbington and Kuipers (1994) carried out an aggregate analysis on all of the data available at that time. An aggregate analysis is where the authors combine together as much of the raw data as they can obtain and carry out a new analysis on this aggregated data. It differs from a meta-analysis in that a meta-analysis only combines information that was reported in the journal articles. Using this method, they managed to obtain an impressive total sample size of 1346. Bebbington and Kuipers discovered a massive difference in the relapse rate between the high-EE group (50.1%) and the low-EE group (21.1%). If people with schizophrenia were also in high contact with the high-EE situation (more than 35 hours per week) then the relapse rate was even higher (54.4%). If the person was not on medication it was, again, higher (57.7%). Bebbington and Kuipers did find some evidence that low-EE was protective as the relapse rate went down when there was high contact in a low-EE situation (18.3%) compared with when there was low contact (23.9%). All in all, they concluded that living in a high-EE environment was likely to make a patient 2.5 times more likely to suffer a relapse. It is worth noting here that whilst most studies have looked only at relatives of the patients (particularly parents), there have been studies that have looked at anyone who has a significant relationship with the patient (e.g. Oliver & Kuipers, 1996) and have found similar results.

A number of researchers have been interested to know more about the relationship between high-EE and relapse. How does high-EE come about? Does high-EE exert its effect over a long period of time? What is the perception of high-EE from the patient's perspective? Subotnik, Goldstein, Nuechterlein, Woo and Mintz (2002) have been interested in the first question, namely, whether or not there is any family history that leads to a parent being high-EE. They interviewed around 100 biological parents of people with schizophrenia concerning a number of different aspects of their family's medical history. They found that there was no link between being high-EE and having a family history of schizophrenia (in other words, having had someone in their family's recent past who had also been a sufferer), but there was a link between low-EE and a family history of depression. This latter finding, they suggested, was due to the fact that having a depressed person in the family leads to the adoption of a tolerant attitude that then manifests in a low-EE.

Is high-EE a good predictor of relapse rate over a long period of time? Marom, Munitz, Jones, Weizman and Hermesh (2005) conducted one of the most recent of a number of studies that have attempted to answer that question. Their study followed a group of 108 people with schizophrenia over a period of seven years and interviewed a total of 151 relatives for EE. This study used the Five Minute Speech Sample method of assessing EE which is a shorter alternative to the Camberwell Family Interview. They examined three elements of the patients' hospitalisation history since the time of their first admission (referred to as the index admission). These were (a) time until the first and second readmissions, (b) total number of admissions since the index admission and (c) total time in hospital since the index admission. They found that high-EE significantly reduced the time until the first and second readmissions. In particular, the criticism element of EE seemed to be the most influential element of the total EE. Higher criticism scores led to a higher number of admissions and a longer total hospitalisation length over the seven-year period. It was also apparent that this increased risk of relapse was not offset by the patient regularly taking their medication and this has important implications for the approach to treatment. It might be that medication alone is insufficient to prevent further psychotic episodes. We will tackle this issue in the last two chapters of this book.

Whilst we can investigate the relationship between EE and the likely relapse profile of the schizophrenic, we can question the degree to which the patient is perceptive to the fact that they are living in a high or low EE environment. After all, we have seen that there are a number of social and cognitive deficits that accompany the condition of schizophrenia. So does the high-EE environment cause the patient stress that then leads to an increased risk of relapse? Tarrier and Turpin (1992) have shown that physiological arousal is increased when high-EE relatives are present. Tompson et al. (1995) have shown that it is the patient's ability to correctly perceive the critical comments that is linked with the chances of relapse and have suggested that this is a better marker than the high-EE scores themselves. In a recent study, Cutting, Aakre and Docherty (2006) asked patients to identify one influential person in their lives. They then asked the patient about the degree to which this person was critical, protective and involved in their lives. They were also asked how stressed they felt when that person was around. These data were then compared with the influential person's scores on the Camberwell Family Interview. Thirty-two patients took part in the study, and it is interesting to note that nearly half of the influential others chosen (14) had received psychiatric treatment themselves at some point in their lives. The patients were very perceptive of the criticisms of the influential others but were less receptive to the emotional over-involvement. Patients also identified being more stressed when they were in the presence of a high-EE person than when in the presence of others. So it seems that patients are able to understand the criticisms of others and it affects their well-being by raising their stress levels. Perhaps they were less able to perceive the emotional over-involvement as this tends to be overly positive (e.g. excessive cuddling). It is important to not that there were some methodological issues with this study. Whilst patients were told that they could choose anyone who was most influential and that this might be a person who nags them a lot, for example, they were also told that this should be the person closest to them and this might have led them to choose someone with a more positive outlook. Perhaps, though, this makes the findings all the more impressive.

There have been criticisms of EE that have suggested that it is a crude measure that uses a dichotomy (high or low) to express a measure that is probably more of a continuum. Hatfield, Spaniol and Zipple (1987) claimed that this invalidated the measure and reduced it to little more than a case of stereotyping. She also cautioned that the approach taken by most researchers has an underlying tenor of blame. This has implications for treatment as we shall see in a later chapter.

◉ Chapter summary

We have looked at a number of different ways in which the psychodynamic approach has been used to try to explain what is causing and/or maintaining the schizophrenic condition. Many of the early ideas, like the schizophrenogenic mother, have been abandoned. In part, this is because they were inadequate theories but it is also because they reflected a more sexist past where the mother was seen as the central carer and therefore most responsible for interactions with the teenager or adolescent at risk from schizophrenia. Even though we would recognise that the environment will be influential over and above any genetic propensities, I think it is fair to say that the framing of the psychodynamic theories has not been seen to provide any insights over and above what we would now derive from a social and cognitive analysis.

Two areas of the psychodynamic approach have been influential in a lasting way. The first is to provide some solid evidence of the role of expressed emotion in the maintenance of schizophrenia and the dangers that high-EE can bring with regard to relapse. The other is to have brought about a whole treatment genre in family therapy. In a later chapter we will assess the efficacy of this form of treatment, but for now we can note that it has been highly influential in providing an alternative perspective to drug treatments.

◉ Further reading

Carley, S.G. (2013) *The Case of Daniel Paul Schreber* (Paranoid Schizophrenia). Boston, MA: SGC Production.

Geekie, J. and Read, J. (2009) Making Sense of Madness: Contesting The Meaning of Schizophrenia (The International Society for the Psychological Treatments of the Schizophrenias and Other Psychoses). London and New York: Routledge.

Gibney, P. (2006) The double bind theory: Still crazy making after all these years. *Psychotherapy in Australia*, 12 (3), 48–55.

Chapter 8

Biological Treatments

👁 Introduction

In this chapter we will explore those treatments that come under the broad heading of biological. For the most part, these are drug treatments and we will chart the time course of developments in this area. However, other

In this chapter we will cover:
- Antipsychotic medication
- First generation antipsychotics
  - Chlorpromazine
  - Haloperidol
  - Fluphenazine
- Side effects of first generation antipsychotics
- Second generation antipsychotics
  - Clozapine
  - Aripiprazole
  - Olanzapine
  - Risperidone
  - Quetiapine
- Comparing first generation and second generation antipsychotics
- Adherence to medication
- Non-drug biological treatments
  - Insulin shock therapy
  - Electroconvulsive therapy
  - Transcranial Magnetic Stimulation
- Psychosurgery and schizophrenia
- Ayurvedic medicine

biological treatments exist or have existed and we will look at a variety of these.

The introduction of a new antipsychotic drug, chlorpromazine, in the 1950s changed the face of schizophrenia dramatically. Whilst it improved symptoms enough to permit discharge from hospital, the medication had horrible side effects that meant patients stopped taking the drug and relapsed, landing them back in hospital. They were given more medication and told to return to their lives, only to be back again sometime later. This became known as 'revolving door psychiatry'. This gave rise to two issues concerning the use of drugs to treat schizophrenia. The first was to begin the search for better and better drugs. The second was to search for ways to ensure that people with schizophrenia took their drugs once they were back in the outside world.

Antipsychotic medication

In this section we will look at some of the more common drug treatments for schizophrenia. These treatments mostly include drugs that are still on the market. The drugs fall into two categories. These are the typical antipsychotics (first generation antipsychotics – FGAs), sometimes called neuroleptics, and the atypical antipsychotics (second generation antipsychotics – SGAs). The first generation antipsychotics are the older drugs and they tend to produce motor control disabilities as a side effect. Users of the newer, second generation drugs do not tend to suffer from this type of problem but, as we shall see, that does not mean they are free from side effects. There are so many different antipsychotic drugs on the market that we just explore a few examples of each type in this chapter.

First generation antipsychotics (neuroleptics)

The term 'typical antipsychotics' captures those drugs that have been around almost since these drugs were first produced. They are often referred to as neuroleptics. What distinguishes these drugs is the degree of motor side effects that often accompany the potent antipsychotic action. For this reason they have been replaced, where possible, in the Western world. However, they are generally cheap to produce and so are still widely used across the world.

Chlorpromazine

The first specific antipsychotic drug was developed in the form of chlor-promazine (also known as Thorazine and Largactil). The drug is actually a member of a class of compounds called phenothiazines and these had first been produced in 1883 as synthetic dyes. On 11th December 1950, Paul Charpentier first synthesised chlorpromazine as a response to work trying to perfect phenothiazines as antihistamines. A year later it was used intrave-nously in a trial conducted by Henri Laborit as an anaesthetic booster. Patients reported improved well-being after taking the drug. Laborit noticed that the drug lowered the body temperature of those taking it and thought that this might be beneficial in reducing shock during surgery. After some attempts to get the drug trialled on psychiatric patients (with minor set-backs), the drug was used on a 24-year-old manic patient in 1952. The results were dramatic and the patient was sent home three weeks later.

The story of chlorpromazine is taken up by Deniker and Delay in 1952. They carried out a clinical trial of daily injections on 38 psychotic patients. Once again, the results were dramatic. The patients showed improvements in both positive symptoms and cognitions (Delay, Deniker & Harl, 1952). Other trials followed and in 1955 it went into full-scale production when the US approved its use. Its efficacy in treating some of the symptoms of psychosis has been compared to the impact penicillin had on infectious diseases.

For a time, chlorpromazine went out of favour, mostly due to its adverse side effects (more of those in a minute). Despite these issues, it remains one of the most commonly used and most inexpensive antipsychotic drugs. It is the drug of choice in almost all parts of the globe, especially in poorer coun-tries. In fact, it is so important worldwide that the drug is included in the latest version of the World Health Organisation's list of essential drugs. Its popularity makes it the benchmark against which to test any other antipsy-chotic drugs.

At the time that chlorpromazine was introduced, no-one knew how the drug worked. They only knew that it seemed to have a calming effect on the behavior of those with schizophrenia. We now know that chlorpromazine acts on the dopamine system to block most types of dopamine receptor, thereby reducing the effect of the excess dopamine in the system. However, the initial effect is the reverse as the dopamine that cannot now bind to its receptors causes the dopamine receptors to release more dopamine. Later, though, this overproduction subsides and chlorpromazine acts to reduce the dopamine effect. Chlorpromazine is considered to be a low potency antipsy-chotic, and so a large amount has to be administered to achieve the desired effect. This has consequences for the side effects as we shall now see.

Chlorpromazine does not only work on the dopamine system. It blocks serotonin receptors, with anxiety-reducing (anxiolytic) consequences, histamine receptors, causing sedation, adrenergic receptors, lowering blood pressure and acetylcholine receptors, causing a dry mouth. In fact, it is its effect on these other systems that gives rise to many of chlorpromazine's side effects. Chlorpromazine has been associated with a vast array of side effects. Among the more common ones are hypotension, dizziness and a dry mouth. In addition, the development of movement disorders is also relatively common. These include acute dystonias (sustained muscle contractions causing twisting and repetitive movements or abnormal postures) and Parkinsonism (movement symptoms similar to those in Parkinson's disease). Finally, there are a number of other side effects that are sometimes reported. These include weight gain, tardive dyskinesia, vertigo, blurred vision and constipation. It is fair to say that chlorpromazine has, by and large, had its day.

Haloperidol

This drug comes from the class of chemicals known as butyrophenones. It is about 50 times more potent than chlorpromazine and so is a very powerful neuroleptic. It was developed in Belgium in 1958 and, like chlorpromazine, was originally for use in preventing surgical shock. Research then indicated that it had a beneficial effect on hallucinations, delusions and other behaviours associated with psychosis (Ayd, 1972). It became obvious quite quickly that haloperidol was an effective and potent antipsychotic. However, some researchers have suggested that its efficacy is dependent on a number of factors, including dosage, age and gender (Settle & Ayd, 1983). In terms of dosage, Donlon et al. (1980) have suggested that acutely ill people with schizophrenia respond to a wide range of doses and that, contrary to some advice, a high initial dose is not necessary. This type of consideration is important because haloperidol has strong motor dysfunction side effects because it blocks dopamine activity in certain motor pathways. The efficacy of haloperidol at low doses can offset some of the adverse side effects associated with the drug. A review by Irving, Adams and Lawrie (2006) explored several features of haloperidol use. They concluded that whilst haloperidol is clearly effective, the side effects may make an alternative treatment more attractive. In addition, the side effects may put people with schizophrenia off taking their medication, a problem we will consider later in the chapter. Haloperidol is a cheap drug and that makes it a popular choice, like chlorpromazine, in poorer countries. The balancing act, in terms of economics, is the cost of the drug versus the cost of treating the many side effects and this is a very real concern with these kinds of antipsychotic treatment.

In a study looking at how effective haloperidol is in treating both positive and negative symptoms, Czobor and Volavka (1996) compared the changes in both during the early phase of treatment. Their participants were 178 chronic people with schizophrenia and they were treated for six weeks. In this study, haloperidol was effective against both positive and negative symptoms and the relative effects were about equal. This did not fit with Crow's (1985) proposal that drugs, like haloperidol, which counteract the excessive dopamine activity, would be ineffective against negative symptoms that have a structural brain deficit as their cause. This disagreement underlines the difficulty of marrying up such a complex condition like schizophrenia with an effective drug regimen.

There have been clinical comparisons of chlorpromazine and haloperidol, but these have only involved 800 patients to date. Both seemed to be as effective as each other in treating the symptoms of schizophrenia. In terms of side effects, haloperidol was more likely to produce motor effects, but chlorpromazine was more likely to produce low blood pressure (C. Leucht, Kitzmantel, Kane, Leucht & Chua, 2010).

Fluphenazine

This is a phenothiazine, like chlorpromazine, but is a slightly different drug to the two described so far in that it is usually administered as an intramuscular injection that lasts for a couple of weeks (an oral version is available). In terms of its potency, it resembles haloperidol more than it resembles chlorpromazine. People with schizophrenia are usually moved over to this form of treatment after they have been stabilised using oral medication. This can be an advantage if a patient is unlikely to remember to take a pill after they leave hospital either because there is some concern about the patient's ability to function in such an organised way or where there is a suspicion that the patient may deliberately not take the pill due to persecution elements of their schizophrenia. Fluphenazine injections have been used in conjunction with non-medical therapies, such as social therapy (see Chapter 9), where they can, together, reduce relapse rates (Hogarty et al., 1979).

In a very recent review of the effectiveness of fluphenazine, Matar, Almerie and Sampson, (2013) concluded that it is a very effective antipsychotic. However, they noted that it is relatively expensive and has a number of adverse side effects so other antipsychotic medications should be considered first. This is a typical pattern for the first generation antipsychotics and is a good reason for us now to turn our attention to the newer antipsychotic treatments.

Side effects of first generation antipsychotics

Whilst there has already been some mention of the side effects of FGAs, some of them are so severe that they are worth a further consideration here.

These severe side effects are a result of disorders of the extrapyramidal system. This is a motor system in the brain and the dysfunction of motor systems can be so severe that these side effects have their own category of disorders under DSM. They are referred to there as medication-induced movement disorders. The most important ones are Parkinsonian symptoms, neuroleptic malignant symptoms and tardive dyskinesia. Parkinson's disease features include tremors and muscle rigidity. It can be understood as a side effect because Parkinson's Disease is the result of too little dopamine being released from the substantia nigra. Given that FGAs reduce the availability of dopamine, these side effects are not really a surprise. Neuroleptic Malignant Syndrome also involves muscle rigidity but, additionally, the patient has a fever and a malfunctioning autonomic nervous system. This can be fatal and as soon as the signs are present, antipsychotic medication is stopped and the neuroleptic syndrome is treated. Finally, tardive dyskinesia does not appear quickly like the other two side effects. In fact it is not usually seen within the first year of medication. The tell-tale signs are tics and jerky movements that are clearly involuntary. However, most cases are relatively mild.

Second generation antipsychotics

Since the 1970s, a different form of antipsychotic drug has been available. These are the atypical antipsychotics, also referred to as the second generation antipsychotics. As already mentioned, these tend not to have such severe movement side effects. In addition, they have other benefits. The speed of treatment once a person has had their first psychotic episode is believed to be important for the long-term management of schizophrenia (Bottlender et al., 2003). Many researchers suggest that the atypical antipsychotics are the best treatment at this stage. Here we will look at a few of these newer drug treatments.

Clozapine

Although developed in 1961, it was not until the 1970s that clozapine started to be used clinically. Although it was clearly a very effective antipsychotic drug, there was one side effect that made physicians wary about its use. This side effect is called agranulocytosis. This disease leads to a decrease in white blood cells to a dangerously low level that can result in death and, indeed, did so in some cases. This led to the drug carrying a requirement that regular blood tests are carried out, and clozapine is only used in cases where a schizophrenic has failed to respond to any other drug treatments. Apart from agranulocytosis, most of the other side effects are relatively minor, including constipation, weight gain and night-time drooling.

In a study by Asenjo Lobos et al. (2010), clozapine was compared with a number of other atypical antipsychotics. It faired very favourably in controlling symptoms, but the risks of serious side effects led to large numbers of patients leaving the studies. However, clozapine does not always remove all of the positive symptoms in those treatment-resistant patients, so other atypical antipsychotic drugs are sometimes prescribed alongside clozapine. There is not sufficient quality data at present to evaluate whether the addition of a second drug leads to any significant improvements (Cipriani, Boso & Barbui, 2009).

When compared with neuroleptics, clozapine appears to be more effective in reducing symptoms (Essali, Al-Haj Haasan, Li & Rathbone, 2009). Furthermore, patients seemed more satisfied with the results of taking clozapine. However, short-term effects were not strong enough regarding global functioning to permit patients to leave hospital or to function at work.

Aripiprazole

Aripiprazole is unique amongst the second generation antipsychotics because its mechanism of action is completely different. All other antipsychotics block dopamine receptors (antagonist). This is good for those regions of the brain where dopamine activity is too high (causing the positive symptoms) but not where it is too low or just right (causing motor, weight gain and other problems). Aripiprazole is a partial agonist. This means that where dopamine activity is too high, it occupies the receptors but only gives rise to a partial response so the net effect is reduced activity. Where there is too little dopamine, aripiprazole can occupy the vacant receptor sites, thereby boosting the level of dopamine activity.

Many of the atypical antipsychotics have weight gain as a side effect and this has been linked to a risk of obesity and diabetes for clozapine and olanzapine. Aripiprazole seems not to suffer from these potential problems (L'Italien, Casey, Kan, Carson & Marcus, 2007). However, there have been isolated incidences where diabetes has developed (Los & Jacob, 2010). The main side effects with Aripiprazole are nausea/vomiting and insomnia.

Olanzapine

Olanzapine is often used in the early stages of psychosis but tends not to be used as a long-term treatment because of its high association with obesity and diabetes. It has also been used with prodromal schizophrenia, that is, with high-risk individuals who have not yet shown schizophrenic symptoms.

McGlashan et al. (2006) showed that it might have some value in this regard as it did reduce the incidence of pre-psychosis positive symptoms. However, even its use here is associated with significant weight gain.

In clinical comparisons with haloperidol for use with first episode schizophrenia (Sanger et al., 1999), olanzapine users were less likely to leave the study early (an indication that either the drug wasn't working or that the side effects were intolerable). In addition, it was reported that olanzapine users had a significantly better improvement. This was for both positive and negative symptoms, but the greater difference was for the positive symptoms. Whether these advantages persist over the course of the schizophrenia has not been investigated.

Risperidone

Risperidone has only been on the market for 20 years, having been approved in the US in 1993. Like most antipsychotics, it acts as a dopamine antagonist. Whilst it does have a number of associated side effects, such as weight gain, type 2 diabetes and tardive dyskinesia, at low doses it has a low incidence of the kind of motor problems associated with the first generation antipsychotics. The drug works by binding to dopamine receptor sites so that effects of the excess dopamine produced by the patient are reduced. Risperidone also acts at serotonin receptors and its actions here might account for the weight gain side effect.

In August 2007, Risperidone was approved as the only drug available to treat people with schizophrenia in adolescents aged 13–17. Like many antipsychotics, it is available as a tablet, an oral solution and as a depot injection. Depot injections are injections of drugs that get released slowly over a period of weeks. The claim made of the drug is that it is effective in alleviating negative symptoms as well as positive symptoms. This is a big advantage as most antipsychotics are not very effective where negative symptoms are concerned, though the second generation drugs generally fair better here.

Quetiapine

Quetiapine is a dopamine, serotonin and adrenergic antagonist. However, it is unusual in that it attaches to the D2 dopamine receptor but then very rapidly detaches again so its dopamine effect is pretty much confined to D1, D3 and D4 antagonism. There are data to suggest that quietapine is better than a placebo, but the data on its effectiveness compared to other antipsychotics is hard to assess because the drop-out rate of trialists has been greater than 50%.

Robles et al. (2011) carried out a study comparing the effectiveness of Quetiapine and Olanzapine in reducing cognitive symptoms in patients with early-onset, first-episode psychosis. Those receiving Quetiapine had marginally better cognitive performance on working memory and executive functions. They also performed marginally better on attention tasks. However, the differences were not large enough for the authors to conclude that Quetiapine was better than Olanzapine. More importantly, neither drug improved cognitive functioning as much as the FGAs.

⊙ Comparing first generation and second generation antipsychotics

From a neurotransmitter perspective we can see why the FGAs and SGAs have different results. The FGAs block dopamine D2 receptors and in doing so decrease the levels of dopamine. However, they block the D2 receptors in brain regions that are the cause of positive symptoms (e.g. the mesolimbic pathway) but also block them in the mesocortical pathway which is in a hypodopaminergic state (not enough dopamine). This latter state of affairs is responsible for the negative, cognitive and affective symptoms, so blocking the D2 receptors here just makes these symptoms worse. In addition, the FGAs also block dopamine D2 receptors in the nigrostriatal pathway. This is a motor area and does not contribute to the schizophrenic symptoms. Furthermore, the dopamine balance in the nigrostriatal pathway was just fine without the drugs so now the balance is now upset. So the consequence of FGAs is that they reduce positive symptoms (mesolimbic), make negative, cognitive and affective symptoms worse (mesocortical) and lead to motor control side effects (nigrostriatal). The SGAs not only block the D2 receptors but they also block serotonin 5-HT2A receptors. These serotonin receptors happen to be found mostly in the mesocortical and nigrostriatal regions. Serotonin acting at these receptors inhibits dopamine release. So by inhibiting these serotonin receptors we inhibit the inhibition of dopamine release. In other words, blocking the serotonin receptors causes a local increase in dopamine release.

Let's put all of that together for the SGAs. They block dopamine functioning in the mesolimbic, mesocortical and nigrostriatal systems by virtue of their direct action on dopamine D2 receptors, and they increase dopamine functioning in the mesocortical and nigrostriatal regions by virtue of their action on serotonin 5-HT2A receptors. So in the mesolimbic system dopamine activity is reduced (good – that reduces the positive symptoms), in the mesocortical system dopamine activity is reduced AND increased (good – if a neutral net effect then it has not made negative, cognitive or affective symptoms worse and if a net dopamine increase this could reverse those symptoms) and in the nigrostriatal system dopamine activity has been reduced AND increased (good – the net effect should be no change in motor control). So does the research evidence support this theoretical framework?

Leucht et al. (2009) carried out a meta-analysis to compare first and second generation antipsychotics (FGAs and SGAs). Their analysis included studies in which nine SGAs had been compared with any of the first generation drugs. After rejecting those studies that did not meet their criteria, they compared the results across 239 studies that had examined 21,533 participants. Nearly half of the studies compared a second generation drug to Haloperidol. Of the nine SGAs looked at, four were more effective than the FGA and the other five showed no difference. The four that yielded better effectiveness were Amisulpride, Clozapine, Olanzapine and Risperidone. Furthermore, they were better at treating both positive and negative symptoms. Amisulpride and Clozapine were the only two of these four that also gave better results for relapse rates and quality of life. It would seem that the common belief that SGAs are better is not true for all of them but is certainly true for a few.

◉ Adherence to medication

It is all very well for us to discuss which drug is better than another, but a very real problem faces all of the drug treatments. That problem is that people with schizophrenia often do not take the drugs they are prescribed. In other words, they do not adhere to their drug regime. Even the new method of delivering the drugs called the depot drug mechanism has not proved to be all that successful. The depot mechanism is a way of reducing the frequency with which medicating must be engaged because, as mentioned earlier, the drug that is administered is slowly released over a number of weeks. However, it seems not to help a lot because at some point a new dose always has to be taken. We have seen one obvious reason why there might be a lack of **adherence** and that is the side effects. If we then add to that the fact that some people with schizophrenia are paranoid and suffering from persecutory delusions then it is even more obvious why the patient is not likely to self-medicate (i.e. take the drug of their own accord).

Valenstein et al. (2004) examined the adherence records of 63,214 patients over a single year. Most, around 49,000 were on just one drug during that period but the rest had changed medication at some point during the year. They examined the adherence rates of those on first generation or second generation antipsychotics (FGAs and SGAs) and they also looked for any differential effects of dosage, ethnicity, sex and age. In their sample 53% of those on just one form of medication during the study period were receiving FGAs. The vast majority of those who had their medication changed (71%) had one FGA and one SGA. The adherence rates for those on one or two drugs were about the same, with 40% and 38% having poor adherence respectively. However, as seen in Box 8.1,

Box 8.1 A Personal Response to Taking Psychoactive Drugs

This is a blog post from a person with schizophrenia. It illustrates a willingness to take medication to control the delusional thoughts but also a desire to take the lowest level of medication that can achieve that goal.

"I saw my psychiatrist today and he is allowing me to try to stop the Latuda and see if I really need to be on 2 antipsychotics or not.

After my relapse he put me on 80 mg to stop some delusional thinking that had resurfaced after my traumatic experience at work. It did the trick but I am always wanting to be on the least medicine possible so I think I need to try it without it. I never do anything with my medicine without my psychiatrist, though. I want him to guide everything although it was my suggestion. He agreed to try because I am doing so well right now.

It is a very expensive medication and my with my insurance it is still around a hundred dollars. I figure I better be sure I really need it at that steep price. There are no side effects I have noticed on this medication. It handled the delusions but I still need to be on Risperdal to counter some of the negative symptoms of Schizophrenia.

Anyway, time will tell. He has cut me down to 40mg for a month and after that I can stop."

(extract from a personal blog by Victoria at mypersonalrecoveryfrom schizophrenia.wordpress.com – accessed 16th January 2014) people with schizophrenia are often reluctant to take too many drugs at one time and desire to reduce their medication. When comparing the types of medication there was little to choose between FGAs and SGAs in terms of the adherence rates (around 40% of both groups having poor adherence), although the FGAs were marginally better adhered to. The exception to this was clozapine which had only 4.6% of patients showing poor adherence. The reason for this is that patients on clozapine are on a strict visit and monitoring regime. When considering age, Valenstein et al found that young people were seen to adhere less than older people. Perhaps younger people are less likely to appreciate the severity of their condition. Valenstein et al. also discovered that many more African-Americans were poorer adherers (54%) than whites (32%) or other ethnicities (45%). It might be that African-Americans are less likely to access the available services such as outpatient visits where checks and reminders about medication would occur.

The most important thing to note about these findings is that, generally, adherence to medication is poor and so there is a significant risk of relapse and rehospitalisation. Furthermore, the reduced side effects associated with the SGAs does not appear to be a critical factor in determining whether or not someone will adhere to their medication. Kikkert et al. (2006) have tried to get a better understanding of why adherence is poor. They wanted to understand the patient's decision-making process by getting the opinions of patients, carers and professionals as to why adherence fails. They were keen to see if they could unpack the quantitative findings of the sort detailed above. Their data collection spanned four European countries and involved 27 patients, 29 carers and 28 professionals. Fischer, Shumway and Owen (2002) had already established that patients, carers and professionals differed in their views on service priorities. Kikkert et al. now wanted to see if they had differing views on the barriers to adherence. It seems that patients and carers placed more emphasis on the positive medication aspects, whereas professionals thought one of the most important factors was side effects. It is encouraging from a treatment perspective that patients and carers picked out similar challenges to adherence.

◉ Non-drug biological treatments

As well as antipsychotic drugs, there are and have been a number of alternative biological treatments. Indeed, some, like insulin-shock and ECT, predate the advent of antipsychotic medication.

Insulin-shock therapy

Even earlier than the realisation that chlorpromazine could be useful as an antipsychotic, Sargant and Slater (1944) published a book in which they referred to the insulin treatment of schizophrenia. This was a treatment first tried in the Vienna Clinic by Manfred Sakel in the 1930s. He used insulin to induce supervised hypoglycaemia to the point of coma which was then followed up with intravenous glucose to counter the effects. Despite being a dangerous operation, Sakel claimed the treatment was extremely successful. Indeed, if treatment was given within six months of diagnosis, the claim was that 59% of patients showed complete or social remission (cessation of symptoms). The timing was critical, it seemed, and treatment was not advised if it was believed that a patient had been suffering for longer even if they had not presented earlier. Whilst this treatment was risky, the mortality rates with treatment were far lower than those where treatment was not given. This treatment had also been used with electroconvulsive therapy, with the latter being relevant to treating the negative symptoms.

Electroconvulsive therapy (ECT)

Electroconvulsive therapy is probably the most controversial therapy in the whole field of mental health care. It involves attaching electrodes to the skull of the patient and passing a current through the head in order to induce a seizure. In modern times it is done under a general anaesthetic and muscle relaxants are given to prevent spasms. Despite the fact that nobody knows really how it works, it is known to be effective in treating depression that is resistant to medication. Furthermore, it is now known that it has no lasting effects on the brain. It has been tried as a treatment for schizophrenia, particularly concerning hallucinations that are not responding to any other forms of treatment (intractable). In fact, it was the treatment of choice from its introduction in 1934 until the advent of antipsychotic drugs in the 1950s and its very inception was based on the fact that dementia praecox was rare in patients with severe epilepsy. ECT made a comeback in the 1970s and there has continued to be some use of ECT as a treatment, but this is usually alongside an antipsychotic drug. It is only in the poorer parts of the globe that ECT is used as a sole treatment because it is extremely inexpensive to administer.

According to the American Psychiatric Association Committee on Electroconvulsive Therapy, ECT for schizophrenia should be used in cases of:

> psychotic exacerbations of an abrupt or recent onset; catatonic schizophrenia (a subtype of schizophrenia where the person becomes

mute and stuporous often adopting bizarre postures, known as catatonic stupor, or demonstrates excessive activity (catatonic excitement);
where a history of a favourable response to ECT is present or for
treating related psychotic disorders such as schizophreniform disorder
(where the symptoms of schizophrenia have been present for less than
six months) and schizoaffective disorder (where there is a mixture of
symptoms of schizophrenia and that of a mood disorder). (Tharyan &
Adams, 2009, p. 3)

In contrast, the **National Institute for Clinical Excellence (NICE)**
in the UK does not recommend the use of ECT for schizophrenia.
We should examine some of the data on ECT and schizophrenia to see how
much of a positive effect it does or does not have. There are no consistent
data regarding the efficacy of ECT. One of the problems is that ECT is
rarely given alone, so the effects of ECT over and above other treatments
are difficult to assess. With that in mind, Tharayn and Adams (2009)
reviewed the literature and found that ECT is not generally as effective as
antipsychotic medication if administered alone. However, a limited set of
studies suggested a faster improvement is achieved if ECT is administered
alongside medication. A further set of studies suggested that ECT can be
useful in patients who do not respond well to medication (e.g. Wu et al.,
1989). Interestingly, these studies make little mention of things like transient memory impairments which is commonplace in the use of ECT alone
to treat, for example, epilepsy. May (1968) carried out a comparison of
ECT and psychotherapy and found that ECT was better. However, if the
psychotherapy was combined with medication then the advantage of ECT
disappeared.

We might consider some issues surrounding this research. Firstly, there
are very few studies and the patients cover a huge range of symptom characteristics, patient characteristics, length of illness and so on. These variables may play a critical role in the outcome of ECT use. Furthermore,
Abrams raised some concern over diagnosis, suggesting that those who
responded to ECT might have been manics rather than people with schizophrenia. Later, though, he did admit that ECT could be useful for patients
with early-onset schizophrenia who show severe negative symptoms
(Abrams, 1992).

Overall it would seem that some improvement has been noted (Tharayan
and Adams, 2009) provided that the ECT accompanies antipsychotic
medication. Given our knowledge that ECT is a treatment more often
associated with chronic depression, the positive effect may not be directly
on the positive symptoms of schizophrenia but a more generalised
improvement in the negative symptoms (e.g. elevated mood). It may be

that ECT is most valuable early on when the effects of medication have not been fully established and when the psychotic episode might be at its most powerful.

Transcranial Magnetic Stimulation (TMS)

This similar to ECT but is not as severe. Instead of directly passing an electric current into the brain, strong pulse of electric current is passed through a coil, and it is the resultant magnetic field that passes into a small targeted area of the brain. Unlike ECT, there are very few side effects. Hoffman et al. (1999) carried out a study in which they directed repetitive TMS (rTMS – delivered as 16 minutes daily for four days) at the left temperoparietal cortex of a group of people with schizophrenia. The results were an improvement in the patients' medication-resistant auditory verbal hallucinations over those who were given a sham procedure (where the procedure is identical but no actual TMS is delivered). However, Slotema et al. (2011) have not been able to replicate this finding. Furthermore, no improvement has been found with TMS delivered to other parts of the brain. If there is any value to this treatment method then it is almost certainly as an addition to pharmacological treatment rather than as a replacement for it.

◉ Psychosurgery and schizophrenia

Psychosurgery is another controversial treatment with an historical past dating back to the 1930s, though the earliest records date back to the 1880s and there are fossil records to suggest that a kind of psychosurgery was carried out by Neanderthal man, presumably to release evil spirits. Our 'modern day' form of psychosurgery was developed by Moniz as an operation known as a leucotomy. The operation, as performed by Moniz, involved making cuts in the frontal lobes of patients with schizophrenia. He did this by inserting a blunt rod through the temples on either side of the head and moving it up and down. This effectively severed the connections between the frontal lobe and the rest of the brain. The result was a calming of the patient's behaviour. He claimed that, *"Prefrontal leukotomy is a simple operation, always safe, which may prove to be an effective surgical treatment in certain cases of mental disorder."* He did recognise that the patients suffered deterioration in their personality but he said that this was a small price to pay for the obvious benefits in the reduction of the illness. His work was so influential that he received the Nobel Prize in 1949.

Walter Freeman was a neuroscientist in the US and he readily took up the new practice developed by Moniz. He tried to improve on the technique and developed the trans-orbital lobotomy. The patient would be rendered unconscious using ECT and then he used an ice pick that was inserted through the orbit of the eye. The ice pick would enter the brain and be moved back and forth to sever the connections. The technique was so popular as a treatment for mental illnesses, including schizophrenia, that by 1949 there were over 5,000 operations being carried out each year. Freeman himself carried out lobotomies on 19 children under the age of 18, including one child who was just four years old. As with ECT, the fate of frontal lobotomies was sealed by the development of antipsychotic medication. Even here, though, such was the popularity of the lobotomy that the new drugs were advertised as a chemical lobotomy. The first British lobotomy was carried out in 1940 and by 1954, when the first antipsychotic drugs were available, the figure in the UK was about 12,000.

Despite the barbarity of the technique, we need to ask whether psychosurgery worked and whether it is still a technique in use today. The effects of the lobotomy were to calm the patient. However, that calmness was in the form of apathy. Patients were also partially paralysed and had a reduced level of intellectual functioning than they had had before. Most dramatically, the patients seemed to lose all of their personality characteristics and became emotionally flat. The characterisation of a lobotomised patient in the film 'One Flew Over The Cuckoo's Nest' is a very good portrayal of the lobotomised patient. These calming symptoms do not constitute any measure of success, but we can reflect on the fact that a number of the deficits faced by the schizophrenic are frontal or prefrontal in origin (as we saw in Chapter 4). However, the principle of removing the damaged area is not the solution. Besides, at the time that lobotomies were being carried out, nobody knew how they 'worked' and there was little knowledge about the role played by the frontal lobes.

Thankfully, lobotomy is no longer used. In the UK, the Mental Health Act of 1983 made it all but impossible for lobotomies to be carried out as they need approval from the Mental Health Act Commission. In the last 10 years in the UK, the number of lobotomies has been in single figures and none of these have been carried out for patients suffering from schizophrenia.

Ayurvedic medicine

Just before we leave the biological treatments, we should consider a biological treatment of a very different kind and one that emphasises the differences in how schizophrenia is seen across the globe. Ayurvedic medicine from India is one of the oldest systems of natural healing and its inclusion in this section because the proposed cures are natural ingredients. Although Ayurveda is both a physical and a spiritual perspective, insanity is seen as being caused by anything from having unhealthy foods to making mistakes in holy worship. The mainstay of the treatment is the use of natural herbs. One such herb is withania somnifera, known in Ayurvedic medicine as ashwagandha. There is probably some truth to the claims that it can help with schizophrenia. One physiological link to the negative symptoms of schizophrenia is high levels of free oxygen radicals. These can cause oxidative stress and this thought to be one factor in the development of the disease. Ashwagandha is a source of antioxidants and, as such, could help to decrease the risk and/or the negative symptoms.

We should not be at all surprised by this finding. We know, within our Western context, that many psychoactive compounds occur naturally and these include those that harm and those that help. Ayurvedic medicine, whilst based within a principle of spirituality and a belief in different kinds of humours, will have remedies that are simply known to work without the practitioners knowing why. Not so very different, then, from our own beginnings with chlorpromazine.

◉ Chapter summary

This chapter has considered many of the drug treatments available to the person with schizophrenia. We have seen that the older, first generation antipsychotics were effective in treating some of the symptoms but the patient paid a high cost of severe side effects. The second generation drugs have been much more effective in reducing these side effects and have also been better able to treat the negative as well as the positive symptoms. A remaining issue surrounding drug treatments is the poor adherence rates and this has serious implications for the prospect of relapse and rehospitalisation.

We also explored in this chapter some of the biologically oriented treatments that do not involve drugs. These were generally used before drug treatments were available and were associated with a much higher risk of failure. We have also examined the practice of psychosurgery and have shown that, despite its popularity, this form of treatment did nothing to help the patient return to a normal life. The final section of the chapter looked at the practice of Ayurvedic medicine and this underlines the need to consider non-Western practices as potential sources of treatment.

◉ Further reading

Bentall, R.P. (2009) *Doctoring The Mind: Why Psychiatric Treatments Fail*. London: Penguin.

Brinkerhoff, S. (2008) *Drug Therapy and Schizophrenia* (Psychiatric Disorders: Drugs and Psychology for the Mind & Body Series) Mason Crest Publishers.

Kikkert, M.J., Schene, A.H., Koeter, M.W.J., Robson, D., Born, A., Helm, H., Nose, M., Goss, C., Thornicroft, G. and Gray, R.J. (2006) Medication adherence in schizophrenia: Exploring patients', carers' and professionals' views. *Schizophrenia Bulletin*, 32 (4), 786–794

Chapter 9

Psychosocial Approaches to Treatment

We have looked at the biological treatments for schizophrenia and it is fair to say that these are generally the psychiatrist's first choice of treatment. However, there are many psychologically oriented therapies and, as we shall see, many practitioners claim that these are underused. Indeed, many claim that these can produce better outcomes than the drug treatments, at least for

In this chapter we will cover:
- Psychodynamic theories
- Psychotherapy
- Psychoeducational therapy
- Family therapy
- Personal therapy
- Single therapies
  - Compassionate mind training
  - Cognitive remediation therapy
  - Social skills training
- Combinatorial therapies
  - Integrated psychological therapy
  - Cognitive behavioural therapy
  - Institutional care
  - Milieu therapy
- Other therapies
  - Art therapy
  - Music therapy
  - Dance therapy

certain cases of schizophrenia. We will explore many of the most popular kinds of psychological treatment and the body of evidence that has been developed around their efficacy.

The chapter is subdivided into four main areas of psychological treatment. The first category is the psychodynamic therapies. These have their basis in the psychodynamic approach and consider that by changing the family dynamics you can change the future outlook for the schizophrenic patient. The second category is the single therapies where the therapy addresses only one dimension of deficit. Two examples are provided, the first of which is Cognitive Remediation Therapy which takes a purely cognitive approach to treatment. This is followed by Social Skills Therapy which takes an alternative view to a single domain and treats the problem of schizophrenia as one stemming from a lack of social skills and social perception. These latter two treatments have more recently been combined into the Integrated Psychological Therapy that we will look at as the first of our third category, the combinatorial therapies. The other combined therapy we will examine is Cognitive Behavioural Therapy. This is probably one of the best known psychological theory used today for a whole range of mental illnesses. The final section looks at a couple of other therapies that have been suggested. They are no less important for being grouped together here; it is just that they have fewer followers and are less widely used. They are Art Therapy and Music Therapy.

As a prelude to discussing these therapies, we might consider a recent document that underlines the gradual move away from a wholly medical approach to the treatment of schizophrenia. It is referred to as the recovery model and has been well articulated in The President's New Freedom Commission on Mental Health: Transforming the Vision (2003). This document defines recovery as "the process by which people are able to live, work, learn, and participate fully in their communities. For some individuals, recovery is the ability to live a fulfilling and productive life despite a disability. For others, recovery implies the reduction or complete remission of symptoms" (p.7). The importance of this model is that it suggests we abandon the idea of a cure, that is implicit in the medical model, and replace it with the idea of recovery, which is both a process and an outcome. So instead of the schizophrenic being a patient (a passive recipient), s/he is seen as a consumer of services (an active participant). Glynn, Cohen, Dixon and Niv (2006) have argued that some of the psychosocial treatments have gone some way towards this recovery model but still talk about patients and have an overly therapist-directed process. After all, we talk about a recovering alcoholic rather than an alcoholic patient. You might like to bear these points in mind as you explore the various kinds of therapies that follow.

Psychodynamic therapies

We start with the psychodynamic therapies. These are based around the belief that many of the problems that interfere with patient recovery concern the way in which the family members interact with each other and react to the patient's behaviours.

Psychotherapy

The history of the use of psychotherapy to treat schizophrenia is not paved with a lot of success. The old methodologies focused on an examination of the patient's past life and was centred on the relationship between the therapist and the patient. Before about 1975, psychotherapy and medication were two ends of a treatment divide. Since then, though, psychotherapy has recognised the importance of medication and has changed towards a more supportive role in the recovery of the patient. During the 1980s, many of the old traditions were still there, but there was an attempt to work in tandem with the pharmacologists. More recently still, new approaches to psychotherapy, such as the personal therapy discussed later, have provided a new role for psychotherapeutic approaches.

Psychoeducational therapy

We start our foray into the world of non-drug treatments with a pivotal issue, namely, how much do people with schizophrenia and their families know about the disorder? It seems obvious in some ways that knowing what the disorder consists of and the kinds of problems faced by the sufferer can help the patient and the rest of the family come to terms with the behaviours that can be expected. It can also help the patient to understand the need to engage with the medication regime they have been given as failing to comply with the medication requirements will present a major barrier to any recovery. As well as being a treatment in its own right, psychoeducation has become a major component of all of the family therapies, so it seems reasonable to start with a description of what it entails and an analysis of its efficacy.

Psychoeducation started in 1980 when Anderson et al. published a new therapy. They argued that even though antipsychotic drug treatments were capable of reducing the symptoms of schizophrenia, as many as 40% of people suffered a relapse within a year of leaving hospital (Hogarty & Ulrich,

1977). In some ways, what Anderson et al were proposing was one of the first ventures into what we now label the biopsychosocial approach to treatment. There was a growing knowledge about the relative successes and failures of family therapies and other psychosocial interventions. Furthermore, there was a growing understanding that interactions within the family had an important role to play in the patient's recovery. We have already seen a number of those influences (e.g. expressed emotion) in Chapter 6. It was becoming obvious that the family's responses needed to be stimulating to avoid apathy and the negative symptoms but not too stimulating or confrontational so as to cause the patient to misinterpret the environment due to their decreased attentional capabilities. Anderson et al. believed that some of the family reactivity was a result of ignorance of what the disease is and how it manifests itself in positive and negative symptoms. The programme they devised was an attempt to increase the stability of the family environment and to do that they sought to increase the family members' self-confidence and knowledge about the illness and to decrease their anxieties.

The principles behind Psychoeducation are that the patient and family should be provided with useful knowledge about the illness, mechanisms to control or deal with the stress that the illness places on the patient and the family, and attainable goals for managing the illness. To see why these principles are important, we should take a moment to try to understand a family's response to discovering that a family member has schizophrenia. Families tend to adopt one of two beliefs when they realise that a family member is a schizophrenic. They either believe the patient to be incurably ill and this produces excessive concern, exaggerated support and a closing of ranks whereby outsiders who might judge are unwelcome. Alternatively, the belief is that the patient has a character defect that is of the patient's own making. This leads to criticism, anger and hostility in the belief that the patient can exercise their will to reverse this behavioural trend.

The evolution of psychoeducation has been slightly different in the UK and the US from that in Germany. In the former psychoeducation is seen as part of a wider family therapy approach whereas in the latter it is seen as a therapy in its own right. The ultimate goal of the therapy is to achieve a situation where the schizophrenic along with their family and health practitioners can come to a well-informed decision about which of the modern pharmacological and/or psychodynamic and/or psychosocial treatment methods should be pursued moving forward. In a study to assess the effectiveness of psychoeducation alone, Pitschel-Walz et al. (2006) showed that when carried out in conjunction with relatives there was a significant decrease in relapse rates requiring hospitalisation compared with controls and their relatives not given the treatment. Indeed the rehospitalisation rate was virtually halved.

Box 9.1 The Psychoeducation Method of Treatment

The treatment devised by Anderson, Hogarty & Reiss (1980) comprises four phases. These phases were labelled: connection with the family, survival skills workshop, re-entry and application and maintenance.

The connection phase usually takes place without the patient as it is desirable to initiate this phase before the patient is in remission. It requires that the clinician interacts with the family in a non-judgmental way and genuinely tries to learn about the family situation and the events leading up to the psychotic episode. The clinician needs to gain the trust of the family as their involvement in the treatment is critical. Through this phase a treatment contract is agreed that sets achievable goals together with an agreement over the scheduling of therapy sessions.

Phase two is usually a day long workshop involving a number of families who are all new to the process. This establishes the realisation that one family is not alone and allows them to compare situations and coping styles. The workshop will provide detailed information about the illness and, most importantly, information about how to manage the illness. Some of this education involves modifying ways of communicating so that an approach is taken to the patient that is more calming and accepting. The last part of this second phase is a reminder that the family must continue with its life and not completely change its life around the patient. After all, it is a marathon and not a sprint. The analogy of coping with something like diabetes is often used to show the family that, whilst they need to make adjustments, life still must go on.

The third phase now introduces the patient back into the family (from a therapeutic perspective). These sessions start as soon as the patient has remitted from the acute phase of the illness. The focus is on reinforcing family boundaries and reintegrating the patient back into family life. Family members will discuss problems with the patient and the patient discusses problems with the family. This helps to establish mutual respect and allows boundaries to be respected. For example, this may include allowing family members time to do something separately from the rest of the family. There is also a gradual reintroduction of the responsibilities of the patient within the family. The long-term goal of this might be for the patient to get a job and find their own apartment but this should be built towards in a gradual and manageable way (remember that most new people with schizophrenia are in their late teens and early twenties).

The final phase allows for the option for the family to move from Psychoeducation to an alternative form of family therapy or for therapy to cease and for the family to disengage with the therapy process altogether. They may, after all, feel that they now have control of the situation and can get back to a more normal existence. The therapy option, of course, always remains open if they decide to resume at a later date.

Bäuml, Froböse, Kraemer, Rentrop and Pitschel-Walz (2006) have suggested that there is a need to provide psychoeducation as early as possible. They describe the sequence of information flow as going from a one-to-one initial diagnosis of schizophrenia for the patient to group information sharing processes that explain the common and basic facets of the condition. Both of these must happen very early on as a prelude to other therapies. The initial explanation is important to deal with the anger, fear and insecurity that comes with being told your recent psychotic episode was a schizophrenic one. The purpose of rapidly moving into a group phase helps to reassure the patient that there are others like them and that they do not have to face their predicament on their own.

Family therapy

Like Psychoeducation, family therapy is designed to allow the whole family to be involved in helping the schizophrenic to avoid a relapse of the psychosis and to lead as normal a life as possible. It usually involves educating the family about the nature of the disorder and providing strategies to reduce the stress that might lead to a relapse. There are different approaches to the therapy itself. Some have involved working with a single family and others have involved a multifamily approach.

Family therapy often proceeds as a phased approach in a similar way to psychoeducation. The first phase is concerned with providing the basic information about what the disorder is and what kinds of cognitions and behaviours the patient can expect to experience and often employs the psychoeducational techniques described above. The provision of good information about the disorder is designed to decrease these feelings of guilt and anger and confusion that often accompany the realisation that a loved one has got schizophrenia. The initial phase is completed when the clinician has established the need to engage with therapy for both the patient and their immediate family. As with Psychoeducation, there is a reassurance that there are sources and mechanisms of help and that the condition can be controlled. One component of this is to reduce the family's stress levels. The clinician will suggest rules to be followed and expectation levels that will simplify the interactions within the family. If they can learn to manage the behaviours that the patient will display then they are less likely to react in an aggressive and critical manner. The other component is to provide social networks and social support. It is known (Brown et al., 1972) that those family members with less social support tend to be more critical of the patient. So it is important that social support networks are provided for family members as well as for the patient. These extra-familial interactions need to serve the purpose of support but also need to provide a source of recreation and even a source of employment if at all possible.

Different kinds of family therapy exist. Some involve a single family and some involve multifamily groups with only selected members from each family being involved. For example, Behavioural Family Therapy (BFT) usually involves the whole family, including the patient, and the therapy sessions are conducted in the patient's home. Relatives Group therapy (RG), on the other hand, usually involves only one or two relatives of patients and they meet as a whole group at the clinic. This latter therapy has, as its principle, the idea that a source of relapse is high expressed emotion (see Chapter 6), so that the relative attending was the person who was central to the patient's everyday interactions. In both cases, the education phase is followed by training in communication skills and problem-solving skills aimed at reducing conflict and increasing the likelihood that amicable solutions to family problems can be worked through in a calm manner. Montero et al. (2001) directly compared these two forms of family therapy. In terms of their ability to prevent relapse, both were found to be equally effective. However, there were other differences between them. BFT gave a better outcome in terms of social adjustment, which included, among other things, the patient's self-care, participation in the household and interest in getting a job. This is not surprising when you think about it as BFT involves the whole family, including the patient, whereas RG only involves the mother and maybe one other family member.

By way of evaluation, Pitschel-Walz, Leucht, Bäuml, Kissling and Engel (2001) carried out a meta-analysis of family intervention studies which had either compared two or more types of family intervention or had compared family intervention with other treatments (such as patient intervention or what is described as 'the usual care'). They analysed a total of 25 studies and concluded that the inclusion of family members in the treatment programme effectively reduces relapse and rehospitalisation rates. However, there were some noteworthy differences between the studies. Family therapy was more effective if the treatment lasted more than three months. When directly compared to Psychoeducation, no differences were found and so the value of the additional elements of family therapy can be called into question, at least as far as relapse rates are concerned. Perhaps, then, the advantages of family therapy lie in the social adjustment elements described by Montero et al. (2001). When compared with psychosocial patient interventions like the Personal Therapy described in the next section, the results are very mixed. Some studies show family therapy to be better, some show patient interventions to be better and one study found no differences. We might simply conclude, therefore, that family therapy is one of a number of methodologies that reduces relapse and rehospitalisation rates in people with schizophrenia.

At the beginning of the chapter, I referred to the recovery model approach to the treatment of mental illness. In a recent study, Glynn et al. (2006) have suggested that family therapy goes some way towards moving us away from a medical model of schizophrenia to the recovery model. However, most of these therapies were devised at a time when the goal was the successful management of schizophrenia rather than an aid to recovery. Furthermore, they are both directed by the therapist rather than by the patient (consumer) and the family. This leads to the process being rather generic so that it fails to recognise that the schizophrenic might be a child in the family or a parent themselves, and that they play different roles within the family (child, parent, sibling, and so on). It will be interesting to see if family therapies can develop to become more individualised or whether that approach is too costly to be differentially effective.

Personal therapy

Personal therapy is a psychosocial patient intervention. It is a therapy that is designed to enhance personal and social adjustment by helping them to respond appropriately to external arousing stimuli. As the name suggests, the therapy is somewhat tailored to the individual patient's needs. Developed by Hoggarty and his colleagues, studies have shown that this therapy can significantly reduce relapse rates (Hogarty et al., 1997). They conducted 3-year trials to test the therapy's efficacy at preventing relapse. Their sample of 151 patients (97 living with their family and 54 living alone) were split roughly equally into personal therapy, family therapy, supportive therapy and personal therapy combined with family therapy. We will just concentrate on the personal therapy here. The personal therapy was provided in three stages. In the first stage (usually delivered within a few months of their being discharged from hospital), patients were introduced to a process called 'internal coping'. This focuses on the patient's experience of stress and allows them to identify their biological response to stress (physiological), their emotional response to stress (affective) and what stress does to their thought processes (cognitive). In addition, they also received some social skills training and help in achieving a stable level of medication. The idea of this basic first stage was to stabilise their symptoms and to get some simple social systems in place. If they achieved this level, they passed to the second stage which continued with the initial themes. More psychoeducation was provided to help them further understand and maintain their drug regimen; relaxation techniques and cognitive reframing (seeing the problem in a different way) were taught to help them deal with the stress and more advanced social skills training was used to improve further their ability to interact with others in an appropriate way. Having successfully navigated this second stage, patients were introduced to the final stage of the therapy. Here they were helped to focus on their role in the community, including a potential vocation. Also introduced now was a consideration of how their own behaviours and social interactions affect the behaviour and interactions of others.

Of 151 patients in Hoggarty et al.'s trial, 52% entered into the final stage of therapy and a further 38% got as far as the second stage. Patients received between two and three therapy sessions a month across the three years. For those living with their family, the personal therapy resulted in significantly fewer relapses than the family therapy or the supportive therapy. Furthermore, a larger percentage (80%) of these patients survived therapy to year three without suffering a relapse However, for those living alone, personal therapy was significantly worse than supportive therapy. It seems that without the support of a family environment, the requirements of the personal therapy are too much of a cognitive overload for patients to deal with on top of their daily survival in their local environment.

With the approach taken by Hoggarty and by others, we can see a pattern emerging where some of these therapies are not being seen as exclusive and a more inclusive approach between psychoeducation, family therapy, supportive therapy and personal therapy is being adopted. Whilst some argue that each one has its own merits, there is a much more integrated approach to treatment being adopted. Next we will look at some therapies in which the individual is treated alone. These will be followed by a method that integrates two of them (albeit more formally than within the psychodynamic forms of therapy discussed so far).

◉ Single therapies

In this section we move away from the strictly psychodynamic approach and concentrate on therapies that focus on just one aspect of schizophrenia. These therapies tend not to involve families and are skills-based therapies to help the patient interact more effectively in the world.

Compassionate mind training

Compassionate mind training is based on the idea that some people find it difficult to be self-supporting because they have never learnt to be so. The training was first developed by Gilbert (2000) for people with high levels of shame as a way of teaching them how to have self-compassion. C. S. Carter (1998) proposed that this ability to feel compassion for yourself, or self-soothing, is usually developed from calming interactions with parents. People suffering from paranoia cannot practice this self soothing as they are constantly alert to the dangers of their hostile world. Mayhew and Gilbert (2008) have tried using compassionate mind training with people with schizophrenia who heard malevolent voices. The compassionate mind training is designed to help the patient to focus on their difficulties and to develop empathy in a nonjudgmental way. Although there were only three patients who managed to complete the course of compassionate mind training, all three found that the training transformed the hostile voices into ones that were more reassuring and less malevolent. It also helped them all to feel safer in their environment. At one-year follow-up the voices had not subsided and in some cases their malevolent nature had returned, but the patients were better able to cope with them by using compassionate thoughts.

Cognitive remediation therapy

As the name suggests, the principle behind cognitive remediation therapy (CRT) is to try to ameliorate the cognitive deficits shown by people with schizophrenia. We have discussed what these are in Chapter 6 but, to remind you, they span all areas of cognitive processing from perception, through attention and memory, to higher order processes such as language and thinking and reasoning. The desire to focus on cognition has arisen from the finding that medication does little to improve cognitive abilities after the initial stabilisation period after the onset of psychosis. Indeed, some have argued that medication can even make cognitive abilities worse (Corrigan & Penn, 1995). In this section we will explore a number of models for cognitive remediation and some of the therapies that they have given rise to.

The origins of CRT go back to Meichenbaum and Cameron (1973) who devised a method of getting people with schizophrenia to talk to themselves as a way of facilitating their ability to control their attentional processes. Even this early method recognised the need to use results obtained in the laboratory to provide the schizophrenic with something that could be managed alone and at home. The technique was self-instructional training. First the therapist carried out a task whilst at the same time talking aloud the components of the task. The patient was then required to firstly repeat what the therapist had done (i.e. complete the task whilst talking the instructions aloud), then repeat the task whilst whispering the instructions and finally to repeat the task whilst covertly saying the instructions (i.e. without any lip movements). The following extract describes one such task

If we examine the speech produced we see that it combines instructional elements (e.g. "fill in these numbers"), attentional focus elements (e.g. "what is it I have to do?") and praise ("Good"). The training progressed by introducing distractions that the patient had to talk through with statements like "just pay attention to what I have to do". (p.520) Finally, patients were taught when to use this self-instruction and, as part of that, to recognise when the expressions of others indicated to them that they were displaying 'schizophrenic behaviours'.

Wykes and van der Gaag (2001) have provided a comprehensive overview of the various models underlying the use of CRT and their relative efficacies. They note that some of the differences between them are due to a more neurocognitive focus in the US (training the brain) and a more cognitive focus in Europe (training information processing strategies). The learning model proposes using behavioural shaping to try to get the patient to be able to focus their attention. Using small incremental goals, the patient is shaped to maintain their attention for a period of longer than a couple of minutes. For example, a reinforcement is provided for maintaining eye contact or for continuing to engage in verbal responding. A variation on this theme is Cognitive Adaptational Training, whereby the required environmental behaviours are made prominent. For example, for dressing correctly, only one shirt and one pair of trousers might be available so that multiple shirts cannot be put on. However, although improvements have been found with this method, it is not clear if those improvements are maintained when the external help is removed (i.e. the person who puts the individual clothes out no longer does this) and the patient is required to perform the tasks themselves.

The other models do not fair particularly well either, according to Wykes and van der Gaag (2001). The retraining model adopts an approach whereby single deficits are retrained individually. For example, verbal memory might be specifically improved using a series of laboratory tasks. The problem here is that the retraining does not generalise to similar tasks. Other models include the neurodevelopmental model (the cognitive deficits are due to a lack of learning because of developmental delay), the energetical model (that patients do not lack the cognitive capability but lack the motivational effort and arousal required to complete cognitive tasks) and the executive functioning model (suggesting that patients show a lack of self-initiated responding and make inappropriate responses to stimuli).

So what of some of the other therapies that have arisen from these models? Cognitive enhancement therapy (CET) is a therapy designed for high functioning people with schizophrenia, that is, those who have good control over their symptoms. It stems from the neurodevelopmental model which suggests that because of their disruption to the normal developmental processes, people with schizophrenia fail to get the 'gist' of what is going on in social situations. Hogarty & Flesher (1999) argue that unaffected adults are able to rapidly and efficiently process social context. In other words, an unaffected adult can quickly appraise the social situation and access their memory to pull down relevant contextual and procedural information (so that they know how to behave appropriately). So the purpose of the therapy is to strengthen the diminished ability to process the gist. To do this, patients are divided into three groups; impoverished, disorganised or rigid on the basis of their cognitive abilities. At first patients who have different cognitive problems are paired up and given computerised exercises, involving attention and/or memory, to collaborate on. After a few months, they join with other pairs to form groups of 6 or 8. These groups socialise together and work together on the programmes. The kinds of tasks are purposeful, for example, to summarise an article in a newspaper for another person. The speaker needs to be clear and the others in the group need to be silent but to take notes. These exercises, then, are designed to encourage both social and cognitive behaviours that are appropriate. Data certainly support a short-term gain in personal and social functioning, but there is not a lot of data on whether this technique produces long-term improvements.

Another therapy is computerised training. Again, this targets attention deficits rather than problem-solving ones. The patients are given a number of attention tasks to carry out using a computer and are trained to produce the correct answers. Whilst these tasks have had some success with patients with closed head injuries, research involving people with schizophrenia has yielded mixed results with only about half of the studies reporting any improvement. As with cognitive enhancement therapy, there is little suggestion that the training provides any kind of generalisation to other tasks.

The picture painted thus far does not provide much support for the use of CRT but a recent analysis by Wykes and Spaulding (2011) has suggested that there may be a place for these kinds of therapy. There has been a rationalisation of what the term 'CRT' means and it was defined by The Cognitive Remediation Experts Workshop of 2010 as "a behavioural-training based intervention that aims to improve cognitive processes (attention, memory, executive function, social cognition, or metacognition) with the goal of durability and generalisation." (cited in Wykes & Spaulding, 2011, p. S84). This was needed as there have been too many methodological variations in studies and too many operational definitions of what constitutes a successful outcome.

The new agreed definition means that we are now in a position to be able to judge treatments from an agreed baseline for efficacy. So it would seem that we should not give up on CRT, but there must be greater clarity over which CRT methods are the best.

Social skills therapy

Alongside cognitive deficits shown by people with schizophrenia, they also display a number of socially inappropriate behaviours. We saw these in detail in Chapter 6. Here we will explore whether or not social skills training can improve these social skills. First let us remind ourselves of what some of these social skills are. According to Bellack, Morrison, Wixted and Mueser (1990), social competence generally includes expressive skills (verbal and non-verbal behaviours), receptive skills (social perception) and conversational skills (the ability to initiate, maintain and terminate a conversation). In addition, the schizophrenic displays problems with assertiveness skills, heterosocial skills (particularly dating and sexual interactions), independent living skills and medication management.

Social skills therapy is derived from a combination of Bandura's (1969) social learning theory and operant conditioning. The goal is to teach accurate social perception, including the norms, rules and expectations of others. For example, one task might be to be able to recognise reliably the emotional expressions shown by others during social interactions. The techniques employed include coaching, goal setting, behavioural rehearsal, positive reinforcement and corrective feedback. In order to embed the training within a normal social setting, the patient will usually be given homework so that they continue to practice the social behaviour beyond the therapy session.

According to Liberman, Glynn, Blair, Ross and Marder (2002) and a number of others, social skills training is capable of helping people with schizophrenia to acquire social skills, maintain those skills and to transfer them to everyday situations. Not all researchers agree about these achievements, and Pilling et al. (2002) claimed that through a meta-analytic review they could find no evidence of the benefit of social skills training on any outcomes. A more recent meta-analysis has questioned this pessimism. Kurtz and Mueser (2008) have suggested that social skills training is effective but not universally across all forms of social competence. According to their analysis, social skills training is effective for those skills directly taught in the sessions, some elements of independent living skills, psychosocial functioning and the reduction of negative symptoms (although here more so for younger patients). However, it proved less effective for reducing relapse rates and for non-negative symptoms. Interestingly, social skills training is recommended by the US health advisors (Patient

Outcomes Research Team) but not by those in the UK (National Institute for Clinical Excellence).

It is clear from these last two sections that there are benefits to providing cognitive remediation and to providing social skills training. It is also fairly obvious that these two dimensions interact with one another. In the next section, therefore, we explore a therapeutic principle that has tried to combine these two domains of therapy.

◉ Combinatorial therapies

The therapies discussed here are ones in which a combination of domains have been used at the same time to create a therapeutic approach. You should bear in mind whether combination is more or less effective than the separate therapies.

Integrated psychological therapy

This therapy first emerged in the 1980s in Germany and was well established a few years later (Brenner et al., 1994). The attraction of Integrated Psychological Therapy (IPT) was that it recognised the importance of cognitive deficits in the manifestation of social inadequacies seen in people with schizophrenia. The therapy was, therefore, a collection of five subprogrammes that combined cognitive therapy with social skills training. The subprogrammes are: cognitive differentiation, social perception, verbal communication, social skills and interpersonal problem solving. These are not new to us, given what we have already explored in this chapter. What was new at the time was the idea of combining these various strands into a coherent therapy. The therapy is designed so that each subprogramme is administered in turn (Figure 9.1), though the subprogrammes have also been used separately. The activities within the programme are delivered in groups via a didactic approach (i.e. through taught sessions). As only one of the subprogrammes is explicitly cognitive, researchers have asked what this component alone contributes to any overall improvements. It would seem that it does provide some improvement to social skills (Spaulding, Reed, Sullivan, Richardson & Weiler, 1999) but does not do very much for cognition itself. In another study, van der Gaag (1992) showed some improvements to the perception of emotion in faces and to executive functioning (mazes, word fluency, and so on) but none to attention and memory capabilities.

Whilst it is fair to question the value of each of the components of IPT so as not to waste time and effort on subprogrammes that are ineffective, it is also important to evaluate the therapy in its entirety. In a meta-analysis by

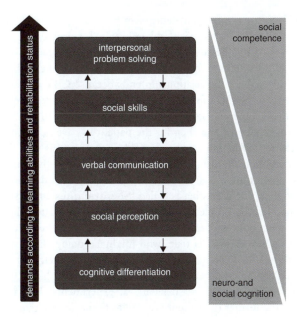

Figure 9.1 Integrated Psychological Therapy (IPT) for Schizophrenia (Roder et al., 2006, p. S82)

Roder, Mueller, Mueser and Brenner (2006) the case for IPT was very strong. From an analysis of high-quality studies (nine in all) covering some 362 patients, Roder et al. concluded that IPT improved patient symptoms, their psychosocial functioning and their neurocognition. Furthermore, the improvements were still present around eight months after treatment.

Roder, Mueller and Schmidt (2011) provided an update to their original meta-analysis and found that with the addition of another six studies in the intervening years there was still the same improvement as before. This is reassuring as it shows that the therapy is robust and reliable. In addition, the full programme gives a better improvement than any single subprogramme, suggesting that there is a combined effect of the component parts.

Cognitive behavioural therapy

We have seen an approach that combines cognitive and social therapies and we will now turn to one that combines two others. As the name suggests, this is a technique that combines a behaviour-based approach with the addition of a cognitive dimension. It is now used as an umbrella term that incorporates Behaviour Therapy and Cognitive Therapy. It was first introduced by

Beck (1952) as a treatment for depression but, as we shall see, it has been successfully adopted for use with schizophrenia. It is interesting to note that this therapy, which is Behaviourist in principle, arose from a psychoanalytic belief that adult beliefs are formulated as a consequence of childhood experiences. However, there the relationship ends because CBT is a collaborative project between the therapist and the patient. The basic technique involves setting a small, achievable goal, deciding on a technique to tackle and practice achieving that goal and then for the patient to have homework to carry out the practice before the next session. The process starts with the collaborative construction of the personal story that explains the current set of problems. When thinking about a current problem, say, a delusion of persecution, the therapist uses what is called '**Socratic questioning**' to explore the evidence for the problem. For example, if a patient thought that their water was being poisoned, the therapist might use a number of questions to explore how they know it is true, who might be doing this and why they would want to, and so on, ending with an analysis of whether they think all of these reasons are good enough to make the scenario likely. Other techniques are reality testing and behavioural experiments. Using our water example, in the former the patient is asked to find evidence that will test the reality of the belief (an exercise for the patient to find out how water gets into the taps) and in the latter it might involve a experiment to rate the taste of the water at home and elsewhere and to try to reason why water might taste slightly different in different places (type of piping, local filtering, etc.). Of course, if the schizophrenic psychosis is so severe that basic daily functioning needs to be achieved first, then CBT can also be used with a more behaviour change emphasis.

Early beliefs were that CBT would not be a useful therapy for schizophrenia as the positive symptoms were outside of healthy psychological functioning and so were inaccessible to the types of questioning techniques required. However, there is now a growing body of evidence that CBT can be an effective treatment for a number of the symptoms of schizophrenia. Sensky et al. (2000) argue that CBT has been used successfully to tackle the hallucinations, delusions, negative symptoms and depression associated with the disease. Using the general structure described above, each patient is given an individualised set of goals based on the question, "why have I changed so much?" The patient is given homework to help them make sense of their thoughts and to reorganise their coping strategies. In this way they come to rethink their thoughts and so learn not to fear them (e.g. their hallucinations may become less important to their behaviour). Perhaps because this therapy is one that includes the patient in agreeing the process, CBT has a very low drop-out rate at only around 12–15% (Turkington & McKenna, 2003).

CBT is not without its critics. Much of the criticism centres around the lack of methodological rigour applied to many of the studies showing positive outcomes. Turkington and McKenna (2003) point out that most of these studies are far less controlled than would be the case for medical research. Cormac, Jones and Campbell (2002) also stated that of 13 studies presented in a meta-analysis, only four used a control and blind testing. So we must exercise some caution over this newer and exciting therapy even though it has become extremely popular amongst health professionals as a panacea for a large number of mental illnesses.

Institutional care

There are two therapies that are most frequently used in institutions with patients who are institutionalised. These therapies arose in the 1950s and were a positive change to the rather barbaric conditions that had previously prevailed within institutions.

Milieu therapy

This therapy is based on humanist principles. The concept is that patients can only improve if they are given responsibilities and a sense of self-respect. In other words, there needs to be the correct social climate (milieu) to promote improvement. The founder of this therapy was Maxwell Jones who, in 1953, converted a ward of patients into a living space with residents (Jones, 1953). They had their own community government and were allowed to make decisions for themselves. They developed rules and also sanctions for those that broke the rules. This approach is used in many institutions, and Paul (2000) claims that this therapy increases the speed and likelihood of a resident leaving the hospital. Unfortunately, as it is the more severely impaired that are institutionalised, their impairments often mean they do not do very well once they leave hospital. Part of the problem may well be that they end up in half-way houses where the responsibilities, rules and residential community are no longer available.

Token economy

This therapy stems from a Behaviourist perspective and is a form of operant conditioning. Patients are rewarded for appropriate behaviour with tokens that they can later exchange for more substantial items such as food, cigarettes or hospital privileges. The tokens themselves are worthless and a single token would not get you much in the way of a reward, so the system encourages continual good behaviour. Token economies have been found to improve behaviours, especially in severely psychotic patients (Wong, 2006). Like milieu therapy, this therapy can result in successful discharge from hospital into a sheltered care facility. Unfortunately, most of the studies on token economy have lacked proper controls, so it is difficult to properly evaluate the success rate. Furthermore, there are ethical questions about the technique. Food and basic needs are a right and some have questioned the use of these basic requirements as rewards for good behaviours. Whilst there are more successful techniques, the token economy was among the first therapies to yield positive changes in behaviour.

◉ Other therapies

In 2008, the BBC published on their web pages a news item suggesting that government advisors were recommending the use of music, art and dance therapy on the NHS as part of the treatment options available for people with schizophrenia. For completeness, and before we summarise the chapter, we will take a brief look at these creative therapies to see if the data supports the claim that they have value in the amelioration of schizophrenic symptoms.

Art therapy

Art therapy is defined by the British Association of Art Therapists as 'a form of psychotherapy that uses art media as its primary mode of communication'. The aim of art therapy is to effect personal change and growth by using art materials in a safe environment. It is somewhat unique in that it is one of only a few therapies that are specifically designed to be used with patients who are extremely disturbed and who reside exclusively in an inpatient setting.

The theory behind art therapy is that doing art is itself a healing process. The quality of the art is not the point, but the expression of inner feelings is at the heart of the purpose of the therapy. Freud believed that it was one of the methods that could be used to tap into the unconscious. The goal of the therapy is to build a closer bond between the patient and the therapist. Sarra (1998) stated that the importance of artwork is in its ability to communicate the rational and the irrational to the patient that the patient can accept and that does not in any way threaten them.

The evidence supporting the effectiveness of art therapy is rather scant. A review by Ruddy and Milnes (2009) could find only one study that was well enough controlled to provide some level of evaluation of the therapy. This study (Richardson, 2002, unpublished) found that art therapy had a beneficial effect on mental state in the short term. However, it found no significant benefit on social functioning or quality of life. Even the positive result must be treated with some caution as 50% of the sample had dropped out before the six-month follow-up was completed. Ruddy and Milnes concluded that art therapy can only be used experimentally with people with schizophrenia as there is not yet sufficient data as to whether it helps or harms the patient in the long term.

Music therapy

As the name suggests, music therapy is aimed at using both the experience and the production of music to help those with a mental illness. Its value claim is that it helps patients to develop relationships that they might not be able to develop using speech alone. It has a wide usage generally in the treatment of mental health problems, so it is appropriate to ask what track record it has in the treatment of schizophrenia. Music therapy usually involves the patient in both listening to music (receptive mode) and producing music (active mode), but competence in music is not a requirement for patients to gain any available benefits. Different models for music therapy practice will use different levels of structure within the therapy sessions. These levels of structure might, for example, differ in the type of rhythm being employed. Often the structure is determined by the therapist on the basis of the needs of the client. American and European approaches to music therapy can show some large differences in approach (Wigram, 2002). From a review of the limited data available, Gold, To, Dahle, and Wigram (2008) suggest that his type of therapy can have a strong effect on global functioning but might require a high number of sessions (20 or more) to achieve this. With fewer sessions there seems to only be an improvement to negative symptoms.

Dance therapy

Also known as Dance Movement Therapy (DMT), this is the psychotherapeutic practice of using dance to aid a person's emotional, cognitive, social and physical well-being. The principle behind it is that a person's movements reflect their patterns of thinking and feeling. The exact process of dance therapy is ill-defined and is very much in the hands of the therapist. However, the principles behind the therapy are constant and there is a relationship between movement and emotion. Dance therapists argue that dance movements stimulate emotions that enable a person to communicate nonverbally. As the therapy session is non-critical, the client feels less anxious and is allowed to enjoy the dance. In a review of the therapy by Xia and Grant (2012) it was found that clients did report a reduction in negative symptoms by, on average, 20%. However, there was little other significant benefit found. Xia and Grant concluded that there was not good reason to recommend dance therapy but, equally, there was no good reason to recommend against it.

◉ Chapter summary

In this final chapter we have looked at those therapies that are not derived directly from a biological perspective. None of them deny the biological underpinnings of schizophrenia and none propose themselves as a replacement for medication. We have seen that some try to involve the family as a central component of the recovery programme whilst others are focused on the patient and trying to improve their ability to function in the real world. It is probably the case that neither approach is sufficient on its own and that a combination of therapies and approaches needs to be sought to cater for the patient's recovery needs. It is becoming increasingly clear that the therapy set for any given patient must be derived on an individual basis. Whilst this is costly, it is probably the only way to ensure the best possible outcome for the patient. If a combination of therapies provides a better quality of life and reduces the chances of a relapse then, in the long term, it will probably represent a cost saving. Currently, though, not enough research data exists to support this view, and so clinicians are forced to provide therapy according to their personal preferences.

◉ Further reading

McDonald, C., Schulze, K., Murray, R.M. and Wright, P. (2007) *Schizophrenia: Challenging the Orthodox* (European Foundation for Psychiatry at the Maudsley). Martin Dunitz.

Williams, P. (2012) *Rethinking Madness: Towards a Paradigm Shift in Our Understanding and Treatment of Psychosis*. San Rafael, CA: Sky's Edge Publishing.

Wigram, T., Pedersen, I.N. and Bonde, L.O. (2002) *A Comprehensive Guide To Music Therapy: Theory, Clinical Practice, Research and Training*. London: Jessica Kingsley Publishers.

Glossary

adherence Adherence refers to whether or not a patient takes the medicine they have been prescribed. Lack of adherence is a major barrier to successful drug treatment in schizophrenia.

anhedonia A lack of the ability to experience pleasure.

antipsychotic A drug used to treat psychosis

auditory hallucination The phenomenon of hearing voices. The voices can be friendly or malicious and are most often perceived as originating from outside of the person's own body. This is one of the defining characteristics of schizophrenia but is not sufficient, alone, to denote the disorder. There are many people who hear voices but are not suffering from schizophrenia. Indeed, there are numerous hearing voices support networks around the world.

concordance rate This is the rate at which two things coincide. In our context, the concordance rate is a measure of how likely it is for a person to have schizophrenia if a defined other (parent, sibling, twin, etc.) also has schizophrenia.

delusional thinking This is when a person holds false beliefs. In schizophrenia, these usually come in one of two forms. One kind of delusions are delusions of grandeur, where the person believes they are more important than they really are (e.g. believing they are God). The other kind are paranoid delusions or delusions of persecution, where the person believes they are being plotted against (for example, believing people are trying to kill them).

dizygotic This refers to a situation where there are two fertilised eggs (or zygotes) in the womb at the same time. This leads to the birth of non-identical twins. Such twins will share, on average, 50% of their genes.

dopamine This is a neurotransmitter substance that is present in the brain. Among its functions is an involvement in the pleasure and reward systems of the brain. One theory of schizophrenia is that the disorder is caused by the presence of an excess of dopamine.

dorsolateral prefrontal cortex This is a region of the brain that lies at the front of the brain towards the top. It connects with a number of other parts of the brain (for instance, the thalamus and hippocampus) and provides a decision-making role. In particular, it is important in working out how to interact with a stimulus, something that is problematic for people with schizophrenia.

DSM-5 The Diagnostic and Statistical Manual version 5. This manual contains the criteria for all mental illnesses. It was revised in 2013 and the criteria for schizophrenia underwent some small changes from the previous version.

double bind This is a situation in which a person is given conflicting instructions, such that to obey one instruction would be to disobey the other. With schizophrenia, this has been a criticism launched at parents and some believe it to be a contributing factor to the development of schizophrenia.

endophenotype An endophenotype is the genetic basis of a behavioural trait that is a component of a higher level trait. In schizophrenia, the higher level trait is psychosis. The endophenotypes might be a lack of perceptual ability and a deficit in working memory. The value of endophenotypes is that they are, individually, easier to identify with genetic changes than the higher level trait.

epigenetics This is the study of how different genes come to be active or inactive in different cells in our body. The process of chemical changes that causes genes to become active or inactive is responsive to things that happen in our environment, for example, the food that we eat. For the study of schizophrenia, epigenetics tries to understand how environmental events can lead to the manifestation of psychotic behaviour.

episode Within the context of schizophrenia, this corresponds to an instance of psychosis. The number of psychotic episodes is one marker of the severity of the schizophrenia.

expressed emotion This is a measure of how the family environment, particularly the interactions between the person with schizophrenia and their immediate family members, can affect the likelihood that a relapse will occur. Families with high expressed emotion pose a greater risk of relapse.

glutamate This is believed by many to be the most important neurotransmitter substance in the brain. It is the neurotransmitter that binds to NMDA receptors and these, in turn, have a regulatory function on dopaminergic neurons. It is possible, therefore, that glutamate dysfunction is the underlying cause of the dopamine dysfunction seen in schizophrenia.

monozygotic This refers to a situation where a single fertilised egg has split into two (or more) within the womb. The result is the birth of identical twins that share exactly the same genetic constitution. Monozygotic twins are useful in helping to distinguish between inherited and learned traits and behaviours.

negative symptoms These are the symptoms accompanying schizophrenia whereby there is a lack of normal functioning. Chiefly, these symptoms are withdrawal, a reduced affect and reduced motivation.

neurodegeneration A term that implies the loss of the structure or function of neurons. It can also include the death of some neurons.

neurodevelopment In the context of schizophrenia, this term is used to refer to the continuing development of the nervous system that occurs during infancy, childhood and, up to and including, adolescence.

neuroleptic This is another term for antipsychotic and refers to any drug used to treat psychosis.

neuropile This is any region of the brain that consists mostly of unmyelinated axons, dendrites and glial cells. There tend to be few cell bodies here.

NICE This is the abbreviation for the National Institute for Health and Care Excellence. This body aims to provide help and advice about all aspects of health care.

NMDA receptor This is a brain receptor that is responsive to the glutamate neurotransmitter. The abbreviation stands for N-methyl-D-aspartate.

positive symptoms This describes the classic symptoms of schizophrenia that are noticeable by their presence. They include delusions, auditory hallucinations and confused thinking.

psychodynamic This is an approach to psychology that views human activity as a function of the drives and forces acting on that person in tandem with both conscious and unconscious desires and beliefs. As well as attempting to explain human behaviour, the approach also gives rise to a perspective on therapy.

psychosis This is a general medical term used to describe a state of mental health that gives rise to the positive symptoms associated with, but not exclusive to, schizophrenia.

relapse This defines the return of symptoms from a period that was symptom free. In schizophrenia this is usually noted by a return of positive symptoms that had been in remission.

remission This describes a period during which symptoms have either significantly decreased or have disappeared altogether.

schizophrenia spectrum personality disorders These are a set of disorders where the person shows many of the personality signs and symptoms of schizophrenia but who may not display enough of the DSM criteria to be classified as a person with schizophrenia.

schizophrenogenic This is a term usually used to describe mothers whose behaviour leads to the development of schizophrenia. At one extreme the blame rests entirely on the schizophrenogenic mother but a less extreme idea is that the mother's behaviour significantly contributes to the manifestation of the disorder in a vulnerable person.

schizotypal This is a term used to describe a person who shows many of the personality traits of schizophrenia such as hallucinations and delusions. A person displaying these characteristics is often referred to as having a schizotypal personality disorder.

serotonin Serotonin is a monoamine neurotransmitter substance and is found mostly in the gut. However, it also functions in the brain where it is linked to depression as a result of too little serotonin being present and hallucinations if an excessive amount is present. The pathways for serotonin include the prefrontal cortex which is known to be damaged in schizophrenia.

social cognition This refers to the way in which we use information to make judgements about a social situation. This information includes perception, memory and reasoning and helps us to appraise the social environment. A failure of social cognition could account for some of the symptoms of schizophrenia.

social functioning This refers to how well a person is able to function in their social environment. It includes the ability to behave appropriately according to the social situation and is closely related to a person's social cognitive abilities.

socratic questioning This is a philosophical method of asking question after question designed to uncover holes in an argument. It can be used by a therapist to uncover for the schizophrenic person the irrational elements of their reasoning.

speciation This is the evolutionary process that enables new species to emerge.

theory of mind This is the ability to attribute mental states, such as beliefs and desires, to others and to recognise that the mental states of others may not be the same as your own mental state.

working memory This is the system of memory that holds information for a short period of time whilst it is actively needed. This concept of memory replaced the idea of short-term memory in the mid-1970s.

References

Abrams, R. (1992). *Electroconvulsive Therapy* (p. 344). Oxford University Press, USA. Retrieved from http://www.amazon.com/Electroconvulsive-Therapy-Richard-Abrams/dp/0195148207.

Aleman, A., Hijman, R., Haan, E. H. F. de & Kahn, R. S. (1999). Memory impairment in schizophrenia: A meta-analysis. *American Journal of Psychiatry*, 156 (9), 1358–1366. Retrieved from http://ajp.psychiatryonline.org/article. aspx?articleid=173684.

Anderson, C. M., Hogarty, G. E. & Reiss, D. J. (1980). Family treatment of adult schizophrenic patients: A psycho-educational approach. *Schizophrenia Bulletin*, 6 (3), 490–505. Retrieved from http://www.ncbi.nlm.nih.gov/pubmed/7403810.

Andreasen, N. C., Arndt, S., Swayze, V., Cizadlo, T., Flaum, M., O'Leary, D., … Yuh, W. T. (1994). Thalamic abnormalities in schizophrenia visualized through magnetic resonance image averaging. *Science (New York, N.Y.)*, *266*(5183), 294–298, doi:10.1126/science.7939669.

Ansari, M. A., Rahman, R., Siddiqui, A. A. & Zaidi, S. Z. H. (2010). Association of order of birth with schizophrenia. *Pakistani Journal of Medical Science*, 26 (1), 49–53.

Arieti, S. (1955). *Interpretation of Schizophrenia* (p. 522). New York: R. Brunner. Retrieved from http://books.google.co.uk/books/about/Interpretation_of_ schizophrenia.html?id=4dRLAAAAMAAJ&pgis=1.

Arseneault, L., Cannon, M., Witton, J. & Murray, R. M. (2004). Causal association between cannabis and psychosis: Examination of the evidence. *The British Journal of Psychiatry: The Journal of Mental Science*, 184, 110–117. Retrieved from http://www.ncbi.nlm.nih.gov/pubmed/14754822.

Asarnow, R. F., Granholm, E., & Sherman, T. (1991). Span of apprehension in schizophrenia. In S. R. Steinhauer, J. H. Gruzelier & J. Zubin (eds), *Handbook of Schizophrenia: Nueropsychology, Psychophysiology and Information Processing* (pp. 335–370).

Asenjo Lobos, C., Komossa, K., Rummel-Kluge, C., Hunger, H., Schmid, F., Schwarz, S. & Leucht, S. (2010). Clozapine versus other atypical antipsychotics for schizophrenia. *The Cochrane Database of Systematic Reviews* (11), CD006633. doi:10.1002/14651858.CD006633.pub2.

Ayd, F. J. (1972). Comparative trial of low dose haloperidol and fluphenazine in office patients. *Diseases of the Nervous System*, 32, 192–195.

Baddeley, A. (1992). Working memory. *Science*, 255 (5044), 556–559. doi:10.1126/science.1736359.

Baddeley, A. D. & Hitch, G. J. (1974). Working Memory. In G. H. Bower (ed.), *The Psychology of Learning and Motivation*, Vol. 8 (pp. 47–89). New York: Academic Press.

Bandura, A. (1969). Social learning theory of idenitificatory processes. In D. A. Goslin (ed.), *Handbook of Socialization Theory and Research* (pp. 213–262). Rand McNally and Company.

Barch, D. M., Csernansky, J. G., Conturo, T. & Snyder, A. Z. (2002). Working and long-term memory deficits in schizophrenia: Is there a common prefrontal mechanism? *Journal of Abnormal Psychology*, 111 (3), 478–494. doi:10.1037/0021-843X.111.3.478.

Barham, P. & Hayward, R. (1991). *From the Mental Patient to the Person*. London: Routledge.

Bartzokis, G. & Altshuler, L. (2005). Reduced intracortical myelination in schizophrenia. *The American Journal of Psychiatry*, 162 (6), 1229–30. doi:10.1176/appi.ajp.162.6.1229-a.

Bateson, G., Jackson, D. D., Haley, J. & Weakland, J. (1956). Toward a theory of schizophrenia. *Behavioral Science*, 1 (4), 251–254. Retrieved from http://onlinelibrary.wiley.com/doi/10.1002/bs.3830010402/full.

Bäuml, J., Fröböse, T., Kraemer, S., Rentrop, M. & Pitschel-Walz, G. (2006). Psychoeducation: A basic psychotherapeutic intervention for patients with schizophrenia and their families. *Schizophrenia bulletin*, 32 Suppl 1, S1–9. doi:10.1093/schbul/sbl017.

Bearden, C. E., Rosso, I. M., Hollister, J. M., Sanchez, L. E., Hadley, T. & Cannon, T. D. (2000). A prospective cohort study of childhood behavioral deviance and language abnormalities as predictors of adult schizophrenia. *Schizophrenia Bulletin*, 26 (2), 395–410. Retrieved from http://www.ncbi.nlm.nih.gov/pubmed/10885639.

Bebbington, P. E., Bhugra, D., Brugha, T., Singleton, N., Farrell, M., Jenkins, R., … Meltzer, H. (2004). Psychosis, victimisation and childhood disadvantage: Evidence from the second British National Survey of Psychiatric Morbidity. *The British Journal of Psychiatry: The Journal of Mental Science*, 185, 220–226. doi:10.1192/bjp.185.3.220.

Bebbington, P. & Kuipers, L. (1994). The predictive utility of expressed emotion in schizophrenia: An aggregate analysis. *Psychological Medicine*, 24 (3), 707–718. Retrieved from http://www.ncbi.nlm.nih.gov/pubmed/7991753.

Beck, A. T. (1952). Successful outpatient psychotherapy of a chronic schizophrenic with a delusion based on borrowed guilt. *Psychiatry*, 15 (3), 305–312. Retrieved from http://www.ncbi.nlm.nih.gov/pubmed/12983446.

Bell, M. D., Corbera, S., Johannesen, J. K., Fiszdon, J. M. & Wexler, B. E. (2013). Social cognitive impairments and negative symptoms in schizophrenia: Are there subtypes with distinct functional correlates? *Schizophrenia Bulletin*, 39 (1), 186–196. doi:10.1093/schbul/sbr125.

Bellack, A. S., Morrison, R. L., Wixted, J. T. & Mueser, K. T. (1990). An analysis of social competence in schizophrenia. *The British Journal of Psychiatry: The Journal of Mental Science*, 156, 809–818. Retrieved from http://www.ncbi.nlm. nih.gov/pubmed/2207511.

Benjamin, L. S. (1976). A reconsideration of the Kety and associates study of genetic factors in the transmission of schizophrenia. *American Journal of Psychiatry*, 133 (10), 1129–1133. Retrieved from http://www.ncbi.nlm.nih.gov/pmc/ articles/PMC1685944/.

Bennedsen, B. E., Mortensen, P. B., Olesen, A. V & Henriksen, T. B. (1999). Preterm birth and intra-uterine growth retardation among children of women with schizophrenia. *The British Aournal of Psychiatry: The Journal of Mental Science*, 175, 239–245. doi:10.1192/bjp.175.3.239.

Berlim, M. T., Mattevi, B. S., Belmonte-de-Abreu, P. & Crow, T. J. (2003). The etiology of schizophrenia and the origin of language: Overview of a theory. *Comprehensive Psychiatry*, 44 (1), 7–14. doi:10.1053/comp.2003.50003.

Birchwood, M. & Smith, J. (1987). Schizophrenia and the family. In J. Orford (ed.), *Coping with Disorder in the Family* (pp. 7–38). London: Croom Helm Ltd.

Bleuler, E. (1950). *Dementia Praecox or the Group of Schizophrenias*. (J. Zinkin, Ed.) (translated.). New York: International Universities Press.

Bleuler, M. (1972). *The Schizophrenic Disorders: Long-Term Patient and Family Studies*. London: Yale University Press.

Boksa, P. & El-Khodor, B. F. (2003). Birth insult interacts with stress at adulthood to alter dopaminergic function in animal models: Possible implications for schizophrenia and other disorders. *Neuroscience and Biobehavioral Reviews*, 27 (1–2), 91–101. Retrieved from http://www.ncbi.nlm.nih.gov/pubmed/12732226.

Bonner-Jackson, A., Haut, K., Csernansky, J. G. & Barch, D. M. (2005). The influence of encoding strategy on episodic memory and cortical activity in schizophrenia. *Biological psychiatry*, 58 (1), 47–55. doi:10.1016/ j.biopsych.2005.05.011.

Bora, E., Eryavuz, A., Kayahan, B., Sungu, G. & Veznedaroglu, B. (2006). Social functioning, theory of mind and neurocognition in outpatients with schizophrenia; mental state decoding may be a better predictor of social functioning than mental state reasoning. *Psychiatry Research*, 145 (2), 95–103. Retrieved from http://www.sciencedirect.com/science/article/pii/ S0165178105003689.

Bottlender, R., Sato, T., Jäger, M., Wegener, U., Wittmann, J., Strauß, A. & Möller, H.-J. (2003). The impact of the duration of untreated psychosis prior to first psychiatric admission on the 15-year outcome in schizophrenia. *Schizophrenia Research*, 62 (1–2), 37–44. doi:10.1016/S0920-9964(02)00348-1.

Boydell, J., van Os, J., McKenzie, K. & Murray, R. M. (2004). The association of inequality with the incidence of schizophrenia – An ecological study. *Social Psychiatry and Psychiatric Epidemiology*, 39 (8), 597–599. doi:10.1007/ s00127-004-0789-6.

Bradbury, T. N. & Miller, G. A. (1985). Season of birth in schizophrenia: A review of evidence, methodology, and etiology. *Psychological Bulletin*, 98 (3), 569–594. doi:10.1037/0033-2909.98.3.569.

Braff, D. L. (1993). Information processing and attention dysfunctions in schizophrenia. *Schizophrenia Bulletin*, 19 (2), 233–259. Retrieved from http://www.ncbi.nlm.nih.gov/pubmed/8322034.

Braver, T. S., Barch, D. M. & Cohen, J. D. (1999). Cognition and control in schizophrenia: A computational model of dopamine and prefrontal function. *Biological Psychiatry*, 46 (3), 312–328. Retrieved from http://www.ncbi.nlm.nih.gov/pubmed/10435197.

Breier, A. (1995). Serotonin, schizophrenia and antipsychotic drug action. *Schizophrenia Research*, 14 (3), 187–202. Retrieved from http://www.ncbi.nlm.nih.gov/pubmed/7539288.

Brenner, H., Roder, V., Hodel, B., Kienzie, N., Reed, D. & Liberman, R. (1994). *Integrated Psychological Therapy for Schizophrenic Patients.* Seattle: Hogrefe & Huber.

Brewer, W. J., Francey, S. M., Wood, S. J., Jackson, H. J., Pantelis, C., Phillips, L. J., Yung, A.R., Anderson, V.A. & McGorry, P. D. (2005). Memory impairments identified in people at ultra-high risk for psychosis who later develop first-episode psychosis. *The American Journal of Psychiatry*, 162 (1), 71–78. doi:10.1176/appi.ajp.162.1.71.

Brown, A. S. (2011). The environment and susceptibility to schizophrenia. *Progress in Neurobiology*, 93 (1), 23–58. Retrieved from http://www.sciencedirect.com/science/article/pii/S0301008210001681.

Brown, G. W., Birley, J. L. T. & Wing, J. K. (1972). Influence of family life on the course of schizophrenic disorders: A replication. *The British Journal of Psychiatry*, 121 (3), 241–258. doi:10.1192/bjp.121.3.241.

Brown, A. S. & Derkits, E. J. (2010). Prenatal infection and schizophrenia: A review of epidemiologic and translational studies. *The American Journal of Psychiatry*, 167 (3), 261–280. doi:10.1176/appi.ajp.2009.09030361.

Brown, A. S. & Patterson, P. H. (2011). Maternal infection and schizophrenia: Implications for prevention. *Schizophrenia Bulletin*, 37 (2), 284–290. doi:10.1093/schbul/sbq146.

Brown, G. W. & Rutter, M. (1966). The measurement of family activities and relationships: A methodological study. *Human Relations*, 19 (3), 241–263. doi:10.1177/001872676601900301.

Bruce, V. & Young, A. (1986). Understanding face recognition. *British Journal of Psychology*, 77 (3), 305–327. doi:10.1111/j.2044-8295.1986.tb02199.x.

Buka, S. L., Tsuang, M. T., Torrey, E. F., Klebanoff, M. A., Bernstein, D. & Yolken, R. H. (2001). Maternal infections and subsequent psychosis among offspring. *Archives of General Psychiatry*, 58 (11), 1032–1037. Retrieved from http://www.ncbi.nlm.nih.gov/pubmed/11695949.

Burns, J. K. (2004). An evolutionary theory of schizophrenia: Cortical connectivity, metarepresentation, and the social brain. *The Behavioral and Brain Sciences*, 27 (6), 831–55; discussion 855–885. Retrieved from http://www.ncbi.nlm.nih.gov/pubmed/16035403.

Byrne, M., Agerbo, E., Bennedsen, B., Eaton, W. W. & Mortensen, P. B. (2007). Obstetric conditions and risk of first admission with schizophrenia: A Danish national register based study. *Schizophrenia Research*, 97 (1), 51–59. Retrieved from http://www.sciencedirect.com/science/article/pii/S0920996407003167.

Cammer, L. (1970). Schizophrenic children of manic-depressive parents. *Diseases of the Nervous System*, 31 (3), 177–180.

Cannon, M., Jones, P. B. & Murray, R. M. (2002). Reviews and overviews obstetric complications and schizophrenia: Historical and meta-analytic review. *Psychiatry: Interpersonal and Biological Processes*, (July), 1080–1092.

Carlsson, A. & Lindqvist, M. (1963). Effect of chlorpromazine or haloperidol on formation of 3methoxytyramine and normetanephrine in mouse brain. *Acta Pharmacologica et Toxicologica*, 20, 140–144. Retrieved from http://www.ncbi.nlm.nih.gov/pubmed/14060771.

Carter, C., Robertson, L., Nordahl, T., Chaderjian, M., Kraft, L. & O'Shora-Celaya, L. (1996). Spatial working memory deficits and their relationship to negative symptoms in unmedicated schizophrenia patients. *Biological Psychiatry*, 40 (9), 930–932. Retrieved from http://www.sciencedirect.com/science/article/pii/S0006322396003502.

Carter, C. S. (1998). Neuroendocrine perspectives on social attachment and love. *Psychoneuroendocrinology*, 23, 779–818.

Caspi, A., Moffitt, T. E., Cannon, M., McClay, J., Murray, R., Harrington, H., … Craig, I. W. (2005). Moderation of the effect of adolescent-onset cannabis use on adult psychosis by a functional polymorphism in the catechol-O-methyltransferase gene: longitudinal evidence of a gene X environment interaction. *Biological Psychiatry*, 57 (10), 1117–1127. doi:10.1016/j.biopsych.2005.01.026.

Chan, R. C. K., Di, X., McAlonan, G. M. & Gong, Q. (2011). Brain anatomical abnormalities in high-risk individuals, first-episode, and chronic schizophrenia: An activation likelihood estimation meta-analysis of illness progression. *Schizophrenia Bulletin*, 37 (1), 177–188. doi:10.1093/schbul/sbp073.

Chen, E. Y. H., Wilkins, A. J. & McKenna, P. J. (1994). Semantic memory is both impaired and anomalous in schizophrenia. *Psychological Medicine*, 24, 193–202. Retrieved from http://journals.cambridge.org/abstract_S0033291700026957.

Chen, Y., Nakayama, K., Levy, D. L., Matthysse, S. & Holzman, P. S. (1999). Psychophysical isolation of a motion-processing deficit in schizophrenics and their relatives and its association with impaired smooth pursuit. *Proceedings of the National Academy of Sciences*, 96 (8), 4724–4729. doi:10.1073/pnas.96.8.4724.

Chen, Yue, Norton, D., Ongur, D. & Heckers, S. (2008). Inefficient face detection in schizophrenia. *Schizophrenia Bulletin*, 34 (2), 367–374. doi:10.1093/schbul/sbm071.

Cipriani, A., Boso, M. & Barbui, C. (2009). Clozapine combined with different antipsychotic drugs for treatment resistant schizophrenia. *The Cochrane Database of Systematic Reviews* (3), CD006324. doi:10.1002/14651858.CD006324.pub2.

Clinton, S. M. & Meador-Woodruff, J. H. (2004). Abnormalities of the NMDA receptor and associated intracellular molecules in the thalamus in schizophrenia and bipolar disorder. *Neuropsychopharmacology: Official Publication of the American College of Neuropsychopharmacology*, 29 (7), 1353–1362. doi:10.1038/sj.npp.1300451.

Cohen, J. D. & Servan-Schreiber, D. (1992). Context, cortex, and dopamine: A connectionist approach to behavior and biology in schizophrenia. *Psychological Review*, 99 (1), 45–77. doi:10.1037/0033-295X.99.1.45.

Combs, D. R. & Gouvier, W. D. (2004). The role of attention in affect perception: An examination of Mirsky's four factor model of attention in chronic schizophrenia. *Schizophrenia Bulletin*, 30 (4), 727–738. Retrieved from http://www.ncbi.nlm. nih.gov/pubmed/15954187.

Condray, R., Steinhauer, S. R., van Kammen, D. P. & Kasparek, A. (1996). Working memory capacity predicts language comprehension in schizophrenic patients. *Schizophrenia Research*, 20 (1), 1–13. Retrieved from http://www.sciencedirect. com/science/article/pii/0920996495000615.

Condray, R., Steinhauer, S. R., van Kammen, D. P. & Kasparek, A. (2002). The language system in schizophrenia: Effects of capacity and linguistic structure. *Schizophrenia Bulletin*, 28 (3), 475–490. Retrieved from http://www.ncbi.nlm. nih.gov/pubmed/12645679.

Cormac, I., Jones, C. & Campbell, C. (2002). Cognitive behaviour therapy for schizophrenia. In *Cochrane Library* (Issue 3.). Oxford.

Cornblatt, B. A., Lenzenweger, M. F., Dworkin, R. H. & Erlenmeyer-Kimling, L. (1992). Childhood attentional dysfunctions predict social deficits in unaffected adults at risk for schizophrenia. *British Jornal of Psychiatry*, *Supplement*, 59–64.

Corrigan, P. W. & Penn, D. L. (1995). The effects of antipsychotic and antiparkinsonian medication on psychosocial skill learning. *Clinical Psychology – Science and Practice*, 2, 251–262.

Couture, S. M., Penn, D. L. & Roberts, D. L. (2006). The functional significance of social cognition in schizophrenia: A review. *Schizophrenia Bulletin*, 32 Suppl 1, S44–63. doi:10.1093/schbul/sbl029.

Coyle, J. T. (1996). The glutamatergic dysfunction hypothesis for schizophrenia. *Harvard Review of Psychiatry*, 3 (5), 241–253. Retrieved from http:// informahealthcare.com/doi/abs/10.3109/10673229609017192.

Crow, T. J. (1985). The two-syndrome concept: Origins and current status. *Schizophrenia Bulletin*, 11 (3), 471–486. Retrieved from http://www.ncbi.nlm. nih.gov/pubmed/2863873.

Crow, T. J. (1997). Schizophrenia as failure of hemispheric dominance for language. *Trends in neurosciences*, 20 (8), 339–343. Retrieved from http://www. pubmedcentral.nih.gov/articlerender.fcgi?artid=2637431&tool=pmcentrez&ren dertype=abstract.

Crow, Timothy J. (2004a). Auditory hallucinations as primary disorders of syntax: An evolutionary theory of the origins of language. *Cognitive Neuropsychiatry*, 9 (1–2), 125–45. doi:10.1080/13546800344000192.

Crow, Timothy J. (2004b). *The Speciation of Modern Homo Sapiens* (p. 272). Oxford University Press.

Cullen, T. J., Walker, M. A., Eastwood, S. L., Esiri, M. M., Harrison, P. J. & Crow, T. J. (2006). Anomalies of asymmetry of pyramidal cell density and structure in dorsolateral prefrontal cortex in schizophrenia. *The British Journal of Psychiatry: The Journal of Mental Science*, 188 (1), 26–31. doi:10.1192/bjp.bp.104.008169.

Culver, L. C., Kunen, S. & Zinkgraf, S. . (1986). Patterns of recall in schizophrenics and normal subjects. *Journal of Nervous and Mental Disease*, 174, 620–623.

Cutting, L. P., Aakre, J. M. & Docherty, N. M. (2006). Schizophrenic patients' perceptions of stress, expressed emotion, and sensitivity to criticism. *Schizophrenia Bulletin*, 32 (4), 743–750. doi:10.1093/schbul/sbl001.

Czobor, P. & Volavka, J. (1996). Positive and negative symptoms: Is their change related? *Schizophrenia Bulletin*, 22 (4), 577–590. Retrieved from http://www.ncbi.nlm.nih.gov/pubmed/8938912.

Davis, K. L., Kahn, R. S., Ko, G. & Davidson, M. (1991). Dopamine in schizophrenia: A review and reconceptualization. *The American Journal of Psychiatry*, 148 (11), 1474–1486. Retrieved from http://www.ncbi.nlm.nih.gov/pubmed/1681750.

Delay, J., Deniker, P. & Harl J. M. (1952). Therapeutic method derived from hiberno-therapy in excitation and agitation states. *Annales médico-psychologiques*, *110*(2 2), 267–73. Retrieved from http://www.ncbi.nlm.nih.gov/pubmed/13008201.

DeLisi, L. E. (2001). Speech disorder in schizophrenia: review of the literature and exploration of its relation to the uniquely human capacity for language. *Schizophrenia Bulletin*, 27 (3), 481–496. Retrieved from http://www.ncbi.nlm.nih.gov/pubmed/11596849.

Dempster, E., Viana, J., Pidsley, R. & Mill, J. (2013). Epigenetic studies of schizophrenia: Progress, predicaments, and promises for the future. *Schizophrenia Bulletin*, 39 (1), 11–16. doi:10.1093/schbul/sbs139.

Dichter, G. S., Bellion, C., Casp, M. & Belger, A. (2010). Impaired modulation of attention and emotion in schizophrenia. *Schizophrenia Bulletin*, 36 (3), 595–606. doi:10.1093/schbul/sbn118.

Dickinson, D. & Harvey, P. D. (2009). Systemic hypotheses for generalized cognitive deficits in schizophrenia: A new take on an old problem. *Schizophrenia Bulletin*, 35 (2), 403–414. doi:10.1093/schbul/sbn097.

Doane, J. A., West, K. L., Goldstein, M. J., Rodnick, H., E. & Jones, J. E. (1981). Reviews experimental and clinical findings on the possibility that disordered family relationships may be a significant factor in the development of schizophrenia. These studies tested models which are summarized as a series of assumptions: (a) Difference. *Archives of General Psychiatry*, 38, 679–685.

Dohrenwend, B., Levav, I., Shrout, P., Schwartz, S., Naveh, G., Link, B., … Stueve, A. (1992). Socioeconomic status and psychiatric disorders: The causation-selection issue. *Science*, 255 (5047), 946–952. doi:10.1126/science.1546291.

Donlon, P. T., Hopkin, J. T., Tupin, Joe, P., Wicks, John, J., Wahba, M. & Meadow, A. (1980). Haloperidol for acute schizophrenic patients. *Archives of General Psychiatry*, 37 (6), 691. doi:10.1001/archpsyc.1980.01780190089011.

Eack, S. M., Mermon, D. E., Montrose, D. M., Miewald, J., Gur, R. E., Gur, R. C., … Keshavan, M. S. (2010). Social cognition deficits among individuals at familial high risk for schizophrenia. *Schizophrenia Bulletin*, 36 (6), 1081–1088. doi:10.1093/schbul/sbp026.

Eack, S. M. & Newhill, C. E. (2007). Psychiatric symptoms and quality of life in schizophrenia: A meta-analysis. *Schizophrenia Bulletin*, 33 (5), 1225–1237. doi:10.1093/schbul/sbl071.

Ekman, P. & Friesen, W. P. (1978). *The Facial Action Coding System*. Palo Alto, CA: Consulting Psychological Press.

Erlenmyer-Kimling, L. & Paradowski, W. (1966). Selection and schizophrenia. *The American Naturalist*, 100 (916), 651–665.

Essali, A., Al-Haj Haasan, N., Li, C. & Rathbone, J. (2009). Clozapine versus typical neuroleptic medication for schizophrenia. *The Cochrane Database of Systematic Reviews*, (1), CD000059. doi:10.1002/14651858.CD000059.pub2.

Essen-Moller, E. (1963). Twin research and psychiatry. *Acta Psychiatrica Scandinavica*, 39, 65–77.

Falkai, P. & Bogerts, B. (1986). Cell loss in the hippocampus of schizophrenics. *Archives of Psychiatry and Neurological Sciences*, 236, 154–161.

Faris, R. E. L. & Dunham, H. W. (1939). *Mental Disorders in Urban Areas: An Ecological Study of Schizophrenia and Other Psychoses*. Oxford, England: University of Chicago Press.

Fatemi, S. H. & Folsom, T. D. (2009). The neurodevelopmental hypothesis of schizophrenia, revisited. *Schizophrenia Bulletin*, 35 (3), 528–548. doi:10.1093/schbul/sbn187.

Feinberg, I. (1982). Schizophrenia and late maturational brain changes in man. *Psychopharmacology Bulletin*, 18 (3), 29–31.

Fink, H., Morgenstern, R. & Oetssner, W. (1984). Clozapine – A serotonin antagonist? *Pharmacology Biochemistry and Behavior*, 20, 513–517.

Fischer, E. P., Shumway, M., & Owen, R. R. (2002). Priorities of consumers, providers, and family members in the treatment of schizophrenia. *Psychiatric Services (Washington, D.C.)*, 53 (6), 724–729. Retrieved from http://www.ncbi.nlm.nih.gov/pubmed/12045310.

Frankle, W. G. & Laruelle, M. (2002). Neuroreceptor imaging in psychiatric disorders. *Annals of Nuclear Medicine*, 16 (7), 437–446. Retrieved from http://www.ncbi.nlm.nih.gov/pubmed/12508833.

Freud, S. (1911). Psychoanalytic notes on an autobiographical account of a case of paranoia (dementia paranoides). In J. Strachey (ed.), *The Standard Edition of the Complete Psychological Works of Sigmund Freud*. (Volume 12.). London: Hogarth Press.

Friedman, C. J. & Friedman, A. S. (1970). Characteristics of Schizogenic Families during a joint story-telling task. *Family Process*, 9 (3), 333–353. doi:10.1111/j.1545-5300.1970.00333.x.

Frith, C. D. (1992). *The Cognitive Neuropsychology of Schizophrenia*. Hove, UK: Lawrence Erlbaum Associates.

Fromm-Reichmann, F. (1948). Notes on the development of treatment of schizophrenics by psychoanalytic psychotherapy. *Psychiatry*, 11 (3), 263–273. Retrieved from http://www.mendeley.com/catalog/notes-development-treatment-schizophrenics-psychoanalytic-psychotherapy/.

Fuller Torrey, E. & Peterson, M. (1974). Schizophrenia and the limbic system. *The Lancet*, 304 (7886), 942–946. doi:10.1016/S0140-6736(74)91143-X.

Garety, P. A., Freeman, D., Jolley, S., Dunn, G., Bebbington, P. E., Fowler, D. G., … Dudley, R. (2005). Reasoning, emotions, and delusional conviction in psychosis. *Journal of Abnormal Psychology*, 114 (3), 373–384. doi:10.1037/0021-843X. 114.3.373.

Gibney, P. (2006). The double bind theory: Still crazy-making after all these years. *Psychotherapy in Australia*, 12 (3), 48–55.

Gilbert, P. (2000). Social mentalities: Internal "social" conflicts and the role of inner warmth and compassion in cognitive therapy. In P. Gilbert & K. G. Bailey (eds), *Genes on the Couch: Explorations in Evolutionary Psychotherapy* (pp. 118–150). Psychology Press.

Glynn, S. M., Cohen, A. N., Dixon, L. B. & Niv, N. (2006). The potential impact of the recovery movement on family interventions for schizophrenia: Opportunities and obstacles. *Schizophrenia Bulletin*, 32 (3), 451–463. doi:10.1093/schbul/sbj066.

Goghari, V. M., Macdonald, A. W. & Sponheim, S. R. (2011). Temporal lobe structures and facial emotion recognition in schizophrenia patients and nonpsychotic relatives. *Schizophrenia Bulletin*, 37 (6), 1281–1294. doi:10.1093/schbul/sbq046.

Gold, C., To, H., Dahle, T. & Wigram, T. (2008). Music therapy for schizophrenia or schizophrenia-like illnesses (Review), (3).

Goldstein, M. J. & Rodnick, E. H. (1975). The family ' s contribution to the etiology of schizophrenia: Current status, 1 (14), 48–63.

Goodman, N. (1957). Relation between maternal age at the parturition and incidence of mental disorder in the offspring. *British Journal of Preventive and Social Medicine*, 11, 203–213.

Gottesman, Irving I. & Shields, J. (1972). A polygenic theory of schizophrenia. *International Journal of Mental Health*, 1, 107–115.

Gottesman, Irving I. & Shields, J. (1976). A critical review of recent adoption, twin, and family studies of schizophrenia: Behavioral genetics perspectives. *Schizophrenia Bulletin*, 2 (3), 360–401. Retrieved from http://www.ncbi.nlm.nih.gov/pubmed/1034336.

Gottesman, Irving I, Shields, J. & Hanson, D. R. (1982). *Schizophrenia: The Epigenetic Puzzle*. Cambridge: Cambridge University Press.

Gur, R. E., Cowell, P. E., Latshaw, A., Turetsky, B. I., Grossman, R. I., Arnold, S. E., … Gur, R. C. (2000). Reduced dorsal and orbital prefrontal gray matter volumes in schizophrenia. *Archives of General Psychiatry*, 57 (8), 761–768. Retrieved from http://www.ncbi.nlm.nih.gov/pubmed/10920464.

Hall, F. S., Wilkinson, L. S., Humby, T. & Robbins, T. W. (1999, April 1). Maternal deprivation of neonatal rats produces enduring changes in dopamine function. *Synapse*. Wiley-Blackwell. Retrieved from http://orca.cf.ac.uk/35354/.

Hare, E.H. (1956). Mental illness and social conditions in Bristol. *Journal of Mental Science*, 102 (349—357).

Hare, E H. & Moran, P. A. (1979). Raised parental age in psychiatric patients: evidence for the constitutional hypothesis. *The British Journal of Psychiatry: The Journal of*

Mental Science, 134, 169–77. Retrieved from http://www.ncbi.nlm.nih.gov/pubmed/427333.

Hatfield, A. B., Spaniol, L. & Zipple, A. M. (1987). Expressed emotion: A family perspective. *Schizophrenia Bulletin*, 13 (2), 221–226.

Herman, B. F. & Jones, J. E. (1976). Lack of acknowledgment in the family rorschachs of families with a child at risk for schizophrenia. *Family Process*, 15 (3), 289–302. doi:10.1111/j.1545-5300.1976.00289.x.

Herman, D. B., Brown, A. S., Opler, M. G., Desai, M., Malaspina, D., Bresnahan, M., … Susser, E. S. (2006). Does unwantedness of pregnancy predict schizophrenia in the offspring? Findings from a prospective birth cohort study. *Social Psychiatry and Psychiatric Epidemiology*, 41 (8), 605–610. doi:10.1007/s00127-006-0078-7.

Hickling, F. W., McKenzie, K., Mullen, R. & Murray, R. (1999). A Jamaican psychiatrist evaluates diagnoses at a London psychiatric hospital. *The British Journal of Psychiatry*, 175 (3), 283–285. doi:10.1192/bjp.175.3.283.

Highley, J. R., Walker, M. A., Esiri, M. M., McDonald, B., Harrison, P. J. & Crow, T. J. (2001). Schizophrenia and the frontal lobes: Post-mortem stereological study of tissue volume. *The British Journal of Psychiatry*, 178 (4), 337–343. doi:10.1192/bjp.178.4.337.

Hoek, H. W., Brown, A. S. & Susser, E. (1998). The Dutch famine and schizophrenia spectrum disorders. *Social Psychiatry and Psychiatric Epidemiology*, 33 (8), 373–379. Retrieved from http://www.ncbi.nlm.nih.gov/pubmed/9708024.

Hoffman, L. (1981). *Foundations of Family Therapy. A Conceptual Framework for Systems Change.* New York: Basic Books.

Hoffman, R. E., Boutros, N. N., Berman, R. M., Roessler, E., Belger, A., Krystal, J. H. & Charney, D. S. (1999). Transcranial magnetic stimulation of left temporoparietal cortex in three patients reporting hallucinated "voices". *Biological Psychiatry*, 46 (1), 130–132. Retrieved from http://www.ncbi.nlm.nih.gov/pubmed/10394483.

Hoffman, R. E., Hogben, G. L., Smith, H. & Calhoun, W. (1985). Message disruptions during syntactic processing in schizophrenia. *Journal of Communicative Disorders*, 18, 183–202.

Hogarty, G. E. & Flesher, S. (1999). Developmental theory for a cognitive enhancement therapy of schizophrenia. *Schizophrenia Bulletin*, 25 (4), 677–692. Retrieved from http://www.ncbi.nlm.nih.gov/pubmed/10667739.

Hogarty, G. E., Kornblith, S. J., Greenwald, D., DiBarry, A. L., Cooley, S., Ulrich, R. F., … Flesher, S. (1997). Three-year trials of personal therapy among schizophrenic patients living with or independent of family, I: Description of study and effects on relapse rates. *The American journal of Psychiatry*, 154 (11), 1504–1513. Retrieved from http://www.ncbi.nlm.nih.gov/pubmed/9356557.

Hogarty, G. E., Schooler, N. R., Ulrich, R., Mussare, F., Ferro, P. & Herron, E. (1979). Fluphenazine and social therapy in the aftercare of schizophrenic patients. Relapse analyses of a two-year controlled study of fluphenazine decanoate and fluphenazine hydrochloride. *Archives of General Psychiatry*, 36 (12), 1283–1294. Retrieved from http://www.ncbi.nlm.nih.gov/ pubmed/227340.

Hogarty, G. E. & Ulrich, R. F. (1977). Temporal effects of drug and placebo in delaying relapse in schizophrenic outpatients. *Archives of General Psychiatry*, 34 (3), 297–301. Retrieved from http://www.ncbi.nlm.nih.gov/ pubmed/190970.

Honea, R., Sc, B., Crow, T. J., Ph, D., Passingham, D. & Mackay, C. E. (2005). Regional deficits in brain volume in schizophrenia: A meta-analysis of voxel-based morphometry studies, i, 2233–2245.

Howes, O. D., & Kapur, S. (2009). The dopamine hypothesis of schizophrenia: Version III – The final common pathway. *Schizophrenia Bulletin*, 35 (3), 549–562. doi:10.1093/schbul/sbp006

Hultman, C.M., Ohman, A., Cnattingius, S., Wiselgren, I. M., & Lindstrom, L. H. (1997). Prenatal and neonatal risk factors for schizophrenia. *British Jornal of Psychiatry*, 170, 128–133.

Hultman, C M, Sparén, P., Takei, N., Murray, R. M. & Cnattingius, S. (1999). Prenatal and perinatal risk factors for schizophrenia, affective psychosis, and reactive psychosis of early onset: Case-control study. *BMJ (Clinical research ed.)*, 318 (7181), 421–426. Retrieved from http://www.pubmedcentral.nih.gov/ articlerender.fcgi?artid=27730&tool=pmcentrez&rendertype=abstract.

Huxley, J., Mayr, E., Osmond, H. & Hoffer, A. (1964). Schizophrenia as a genetic morphism. *Nature*, 204, 220–221.

Irving, C. B., Adams, C. & Lawrie, S. (2006). Haloperidol versus placebo for schizophrenia (Review). *The Cochrane Database of Systematic Reviews* (4).

Ito, A., Abe, N., Fujii, T., Hayashi, A., Ueno, A., Mugikura, S., … Mori, E. (2012). The contribution of the dorsolateral prefrontal cortex to the preparation for deception and truth-telling. *Brain Research*, 1464, 43–52. doi:10.1016/j. brainres.2012.05.004.

Jackson, D. D. (1960). *The Etiology of Schizophrenia*. New York: Basic Books.

Janssen, I., Krabbendam, L., Bak, M., Hanssen, M., Vollebergh, W., Graaf, R. & Os, J. (2004). Childhood abuse as a risk factor for psychotic experiences. *Acta Psychiatrica Scandinavica*, 109 (1), 38–45. doi:10.1046/j.0001-690X.2003.00217.x.

Janssen, I., Krabbendam, L., Jolles, J. & van Os, J. (2003). Alterations in theory of mind in patients with schizophrenia and non-psychotic relatives. *Acta Psychiatrica Scandinavica*, 108 (2), 110–117. doi:10.1034/j.1600-0447.2003.00092.x.

Jaspers, K. (1923). *General Psychopathology*. (J. (trans) Hoenig & M. W. (trans) Hamilton, eds.) (translation). Chicago: University of Chicago.

Javitt, D. C. & Zukin, S. R. (1991). Recent advances in the phencyclidine model of schizophrenia. *The American Journal of Psychiatry*, 148 (10), 1301–1308. Retrieved from http://www.ncbi.nlm.nih.gov/pubmed/1654746.

Jentsch, J. D. & Roth, R. H. (1999). The neuropsychopharmacology of phencyclidine: From NMDA receptor hypofunction to the dopamine hypothesis of schizophrenia. *Neuropsychopharmacology: Official Publication of the American*

College of Neuropsychopharmacology, 20 (3), 201–225. doi:10.1016/ S0893-133X(98)00060-8.

Jibiki, I., Kubota, T., Fujimoto, K., Yamaguchi, N., Matsuda, H. & Hisada, K. (1991). Regional relationships between focal hypofixation images in 123I-IMP single photon emission computed tomography and epileptic EEG foci in interictal periods in patients with partial epilepsy. *European Neurology*, 31 (6), 360–365. doi:10.1159/000116694.

Johanson, E. (1958). A study of schizophrenia in the male: A psychiatric and social study based on 138 cases with follow up. *Acta Psychiatrica et Neurologica Scandinavica*, 33 (no Suppl 125), 1–132.

Johnstone, E. C., Crow, T. J., Frith, C. D. & Husband, J. (1976). Cerebral ventricular size and cognitive impairment in chronic schizophrenia. *Lancet*, 30, 924–926.

Jones, B. J., Gallagher, B. J., Pisa, A. M. & McFalls, J. A. (2008). Social class, family history and type of schizophrenia. *Psychiatry Research*, 159 (1), 127–132. Retrieved from http://www.sciencedirect.com/science/article/pii/ S0165178107002892.

Jones, J. (1977). Patterns of transactional style deviance in the TAT's of parents of schizophrenics. *Family Process*, 16, 327–337.

Jones, M. (1953). *The Therapeutic Community: A New Treatment Method in Psychiatry*. New York: Basic Books.

Jones, P., Rodgers, B., Murray, R. & Marmot, M. (1994). Child development risk factors for adult schizophrenia in the British 1946 birth cohort. *Lancet*, 344 (8934), 1398–1402. Retrieved from http://www.ncbi.nlm.nih.gov/ pubmed/7968076.

Jones, S. H., Hemsley, D., Ball, S. & Serra, A. (1997). Disruption of the Kamin blocking effect in schizophrenia and in normal subjects following amphetamine. *Behavioural Brain Research*, 88 (1), 103–114. Retrieved from http://www.ncbi. nlm.nih.gov/pubmed/9401714.

Jordan, J. C. (1995). First person account: Schizophrenia – adrift in an anchorless reality. *Schizophrenia Bulletin*, 21 (3), 501–503. Retrieved from http://www.ncbi. nlm.nih.gov/pubmed/7481579.

Kallmann, Franz J. (1938). *The Genetics of Schizophrenia* (p. 291). J. J. Augustin. Retrieved from http://books.google.co.uk/books/about/The_genetics_of_ schizophrenia.html?id=A5wHaAEACAAJ&pgis=1.

Kallmann, Franz J. (1946). The genetic theory of schizophrenia. *American Journal of Psychiatry*, *103*, 309–322.

Karlsson, J. L. (1966). *The Biological Basis of Schizophrenia* (p. 87). Thomas Springfield.

Kee, K. S., Horan, W. P., Mintz, J. & Green, M. F. (2004). Do the siblings of schizophrenia patients demonstrate affect perception deficits? *Schizophrenia Research*, 67 (1), 87–94. Retrieved from http://www.sciencedirect.com/science/ article/pii/S0920996403002172.

Kehoe, P., Clash, K., Skipsey, K. & Shoemaker, W. J. (1996). Brain dopamine response in isolated 10-day-old rats: Assessment using D2 binding and dopamine turnover. *Pharmacology, Biochemistry, and Behavior*, 53 (1), 41–9. Retrieved from http://www.ncbi.nlm.nih.gov/pubmed/8848458.

Kemppainen, L., Veijola, J., Jokelainen, J., Hartikainen, A.-L., Jarvelin, M.-R., Jones, P., ... Isohanni, M. (2001). Birth order and risk for schizophrenia: A 31-year follow-up of the Northern Finland 1966 Birth Cohort. *Acta Psychiatrica Scandinavica*, 104 (2), 148–152. doi:10.1034/j.1600-0447.2001.00258.x.

Kendler, K. S., Karkowski-Shuman, L., O'Neill, F. a, Straub, R. E., MacLean, C. J. & Walsh, D. (1997). Resemblance of psychotic symptoms and syndromes in affected sibling pairs from the Irish Study of High-Density Schizophrenia Families: Evidence for possible etiologic heterogeneity. *The American Journal of Psychiatry*, 154 (2), 191–198. Retrieved from http://www.ncbi.nlm.nih.gov/pubmed/9016267.

Keshavan, M. S. (1999). Development, disease and degeneration in schizophrenia: A unitary pathophysiological model. *Journal of Psychiatric Research*, 33 (6), 513–521. Retrieved from http://www.ncbi.nlm.nih.gov/pubmed/10628528.

Kety, S. S. (1980). The syndrome of schizophrenia: Unresolved questions and opportunities for research. *British Jornal of Psychiatry*, 136, 421–436.

Kety, S. S., Rosenthal, D., Wender, P. H. & Schulsinger, F. (1968). The types and prevalance of mental illness in the biological and adoptive families of adopted schizophrenics. In D. Rosenthal & S. S. Kety (eds), *The Transmission of Schizophrenia* (pp. 345–362). Oxford: Pergamon Press.

Khashan, A. S., Abel, K. M., McNamee, R., Pedersen, M. G., Webb, R. T., Baker, P. N., ... Mortensen, P. B. (2008). Higher risk of offspring schizophrenia following antenatal maternal exposure to severe adverse life events. *Archives of General Psychiatry*, 65 (2), 146–152.

Kikkert, M. J., Schene, A. H., Koeter, M. W. J., Robson, D., Born, A., Helm, H., ... Gray, R. J. (2006). Medication adherence in schizophrenia: Exploring patients', carers" and professionals' views. *Schizophrenia Bulletin*, 32 (4), 786–794. doi:10.1093/schbul/sbl011.

Kim, J. S., Kornhuber, H. H., Schmid-Burgk, W. & Holzmüller, B. (1980). Low cerebrospinal fluid glutamate in schizophrenic patients and a new hypothesis on schizophrenia. *Neuroscience Letters*, 20 (3), 379–382. Retrieved from http://www.ncbi.nlm.nih.gov/pubmed/6108541.

Kinderman, P. & Bentall, R. P. (1997). Causal attributions in paranoia and depression: Internal, personal, and situational attributions for negative events. *Journal of Abnormal Psychology*, 106 (2), 341–345. doi:10.1037/0021-843X.106.2.341.

Kohler, C. G., Bilker, W., Hagendoorn, M., Gur, R. E. & Gur, R. C. (2000). Emotion recognition deficit in schizophrenia: Association with symptomatology and cognition. *Biological Psychiatry*, 48 (2), 127–136. Retrieved from http://www.ncbi.nlm.nih.gov/pubmed/10903409.

Kohler, Christian, G., Walker, J. B., Martin, E. A., Healey, K. M. & Moberg, P. J. (2010). Facial emotion perception in schizophrenia: A meta-analytic review. *Schizophrenia Bulletin*, 36 (5), 1009–1019. doi:10.1093/schbul/sbn192.

Kraepelin, E. (1899). *Psychiatrie. Ein Lehrbuch für Studirende und Aertze*. (J. M. Quen (ed.), H. Metoiu (trans.) & S. Ayed (trans.) (eds) (6th edition). Canton, MA: Science History Publications.

Kurtz, M. M. & Mueser, K. T. (2008). A meta-analysis of controlled research on social skills training for schizophrenia. *Journal of Consulting and Clinical Psychology*, 76 (3), 491–504. doi:10.1037/0022-006X.76.3.491.

Kuttner, R. E., Lorincz, A. B. & Swan, D. A. (1967). The schizophrenia gene and social evolution. *Psychological Reports*, 20 (2), 407–412. Retrieved from http://www.ncbi.nlm.nih.gov/pubmed/6042998.

L'Italien, G. J., Casey, D. E., Kan, H. J., Carson, W. H. & Marcus, R. N. (2007). Comparison of metabolic syndrome incidence among schizophrenia patients treated with aripiprazole versus olanzapine or placebo. *The Journal of Clinical Psychiatry*, 68 (10), 1510–1516. Retrieved from http://www.ncbi.nlm.nih.gov/pubmed/17960964.

Lahti, A. C., Koffel, B., LaPorte, D. & Tamminga, C. A. (1995). Subanesthetic doses of ketamine stimulate psychosis in schizophrenia. *Neuropsychopharmacology: Official Publication of the American College of Neuropsychopharmacology*, 13 (1), 9–19. doi:10.1016/0893-133X(94)00131-I.

Langdon, R. & Coltheart, M. (1999). Mentalising, schizotypy, and schizophrenia. *Cognition*, 71 (1), 43–71. Retrieved from http://www.sciencedirect.com/science/article/pii/S0010027799000189.

Langdon, R., Coltheart, M., Ward, P. B. & Catts, S. V. (2001). Mentalising, executive planning and disengagement in schizophrenia. *Cognitive Neuropsychiatry*, 6 (2), 81–108. doi:10.1080/13546800042000061.

Langdon, R., Ward, P. B. & Coltheart, M. (2010). Reasoning anomalies associated with delusions in schizophrenia. *Schizophrenia Bulletin*, 36 (2), 321–330. doi:10.1093/schbul/sbn069.

Larson, C. A. & Nyman, G. E. (1974). Schizophrenia: Outcome in a birth year cohort. *Psychopathology*, 7 (1), 50–55. doi:10.1159/000283371.

Lee, J. & Park, S. (2005). Working memory impairments in schizophrenia: A meta-analysis. *Journal of Abnormal Psychology*, 114 (4), 599–611. doi:10.1037/0021-843X.114.4.599.

Leeson, V. C., Barnes, T. R. E., Harrison, M., Matheson, E., Harrison, I., Mutsatsa, S. H., … Joyce, E. M. (2010). The relationship between IQ, memory, executive function, and processing speed in recent-onset psychosis: 1-year stability and clinical outcome. *Schizophrenia Bulletin*, 36 (2), 400–9. doi:10.1093/schbul/sbn100.

Leppänen, J. M., Niehaus, D. J. H., Koen, L., Du Toit, E., Schoeman, R. & Emsley, R. (2008). Deficits in facial affect recognition in unaffected siblings of Xhosa schizophrenia patients: Evidence for a neurocognitive endophenotype. *Schizophrenia Research*. Retrieved from http://www.sciencedirect.com/science/article/pii/S0920996407005105.

Leucht, C., Kitzmantel, M., Kane, J., Leucht, S. & Chua, W. L. L. C. (2010). Haloperidol versus chlorpromazine for schizophrenia (Review). *Cochrane Database of Systematic Reviews (Online)*, (3).

Leucht, S., Corves, C., Arbter, D., Engel, R. R., Li, C. & Davis, J. M. (2009). Second-generation versus first-generation antipsychotic drugs for schizophrenia: A meta-analysis. *Lancet*, 373 (9657), 31–41. doi:10.1016/S0140-6736(08)61764-X.

Levin, S., Luebke, A., Zee, D. S., Hain, T. C., Robinson, D. A. & Holzman, P. S. (1988). Smooth pursuit eye movements in schizophrenics: Quantitative measurements with the search-coil technique. *Journal of Psychiatric Research*, 22 (3), 195–206. Retrieved from http://www.sciencedirect.com/science/article/pii/0022395688900052.

Lewis, J. M. (1979). *Family Interaction Behaviors Associated with a Communication Disorder Index of Risk for Schizophrenia*. University of California.

Liberman, R. P., Glynn, S., Blair, K. E., Ross, D. & Marder, S. R. (2002). In vivo amplified skills training: Promoting generalization of independent living skills for clients with schizophrenia. *Psychiatry*, 65 (2), 137–155. Retrieved from http://www.ncbi.nlm.nih.gov/pubmed/12108138.

Lidz, R. W. & Lidz, T. (1949). The family environment of schizophrenic patients. *American Journal of Psychiatry*, 106, 332–345.

Lidz, T., Cornelison, A. R., Fleck, S. & Terry, D. (1957). The intrafamilial environment of schizophrenic patients. II. Marital schism and marital skew. *The American Journal of Psychiatry*, 114 (3), 241–248.

Lidz, T., Fleck, S., Alanen, Y. O. & Cornelison, A. (1963). Schizophrenic patients and their siblings. *Psychiatry*, 26, 1–18.

Lieber, D. J. (1977). Parental focus of attention in a videotape feedback task as a function of hypothesized risk for offspring schizophrenia. *Family Process*, 16 (4), 467–475. doi:10.1111/j.1545-5300.1977.00467.x.

Lincoln, T. M., Lange, J., Burau, J., Exner, C. & Moritz, S. (2010). The effect of state anxiety on paranoid ideation and jumping to conclusions. An experimental investigation. *Schizophrenia Bulletin*, 36 (6), 1140–1148. doi:10.1093/schbul/sbp029.

Lindamer, L. A., Lohr, J. B., Harris, M. J. & Jeste, D. V. (1997). Gender, estrogen, and schizophrenia. *Psychopharmacology Bulletin*, 33 (2), 221–228. Retrieved from http://www.ncbi.nlm.nih.gov/pubmed/9230634.

Lipton, R. B., Levy, D. L., Holzman, P. S. & Levin, S. (1983). Eye movement dysfunctions in psychiatric patients: A review. *Schizophrenia Bulletin*, 9 (1), 13–32. Retrieved from http://www.ncbi.nlm.nih.gov/pubmed/6844884.

Los, I. & Jacob, R. (2010). Metabolic Complications with Aripiprazole. *German Psychiatry*, 13, 49–50.

Loughland, C. M., Williams, L. M. & Gordon, E. (2002). Schizophrenia and affective disorder show different visual scanning behavior for faces: A trait versus state-based distinction? *Biological Psychiatry*, 52 (4), 338–348. Retrieved from http://www.sciencedirect.com/science/article/pii/S0006322302013562.

Luxenburger, H. (1928). Demographische und psychiatrische Untersuchungen in der engeren biologischen Familie von Paralytikerehegatten Versuch einer Belastungsstatistik der Durchschnittsbevölkerung. *Zeitschrift für die gesamte Neurologie und Psychiatrie*, 112 (1), 331–491.

MacDonald, A. W. & Schulz, S. C. (2009). What we know: Findings that every theory of schizophrenia should explain. *Schizophrenia Bulletin*, 35 (3), 493–508. doi:10.1093/schbul/sbp017.

Manglam, M. K., Ram, D., Praharaj, S. K. & Sarkhel, S. (2010). Working memory in schizophrenia. *German Jornal of Psychiatry*, 13 (3), 116–120.

Marom, S., Munitz, H., Jones, P. B., Weizman, A. & Hermesh, H. (2005). Expressed emotion: Relevance to rehospitalization in schizophrenia over 7 years. *Schizophrenia Bulletin*, 31 (3), 751–758. doi:10.1093/schbul/sbi016.

Martin, J. A & Penn, D. L. (2002). Attributional style in schizophrenia: An investigation in outpatients with and without persecutory delusions. *Schizophrenia Bulletin*, 28 (1), 131–141. Retrieved from http://www.ncbi.nlm.nih.gov/pubmed/12047013.

Maslow, A. H. (1954). *Motivation and Personality*. New York: Harper and Row.

Matar, H. E., Almerie, M. Q. & Sampson, S. (2013). Fluphenazine (Oral) versus placebo for schizophrenia. *Schizophrenia Bulletin*, 39 (6), 1187–1188.

May, P. R. (1968). *Treatment of Schizophrenia*. New York: Science House.

Mayer-Gross, W., Roth, M. & Slater, E. (1969). *Clinical Psychiatry, [by] Mayer-Gross, Slater and Roth: 3d Ed. by Eliot Slater and Martin Roth* (p. 904). Baillière, Tindall & Cassell. Retrieved from http://books.google.co.uk/books/about/Clinical_Psychiatry_by_Mayer_Gross_Slate.html?id=dErRNwAACAAJ&pgis=1.

Mayhew, S. L. & Gilbert, P. (2008). Report training with people who hear malevolent voices: A case series report. *Clinical Psychology and Psychotherapy*, 15, 113–138.

Mazza, M., De Risio, A., Tozzini, C., Roncone, R. & Casacchia, M. (2003). Machiavellianism and theory of mind in people affected by schizophrenia. *Brain and Cognition*, 51 (3), 262–269. Retrieved from http://www.sciencedirect.com/science/article/pii/S0278262603000186.

McDonald, B., Highley, J. R., Walker, M. a, Herron, B. M., Cooper, S. J., Esiri, M. M. & Crow, T. J. (2000). Anomalous asymmetry of fusiform and parahippocampal gyrus gray matter in schizophrenia: A postmortem study. *The American Journal of Psychiatry*, 157 (1), 40–47. Retrieved from http://www.ncbi.nlm.nih.gov/pubmed/10618011.

McGlashan, T. H. (2009). Psychosis as a disorder of reduced cathectic capacity: Freud's analysis of the Schreber case revisited. *Schizophrenia Bulletin*, 35 (3), 476–481. doi:10.1093/schbul/sbp019.

McGlashan, T. H., Zipursky, R. B., Perkins, D., Addington, J., Miller, T., Woods, S. W., … Breier, A. (2006). Randomized, double-blind trial of olanzapine versus placebo in patients prodromally symptomatic for psychosis. *The American Journal of Psychiatry*, 163 (5), 790–799. doi:10.1176/appi.ajp.163.5.790.

McKay, Paula, A., McKenna, P. J., Bentham, P., Mortimer, A. M., Holbery, A. & Hodges, J. R. (1996). Semantic memory is impaired in schizophrenia. *Biological Psychiatry*, 39 (11), 929–937. Retrieved from http://www.sciencedirect.com/science/article/pii/0006322395002502.

McKenna, P. J., Tamlyn, D., Lund, C. E., Mortimer, A. M., Hammond, S. & Baddeley, A. D. (1990). Amnesic syndrome in schizophrenia. *Psychological Medicine*, 20 (04), 967–972. doi:10.1017/S0033291700036667.

Mednick, S. A., Machon, R. A., Huttunen, M. O. & Bonett, D. (1988). Adult schizophrenia Following prenatal exposure to an influenza epidemic. *Archives of General Psychiatry*, 45 (2), 189–192. Retrieved from http://www.ncbi.nlm.nih.gov/pubmed/3337616.

Meichenbaum, D. & Cameron, R. O. Y. (1973). Training schizophrenics to talk to themselves: A means of developing attentional controls. *Behavior Therapy*, 4, 515–534.

Miller, W. K, & Phelan, J. G. (1980). Comparison of adult schizophrenics with matched normal native speakers of English as to acceptability of English sentences. *Journal of Psycholinguistic Research*, 9 (6), 579–593. doi:10.1007/BF01068118.

Minnis, H., McMillan, A., Gillies, M. & Smith, S. (2001). Racial stereotyping: Survey of psychiatrists in the United Kingdom. *BMJ*, 323 (7318), 905–906. doi:10.1136/bmj.323.7318.905.

Mishler, E. G. & Waxler-Morrison, N. (1968). *Interaction in Families: An Experimental Study of Family Processes and Schizophrenia* (p. 436). New York: Wiley.

Moghaddam, B., Adams, B., Verma, A. & Daly, D. (1997). Activation of glutamatergic neurotransmission by ketamine: a novel step in the pathway from NMDA receptor blockade to dopaminergic and cognitive disruptions associated with the prefrontal cortex. *The Journal of neuroscience: the official journal of the Society for Neuroscience*, *17*(8), 2921–7. Retrieved from http://www.ncbi.nlm.nih.gov/pubmed/9092613.

Moghaddam, Bita. (2003). Bringing order to the glutamate chaos in schizophrenia. *Neuron*, 40 (5), 881–884. Retrieved from http://www.ncbi.nlm.nih.gov/pubmed/14659087.

Montero, I., Asencio, A., Hernández, I., Masanet, M. J., Lacruz, M., Bellver, F., ... Ruiz, I. (2001). Two strategies for family intervention in schizophrenia: A randomized trial in a Mediterranean environment. *Schizophrenia Bulletin*, 27 (4), 661–670.

Morgan, C., Charalambides, M., Hutchinson, G. & Murray, R. M. (2010). Migration, ethnicity, and psychosis: Toward a sociodevelopmental model. *Schizophrenia Bulletin*, 36 (4), 655–64. doi:10.1093/schbul/sbq051.

Morris, R., Griffiths, O., Le Pelley, M. E. & Weickert, T. W. (2012). Attention to irrelevant cues is related to positive symptoms in schizophrenia. *Schizophrenia Bulletin*, 39 (3), 575–582. doi:10.1093/schbul/sbr192.

Murray, R. M., O'Callaghan, E., Castle, D. J. & Lewis, S. W. (1992). A neurodevelopmental approach to the classification of schizophrenia. *Schizophrenia Bulletin*, 18 (2), 319–332. Retrieved from http://www.ncbi.nlm.nih.gov/pubmed/1377834.

Myers, David G.Diener, E. (1996). The pursuit of happiness. *Scientific American. May96*, 274 (5), 70. 3p. 6 Graphs.

Newsome, W., Wurtz, R., Dursteler, M. & Mikami, A. (1985). Deficits in visual motion processing following ibotenic acid lesions of the middle temporal visual area of the macaque monkey. *J. Neurosci.*, 5 (3), 825–840. Retrieved from http://www.jneurosci.org/content/5/3/825.short.

Olabi, B., Ellison-Wright, I., McIntosh, A. M., Wood, S. J., Bullmore, E. & Lawrie, S. M. (2011). Are there progressive brain changes in schizophrenia? A meta-analysis of structural magnetic resonance imaging studies. *Biological Psychiatry*, 70 (1), 88–96. doi:10.1016/j.biopsych.2011.01.032.

Oliver, N. & Kuipers, E. (1996). Stress and its relationship to expressed emotion in community mental health workers. *International Journal of Social Psychiatry*, 42, 150–159.

Olney, J. W., Newcomer, J. W. & Farber, N. B. (1999). NMDA receptor hypofunction model of schizophrenia. *Journal of Psychiatric Research*, 33 (6), 523–533. Retrieved from http://www.ncbi.nlm.nih.gov/pubmed/10628529.

Pantelis, C., Yücel, M., Wood, S. J., Velakoulis, D., Sun, D., Berger, G., … McGorry, P. D. (2005). Structural brain imaging evidence for multiple pathological processes at different stages of brain development in schizophrenia. *Schizophrenia Bulletin*, 31 (3), 672–696. doi:10.1093/schbul/sbi034.

Park, S. & Holzman, P. S. (1992). Schizophrenics show spatial working memory deficits. *Archives of General Psychiatry*, 49 (12), 975–982. Retrieved from http://www.ncbi.nlm.nih.gov/pubmed/1449384.

Paul, G. L. (2000). Milieu Therapy. In A. E. Kazdin (ed.), *Encyclopedia of Psychology*. American Psychological Association and Oxford University Press.

Paulsen, J. S., Heaton, R. K., Sadek, J. R., Perry, W., Delis, D. C., Braff, D., … Jeste, D. V. (2009). The nature of learning and memory impairments in schizophrenia. *Journal of the International Neuropsychological Society*, 1 (01), 88. doi:10.1017/S135561770000014X.

Pedersen, C. B. & Mortensen, P. B. (2006). Urbanization and traffic related exposures as risk factors for schizophrenia. *BMC Psychiatry*, 6 (1), 2. doi:10.1186/1471-244X-6-2.

Perris, C. (1974). A study of cycloid psychoses. *Acta Psychiatrica Scandinavica*, 50, 7–79. doi:10.1111/j.1600-0447.1975.tb10436.x.

Perry, W., Heaton, R. K., Potterat, E., Roebuck, T., Minassian, A. & Braff, D. L. (2001). Working memory in schizophrenia: Transient "online" storage versus executive functioning. *Schizophrenia Bulletin*, 27 (1), 157–176. Retrieved from http://www.ncbi.nlm.nih.gov/pubmed/11215544.

Phillips, M. L. & David, A. S. (1998). Abnormal visual scan paths: A psychophysiological marker of delusions in schizophrenia. *Schizophrenia Research*, 29 (3), 235–245. Retrieved from http://www.ncbi.nlm.nih.gov/pubmed/9516664.

Pilling, S., Bebbington, P., Kuipers, E., Garety, P., Geddes, J., Martindale, B., … Morgan, C. (2002). Psychological treatments in schizophrenia: II. Meta-analyses of randomized controlled trials of social skills training and cognitive remediation. *Psychological Medicine*, 32 (5), 783–791. Retrieved from http://www.ncbi.nlm.nih.gov/pubmed/12171373.

Pilowsky, L. S., Bressan, R. A., Stone, J. M., Erlandsson, K., Mulligan, R. S., Krystal, J. H. & Ell, P. J. (2006). First in vivo evidence of an NMDA receptor deficit in medication-free schizophrenic patients. *Molecular Psychiatry*, 11 (2), 118–119.

Pitschel-Walz, Gabriele, Bäuml, J., Bender, W., Engel, R. R., Wagner, M. & Kissling, W. (2006). Psychoeducation and compliance in the treatment of schizophrenia: Results of the Munich Psychosis Information Project Study.

The Journal of Clinical Psychiatry, 67 (3), 443–452. Retrieved from http://cirrie. buffalo.edu/database/30710/.

Pitschel-Walz, G., Leucht, S., Bäuml, J., Kissling, W. & Engel, R. R. (2001). The effect of family interventions on relapse and rehospitalization in schizophrenia – A meta-analysis. *Schizophrenia Bulletin*, 27 (1), 73–92. Retrieved from http:// www.ncbi.nlm.nih.gov/pubmed/11215551.

Plaze, M., Paillère-Martinot, M.-L., Penttilä, J., Januel, D., de Beaurepaire, R., Bellivier, F., … Cachia, A. (2011). "Where do auditory hallucinations come from?" – A brain morphometry study of schizophrenia patients with inner or outer space hallucinations. *Schizophrenia Bulletin*, 37 (1), 212–221. doi:10.1093/schbul/sbp081.

Popken, G. J., Bunney, W. E., Potkin, S. G. & Jones, E. G. (2000). Subnucleus-specific loss of neurons in medial thalamus of schizophrenics. *Proceedings of the National Academy of Sciences of the United States of America*, 97 (16), 9276–9280. doi:10.1073/pnas.150243397.

Price, J. S. & Stevens, A. (1998). The human male socialization strategy set: Cooperation, defection, individualism, and schizotypy, 70, 57–70.

Reed, S. C., Hartley, C., Anderson, V. E., Phillips, V. P. & Johnson, N. A. (1973). *The Psychoses: Family Studies*. Philadelphia: Saunders.

Reichenberg, A. & Harvey, P. D. (2007). Neuropsychological impairments in schizophrenia: Integration of performance-based and brain imaging findings. *Psychological Bulletin*, 133 (5), 833–858. doi:10.1037/0033-2909.133.5.833.

Reiss, D. (1976). The family and schizophrenia. *The American Journal of Psychiatry*, 133 (2), 181–185. Retrieved from http://www.ncbi.nlm.nih.gov/pubmed/1082721.

Reiss, D. (1981). *The Family's Construction of Reality*. Cambridge, MA: Harvard University Press.

Richardson, P. (2002). A randomised trial of group based art therapy as an adjunctive treatment in severe mental illness. *unpublished*.

Ringuette, E. L. & Kennedy, T. (1966). An experimental study of the double bind hypothesis. *Journal of Abnormal Psychology*, 71 (2), 136–141.

Robles, O., Zabala, A., Bombín, I., Parellada, M., Moreno, D., Ruiz-Sancho, A. & Arango, C. (2011). Cognitive efficacy of quetiapine and olanzapine in early-onset first-episode psychosis. *Schizophrenia Bulletin*, 37 (2), 405–415. doi:10.1093/schbul/sbp062.

Roder, V., Mueller, D. R., Mueser, K. T. & Brenner, H. D. (2006). Integrated psychological therapy (IPT) for schizophrenia: Is it effective? *Schizophrenia Bulletin*, 32 Suppl 1, S81–93. doi:10.1093/schbul/sbl021.

Roder, V., Mueller, D. R. & Schmidt, S. J. (2011). Effectiveness of integrated psychological therapy (IPT) for schizophrenia patients: A research update. *Schizophrenia Bulletin*, 37 Suppl 2 (suppl_2), S71–9. doi:10.1093/schbul/sbr072.

Rosenthal, David, Wender, P. H., Kety, S. S., Schulsinger, F., Welner, J. & Ostergaard, L. (1968). Schizophrenics' offspring reared in adoptive homes. In D. Rosenthal & S. S. Kety (eds), *The Transmission of Schizophrenia* (pp. 377–391). Oxford: Pergamon Press.

Ruddy, R. & Milnes, D. (2009). Art therapy for schizophrenia or schizophrenia-like illnesses (Review), (1).

Sanger, T. M., Lieberman, J. A., Tohen, M., Grundy, S., Beasley, C. & Tollefson, G. D. (1999). Olanzapine versus haloperidol treatment in first-episode psychosis. *The American Journal of Psychiatry*, 156 (1), 79–87. Retrieved from http://www.ncbi. nlm.nih.gov/pubmed/9892301.

Saperstein, A. M., Fuller, R. L., Avila, M. T., Adami, H., McMahon, R. P., Thaker, G. K. & Gold, J. M. (2006). Spatial working memory as a cognitive endophenotype of schizophrenia: Assessing risk for pathophysiological dysfunction. *Schizophrenia Bulletin*, 32 (3), 498–506. doi:10.1093/schbul/sbj072.

Sargant, W. & Slater, E. (1944). *An Introduction to Physical Methods of Treatment in Psychiatry* (E & S Livi.). Edinburgh.

Sarra, N. (1998). Connection & disconnection in the art therapy group: Working with forensic patients in acute states on a locked ward. In S. Skaife & V. Huet (eds), *Art Psychotherapy Groups: Between Pictures and Words*. London: Routledge.

Schneider, F., Gur, R. C., Koch, K., Backes, V., Amunts, K., Shah, N. J., ... Habel, U. (2006). Impairment in the specificity of emotion processing in schizophrenia. *The American Journal of Psychiatry*, 163 (3), 442–447. doi:10.1176/appi. ajp.163.3.442.

Schobel, S. A., Kelly, M. A., Corcoran, C. M., Van Heertum, K., Seckinger, R., Goetz, R., ... Malaspina, D. (2009). Anterior hippocampal and orbitofrontal cortical structural brain abnormalities in association with cognitive deficits in schizophrenia. *Schizophrenia Research*, 114 (1–3), 110–118. doi:10.1016/ j.schres.2009.07.016.

Schooler, C. (1964). Birth order and hospitalization for schizophrenia. *The Journal of Abnormal and Social Psychology*, 69 (5), 574–579.

Schuham, A. I. (1967). The double-bind hypothesis a decade later. *Psychological Bulletin*, 68 (6), 409–416. Retrieved from http://www.ncbi.nlm.nih.gov/ pubmed/4869090.

Schwartz, B. L., Rosse, R. B., Johri, S. & Deutsch, S. I. (1999). Visual scanning of facial expressions in schizophrenia. *The Journal of Neuropsychiatry and Clinical Neurosciences*, 11 (1), 103–106. Retrieved from http://www.ncbi.nlm.nih.gov/ pubmed/9990565.

Selemon, L. D. (2001). Regionally diverse cortical pathology in schizophrenia: Clues to the etiology of the disease. *Schizophrenia Bulletin*, 27 (3), 349–377. Retrieved from http://www.ncbi.nlm.nih.gov/pubmed/11596841.

Sensky, T., Turkington, D., Kingdon, D., Scott, J. L., Scott, J., Siddle, R., ... Barnes, T. R. (2000). A randomized controlled trial of cognitive-behavioral therapy for persistent symptoms in schizophrenia resistant to medication. *Archives of General Psychiatry*, 57 (2), 165–172. Retrieved from http://www. ncbi.nlm.nih.gov/pubmed/10665619.

Settle, E. C. & Ayd, F. J. (1983). Haloperidol: A quarter century of experience. *The Journal of Clinical Psychiatry*, 44 (12), 440–448. Retrieved from http://www. ncbi.nlm.nih.gov/pubmed/6418723.

Shin, Y.-W., Na, M. H., Ha, T. H., Kang, D.-H., Yoo, S.-Y. & Kwon, J. S. (2008). Dysfunction in configural face processing in patients with schizophrenia. *Schizophrenia Bulletin*, 34 (3), 538–543. doi:10.1093/schbul/sbm118.

Shum, D., Ungvari, Q. S., Tang, W. K. & Leung, J. P. (2004). Performance of schizophrenia patients on time-, event-, and activity-based prospective memory tasks. *Schizophrenia Bulletin*, 30 (4), 693–702.

Silver, E., Mulvey, E. P. & Swanson, J. W. (2002). Neighborhood structural characteristics and mental disorder: Faris and Dunham revisited. *Social Science & Medicine*, 55(8), 1457–1470. Retrieved from http://www.sciencedirect.com/science/article/pii/S0277953601002660.

Singer, M. T. (1968). The consensus Rorschach and family transaction. *Journal of Projective Techniques*, 32, 348–351.

Singer, M. T. & Wynne, L. C. (1965a). Thought disorder and family relations of schizophrenics. III. Methodology using projective techniques. *Archives of General Psychiatry*, 12, 187–200.

Singer, M. T. & Wynne, L. C. (1965b). Thought disorder and family relations of schizophrenics. IV. Results and implications. *Archives of General Psychiatry*, 12, 201–212.

Singer, M. T., Wynne, L. C. & Toohey, M. L. (1978). Communication disorders and the families of schizophrenics. In L. C. Wynne, R. L. Cromwell & S. Matthysse (eds), *The Nature of Schizophrenia: New Approaches to Research and Treatment* (pp. 499–511). New York: Wiley.

Slotema, C. W., Blom, J. D., de Weijer, A. D., Diederen, K. M., Goekoop, R., Looijestijn, J., ... Sommer, I. E. C. (2011). Can low-frequency repetitive transcranial magnetic stimulation really relieve medication-resistant auditory verbal hallucinations? Negative results from a large randomized controlled trial. *Biological Psychiatry*, 69 (5), 450–456. doi:10.1016/j.biopsych.2010.09.051.

Sommer, I., Ramsey, N., Kahn, R., Aleman, A. & Bouma, A. (2001). Handedness, language lateralisation and anatomical asymmetry in schizophrenia: Meta-analysis. *The British Journal of Psychiatry: The Journal of Mental Science*, 178, 344–351. Retrieved from http://www.ncbi.nlm.nih.gov/pubmed/11282814.

Spataro, J., Mullen, P. E., Burgess, P. M., Wells, D. L. & Moss, S. A. (2004). Impact of child sexual abuse on mental health: Prospective study in males and females. *The British Journal of Psychiatry*, 184 (5), 416–421. doi:10.1192/bjp.184.5.416.

Spaulding, W. D., Reed, D., Sullivan, M., Richardson, C. & Weiler, M. (1999). Effects of cognitive treatment in psychiatric rehabilitation. *Schizophrenia Bulletin*, 25 (4), 657–676. Retrieved from http://www.ncbi.nlm.nih.gov/pubmed/10667738.

Stevens, A. & Price, J. (1996). *Evolutionary Psychiatry: A New Beginning*. London: Routledge.

Stevens, A. & Price, J. S. (2000). *Prophets, Cults and Madness*. London: Duckworth.

Stilo, S. a, Di Forti, M., Mondelli, V., Falcone, A. M., Russo, M., O'Connor, J., ... Morgan, C. (2013). Social disadvantage: Cause or consequence of impending psychosis? *Schizophrenia Bulletin*, 39 (6), 1288–1295. doi:10.1093/schbul/sbs112.

Stromgren, E. (1975). Genetic factors in the origin of schizophrenia. In H. M. van Praag (ed.), *On the Origin of Schizophrenic Psychoses* (pp. 7–18). Amsterdam: De Erven Bohn.

Subotnik, K. L., Goldstein, M. J., Nuechterlein, K. H., Woo, S. M. & Mintz, J. (2002). Are communication deviance and expressed emotion related to family history of psychiatric disorders in schizophrenia? *Schizophrenia Bulletin*, 28 (4), 719–729. Retrieved from http://www.ncbi.nlm.nih.gov/pubmed/12795501.

Sullivan, R. J. & Allen, J. S. (1999). Social deficits associated with schizophrenia defined in terms of interpersonal Machiavellianism. *Acta Psychiatrica Scandinavica*, 99 (2), 148–154. Retrieved from http://www.ncbi.nlm.nih.gov/pubmed/10082191.

Sun, J., Maller, J. J., Guo, L. & Fitzgerald, P. B. (2009). Superior temporal gyrus volume change in schizophrenia: A review on Region of Interest volumetric studies. *Brain Research Reviews*, 61 (1), 14–32. Retrieved from http://www.sciencedirect.com/science/article/pii/S016501730900037X.

Takahashi, H., Higuchi, M. & Suhara, T. (2006). The role of extrastriatal dopamine D2 receptors in schizophrenia. *Biological Psychiatry*, 59 (10), 919–928. doi:10.1016/j.biopsych.2006.01.022.

Talkowski, M. E., Kirov, G., Bamne, M., Georgieva, L., Torres, G., Mansour, H., ... Nimgaonkar, V. L. (2008). A network of dopaminergic gene variations implicated as risk factors for schizophrenia. *Human molecular Genetics*, 17 (5), 747–758. doi:10.1093/hmg/ddm347.

Tandon, R., Gaebel, W., Barch, D. M., Bustillo, J., Gur, R. E., Heckers, S., ... Carpenter, W. (2013). Definition and description of schizophrenia in the DSM-5. *Schizophrenia Research*, 150 (1), 3–10. doi:10.1016/j.schres.2013.05.028.

Tarrier, N. & Turpin, G. (1992). Psychosocial factors, arousal and schizophrenic relapse: The psychophysiological data. *British Journal of Psychiatry*, 161, 3–11.

Tek, C., Gold, J., Blaxton, T., Wilk, C., McMahon, R. P. & Buchanan, R. W. (2002). Visual Perceptual and Working Memory Impairments in Schizophrenia. *Archives of General Psychiatry*, 59 (2), 146. doi:10.1001/archpsyc.59.2.146.

Tharyan, P. & Adams, C. (2009, October 7). Electroconvulsive therapy for schizophrenia. John Wiley and Sons, Ltd. for The Cochrane Collaboration. Retrieved from http://summaries.cochrane.org/CD000076/electroconvulsive-therapy-for-schizophrenia.

The President's New Freedom Commission on Mental Health: Transforming the Vision. (2003). In *The Nineteenth Annual Rosalynn Carter Symposium on Mental Health Policy*.

Thomas, P., King, K., Fraser, W. I. & Kendell, R. E. (1990). Linguistic performance in schizophrenia: A comparison of acute and chronic patients. *The British Journal of Psychiatry: The Journal of Mental Science*, 156, 204–210, 214–215. Retrieved from http://www.ncbi.nlm.nih.gov/pubmed/2317624.

Tienari, P, Sorri, A., Lahti, I., Naarala, M., Wahlberg, K. E., Moring, J., ... Wynne, L. C. (1987). Genetic and psychosocial factors in schizophrenia: The Finnish adoptive family study. *Schizophrenia Bulletin*, 13 (3), 477–484. Retrieved from http://www.ncbi.nlm.nih.gov/pubmed/3629201.

Tienari, Pekka. (1963). A psychiatric twin study. *Acta Psychiatrica Scandinavica*, 39 (s169), 393–397. doi:10.1111/j.1600-0447.1963.tb07892.x.

Tompson, M. C., Goldstein, M. J., Lebell, M. B., Mintz, L. I., Marder, S. R. & Mintz, J. (1995). Schizophrenic patients' perceptions of their relatives' attitudes. *Psychiatry Research*, 57 (2), 155–167. Retrieved from http://www.sciencedirect.com/science/article/pii/016517819502598Q.

Torrey, E. F. (1994). *Surviving Schizophrenia: A Manual for Families Consumers and Providers* (p. 409). HarperCollins. Retrieved from http://www.amazon.co.uk/Surviving-Schizophrenia-Families-Consumers-Providers/dp/0060950765.

Toulopoulou, T. & Murray, R. (2004). Verbal memory deficit in patients with schizophrenia: An important future target for treatment. *Expert Review of Neurotherapeutics*, 4 (1), 43–52.

Tschacher, W. & Kupper, Z. (2006). Perception of causality in schizophrenia spectrum disorder. *Schizophrenia bulletin*, *32 Suppl 1*, S106–12. doi:10.1093/schbul/sbl018.

Turkington, D. & McKenna, P. J. (2003). Is cognitive-behavioural therapy a worthwhile treatment for psychosis? *The British Journal of Psychiatry: The Journal of Mental Science*, 182, 477–479. Retrieved from http://www.ncbi.nlm.nih.gov/pubmed/12777337.

Valenstein, M., Blow, F. C., Copeland, L. A, McCarthy, J. F., Zeber, J. E., Gillon, L., … Stavenger, T. (2004). Poor antipsychotic adherence among patients with schizophrenia: Medication and patient factors. *Schizophrenia Bulletin*, 30 (2), 255–264. Retrieved from http://www.ncbi.nlm.nih.gov/pubmed/15279044.

Van der Gaag, M. (1992). *The Results of Cognitive Training in Schizophrenic Patients*. Delft, the Netherlands: Eburon.

Van Haren, N. E. M., Pol, H. E. H., Schnack, H. G., Cahn, W., Brans, R., Carati, I., … Kahn, R. S. (2008). Progressive brain volume loss in schizophrenia over the course of the illness: Evidence of maturational abnormalities in early adulthood. *Biological Psychiatry*, 63 (1), 106–113. Retrieved from http://www.sciencedirect.com/science/article/pii/S0006322307000133.

Van Os, J., Driessen, G., Gunther, N. & Delespaul, P. (2000). Neighbourhood variation in incidence of schizophrenia. Evidence for person-environment interaction. *The British Journal of Psychiatry: The Journal of Mental Science*, 176, 243–248. Retrieved from http://www.ncbi.nlm.nih.gov/pubmed/10755071.

Vaughn, C. E. & Leff, J. P. (1976). The influence of family and social factors on the course of psychiatric illness: A comparison of schizophrenic and depressed neurotic patients. *British Journal of Psychiatry*, 129, 125–137.

Veling, W., Susser, E., van Os, J., Mackenbach, J. P., Selten, J. P. & Hoek, H. W. (2008). Ethnic density of neighborhoods and incidence of psychotic disorders among immigrants. *American Journal of Psychiatry*, 165, 66–73.

Wallace, A. F. C. (1970). *Culture and Personality* (2nd edition). University of Pennsylvania, Albany: Random House Inc.

Weinberger, D. R., Berman, K. F. & Zec, R. (1986). Physiological dysfunction of dorsolateral prefrontal cortex in schizophrenia. I. Regional cerebral blood flow evidence. *Archives of General Psychiatry*, 43, 114–124.

Weinberger, D. R, Wagner, R. L. & Wyatt, R. J. (1983). Neuropathological studies of schizophrenia: A selective review. *Schizophrenia Bulletin*, 9 (2), 193–212. Retrieved from http://www.ncbi.nlm.nih.gov/pubmed/6346480.

Weinberger, D. R., Bigclow, L. B., Kleinman, J. . E., Klein, S. T., Roscnblatt, J. . . ., & Wyatt, R. I. (1980). Cerebral ventricular enlargement in chronic schizophrenia: Association with poor response to treatment. *Archives of General Psychiatry*, 37 (1), 11.

Weller, I. & Miller, S. (1978). Birth order, country of origin and schizophrenia in Israel. *International Journal of Social Psychiatry*, 24, 195–198.

Whiten, A. (1999). The evolution of deep social mind in humans. In M. Corballis & S. Lea (eds), *The Descent of Man* (pp. 155–175). Oxford: Oxford University Press.

Wicks, S., Hjern, A., Gunnell, D., Lewis, G. & Dalman, C. (2005). Social adversity in childhood and the risk of developing psychosis: A national cohort study. *American Journal of Psychiatry*, 162 (9), 1652–1657.

Wigram, T. (2002). Indications in music therapy: Evidence from assessment that can Identify the expectations of music therapy as a treatment for autistic spectrum sisorder (ASD): Meeting the challenge of Evidence Based Practice. *British Journal of Music Therapy*, 16, 11–28.

Wild, C. M., Shapiro, L. N. & Abelin, T. (1974). Sampling issues in family studies of schizophrenia. *Archives of General Psychiatry*, 30 (2), 211. doi:10.1001/archpsyc.1974.01760080067011.

Wild, C. M., Shapiro, L. N. & Goldenberg, L. (1975). Transactional communication disturbances in families of male schizophrenics. *Family Process*, 14 (2), 131–160. doi:10.1111/j.1545-5300.1975.00131.x.

Williams, J., McGuffin, P., Nothen, M. M. & Owen, M. J. (1997). Meta-analysis of the association between the 5-HT2A receptor T102C polymorphism and schizophrenia. *Lancet*, 349, 1221.

Wimmer, H. & Perner, J. (1983). Beliefs about beliefs: Representation and constraining function of wrong beliefs in young children's understanding of deception. *Cognition*, 13 (1), 103–128. Retrieved from http://www.sciencedirect.com/science/article/pii/0010027783900045.

Wing, J. K., Cooper, J. E. & Sartorius, N. (1974). *The Description and Classification of Psychiatric Symptoms. An Instruction Manual for the PSE and CATEGO Systems.* Cambridge: Cambridge University Press.

Winokur, G., Morrison, J., Clancy, J. & Crowe, R. (1974). Iowa 500: The clinical and genetic distinction of hebephrenic and paranoid schizophrenia. *The Journal of Nervous and Mental Disease*. Retrieved from http://journals.lww.com/jonmd/Abstract/1974/07000/Iowa_500__the_Clinical_and_Genetic_Distinction_of.2.aspx.

Wong, S. E. (2006). Behavior analysis of psychotic disorders: scientific dead end or casualty of the mental health political economy ? *Behavior and Social Issues*, 15, 152–177.

Wood, N., Brewin, C. R. & McLeod, H. J. (2006). Autobiographical memory deficits in schizophrenia. *Cognition & Emotion*, 20 (3-4), 536–547. doi:10.1080/02699930500342472.

Woolley, D. W. & Shaw, E. (1954). Some neurophysiological aspects of serotonin. *British Medical Journal*, 2 (4880), 122–126. Retrieved from http://www. pubmedcentral.nih.gov/articlerender.fcgi?artid=2079253&tool=pmcentrez&ren dertype=abstract.

Woolley, D. W. & Shaw, E. N. (1956). Antiserotonins in hypertension and the antimetabolite approach to chemotherapy. *Science (New York, N. Y.)*, 124 (3210), 34. Retrieved from http://www.ncbi.nlm.nih.gov/pubmed/13337349.

Wright, I. C., Rabe-Hesketh, S., Woodruff, P. W. R., David, A. S., Murray, R. M. & Bullmore, E. T. (2000). Meta-analysis of regional brain volumes in schizophrenia. *American Journal of Psychiatry*, 157 (1), 16–25. Retrieved from http://journals. psychiatryonline.org/article.aspx?articleid=173894.

Wu, D., She, C. W., Liu, C. Z., Cho, W. L., Quon, M., S.Y., L. & Ai, S. C. (1989). Using BPRS and serial numbers and picture recall to test the effectiveness of ECT versus chlorpromazine versus chlorpromazine alone in the treatment of schizophrenia: 40 cases, single blind observations. *Chinese Journal of Nervous and Mental Disorders*, 15 (1), 26–28.

Wykes, T & van der Gaag, M. (2001). Is it time to develop a new cognitive therapy for psychosis – Cognitive remediation therapy (CRT)? *Clinical Psychology Review*, 21 (8), 1227–1256. Retrieved from http://www.ncbi.nlm.nih.gov/ pubmed/11702514.

Wykes, T. & Spaulding, W. D. (2011). Thinking about the future cognitive remediation therapy – What works and could we do better? *Schizophrenia Bulletin*, 37 Suppl 2, S80–90. doi:10.1093/schbul/sbr064.

Wynne, L. C. & Singer, M. T. (1963a). Thought disorder and family relations of schizophrenics: I. A research strategy. *Archives of General Psychiatry*, 9, 191–198.

Wynne, L. C. & Singer, M. T. (1963b). Thought disorder and family relations of schizophrenics: II. A classification of forms of thinking. *Archives of Ggeneral Psychiatry*, 9, 199–206.

Wynne, L. C., Singer, M. T., Bartko, J. & Toohey, M. L. (1977). Schizophrenics and their families: Recent research on parental communication. In J. M. Tanner (ed.), *Developments in Psychiatric Research*. London: Hodder and Stoughton.

Xia, J. & Grant, T. J. (2012). Dance therapy for schizophrenia (Review). *Cochrane Database of Systematic Reviews (Online)*, (8).

Zammit, S., Allebeck, P., Andreasson, S., Lundberg, I. & Lewis, G. (2002). Self-reported cannabis use as a risk factor for schizophrenia in Swedish conscripts of 1969: Historical cohort study. *British Medical Journal*, 325, 1199–1201.

Ziermans, T. B., Schothorst, P. F., Schnack, H. G., Koolschijn, P. C. M. P., Kahn, R. S., van Engeland, H. & Durston, S. (2012). Progressive structural brain changes during development of psychosis. *Schizophrenia Bulletin*, 38 (3), 519–530. doi:10.1093/ schbul/sbq113.

Index